CONSTITUTIONALISM IN GLOBAL CONSTITUTIONALISATION

Constitutionalism offers a governance order a set of normative values including, amongst others, the rule of law, divisions of power and democratic legitimacy. These normative values regulate the relationship between constituent and constituted power holders. Such normative constitutional legal orders are commonplace in domestic systems but the global constitutionalisation debate seeks to identify a constitutional narrative beyond the state.

This book considers the manner in which the global constitutionalisation debate has neglected constitutionalism within its proposals. It examines the role normative constitutionalism plays within a constitutionalisation process, and considers the use of community at both the domestic and global governance levels to identify the holders of constituent and constituted power within a constitutional order. In doing so this analysis offers an alternative narrative for global constitutionalisation based within normative constitutionalism.

AOIFE O'DONOGHUE is a senior lecturer at Durham Law School, Durham University, where her teaching centres on public international law, international economic law, and law and gender.

CONSTITUTIONALISM IN GLOBAL CONSTITUTIONALISATION

AOIFE O'DONOGHUE

CAMBRIDGE
UNIVERSITY PRESS

CAMBRIDGE
UNIVERSITY PRESS

University Printing House, Cambridge CB2 8BS, United Kingdom

Cambridge University Press is part of the University of Cambridge.

It furthers the University's mission by disseminating knowledge in the pursuit of education, learning and research at the highest international levels of excellence.

www.cambridge.org
Information on this title: www.cambridge.org/9781107050259

First published 2014

A catalogue record for this publication is available from the British Library

Library of Congress Cataloguing in Publication data
O'Donoghue, Aoife, 1981– author.
Constitutionalism in global constitutionalisation / Aoife O'Donoghue.
pages cm
Includes bibliographical references and index.
ISBN 978-1-107-05025-9 (hardback)
1. Constitutional law. 2. Law and globalization. I. Title.
K3165.O32 2014
342–dc23
2013045309

ISBN 978-1-107-05025-9 Hardback

To Colin

CONTENTS

Acknowledgements *page* ix

1 **Introduction** 1

2 **Norms of constitutionalism** 14

2.1 Constitutionalism 15

2.2 The norms of constitutionalism: the rule of law, divisions of power and democratic legitimacy 24

2.3 The relationship between domestic and global constitutionalism 44

2.4 Conclusion 51

3 **Who benefits? Constituent and constituted power** 54

3.1 Constituent and constituted power holders and their relationship with constitutional governance 56

3.2 Community 59

3.3 Constituency 77

3.4 Conclusion: community or constituency? 84

4 **The global constitutionalisation debate in context** 87

4.1 Context of debate 90

4.2 What to do about global governance? 106

4.3 Historical antecedents of global constitutionalisation 108

4.4 Verdross and New Haven within constitutionalisation 132

4.5 Conclusion 133

5 **The structure of global constitutionalisation** 135

5.1 Theories of global constitutionalisation 140

5.2 Coherence, competence, consistency and hierarchy? 151

6 **The development of a constitutional approach** 155

6.1 The rule of law and constitutionalisation theories 156

6.2 Divisions of power 171

6.3 Democratic legitimacy 183
6.4 Constitutional norms in global constitutionalisation 197

7 Whom does global constitutionalism address? 200
7.1 Community 202
7.2 International constituency 225
7.3 The possible use of constituency in international constitutionalism 236
7.4 Conclusion: constituency or community? 241

8 Constitutionalism in global constitutionalisation theories 243

Bibliography 250
Index 266

ACKNOWLEDGEMENTS

Many people were instrumental in enabling me to complete this work. Professor Dr M. M. T. A. Brus was extremely supportive at all stages of my research. His analysis of my work was always insightful, critical and constructive, and without his help it would not have been completed. Thanks to Andrew Hayward, Fiona de Londras, Máiréad Enright, Aoife Nolan, Neil Cobb, Clare McGlynn, Erika Rackley, Gleider Hernández and Roger Masterman, as well as the staff of Durham Law School for their willingness to discuss my ideas and being supportive at all stages of this work. Special thanks to Laura Laffler, Illan rua Wall, Matt Saul, Tom Frost and Richard Collins for reading chapters and offering extremely helpful and astute comments. Thanks also to Monica, Jim, Léan, Martin, Niamh, Brendan, Cormac, Gráinne, Seán, Conor, Eoghan, Fionn, Cian and John who are always supportive. Finally, without Colin Murray's support during this process, from listening to my endless talk about 'constituent power' on the way home from the train station to accepting the arduous task of reading the manuscript in its entirety several times, this project would have never been completed. Most of all I wish to thank him for his wise counsel, which, whenever I need it, is there.

1

Introduction

Tackling a debate contingent upon the interpretation of a contested legal form, particularly one as central as governance, requires innumerable pitfalls to be circumnavigated before a positive contribution to debate is possible. Constitutionalism, while a legal order perceivable everywhere in governance, exemplifies both the contestations and snags typified in such debates. Questions on constitutionalism's presence, absence or potential inculcation into the global legal order ought to stand in the midst of these controversies; yet often, concerns as to its nature are bypassed for the supposed glamour of constitutional global governance. Almost instinctively, global constitutionalisation appears as the epitome of international law's development. Constitutionalism is a form of legal order that is tried and tested in domestic law, proven to indicate the final maturing of domestic governance and a faithful servant of legitimacy. It offers international law its final repose as a 'good' legal order. But, perhaps in rushing towards the idyll of global constitutionalisation a few preliminary questions have been missed. By focusing on the conduct of the debate, this book seeks to consider an aspect of a priori constitutionalisation, the necessary aspects of constitutionalism as a normative legal order.

Constitutionalism, as an ideal legal order, as a documentary source of law, as a historical explanation or justification for the present form of state governance, or as a normative legal order suffused with a particular notion of what governance ought to be, deserves and requires consideration prior to any proposed consolidation of its place within the global legal order. Rather than tackling the entirety of constitutionalism's manifestations, this book concentrates on constitutionalism's normative content and its place in the global constitutionalisation debate. Admittedly, a focus upon constitutionalism as a normative legal order instilled with particular values omits other important questions necessary to a critical consideration of any debate on governance. But in considering its normative form, this work hopes to incite debate as to constitutionalism's worth within the global legal order and beyond, while also pointing to some of the unsatisfactory aspects of global governance as it currently operates. Frankly, the debate on the suitability of global constitutionalisation should not end until all variations of constitutionalism's character are firmly underway and informing the actual process of transformation within the global legal order. Before the contemplation of a global constitutional order can truly begin, this book seeks to understand its meaning.

Underlying much of what follows is the assumption that there is purchase in constitutionalism's operation and that it is not a neutral indicator of legalisation or maturity but rather enjoys substantive form. Thus, to call something constitutionalised means to assert that a particular form of governance, immersed in a specific normative structure, exists. While such a claim could be contested, indeed usefully so, this assertion sets the tone for this discussion of constitutionalisation. To argue that it is something other than normative constitutionalism leads to a debate where constitutionalisation is a metaphor for an entirely different process. By purchase, this work denotes both the means of exercising governance and the advantages gained by those utilising its accoutrements within that governance order. Constitutionalism's purchase derives from both the form of governance order it establishes and the benefits accrued by those making use of its form. Clearly, this idea of purchase is not neutral. Constitutionalism's underlying rationales and values are a critical point that must be tackled. Yet, herein, beyond acknowledging that constitutionalism inculcates particular historical and cultural values that ought to be questioned (and that these form part of its purchase), this book restricts itself to arguing that its normative content ought to be conceded by proponents of constitutionalism's plantation into international law.

The means of exercising governance and the advantages gained by such utilisation must be held and accrued by some body. Thus constitutionalism's purchase requires that the means and advantages of constitutionalism ought to be readily identifiable and further, that those who hold those means, to whom such advantages accrue and their inter-relationship must also be extant. As such, part of the purchase that constitutionalism possesses and an aspect that must also be explored is who within global governance ought to gain from its operation. Constitutionalisation happens to a legal order but what does that legal order contain and whose order is it? If constitutionalism requires particular relational structures, how global constitutionalisation should inculcate these into its structure also forms part of the debate.

Fassbender's statement that 'over the course of the last fifty years the "constitutional predisposition" of the Charter has been confirmed and strengthened in such a way that today the instrument must be referred to as the constitution of the international community', De Wet's claim that there is an 'emerging international constitutional order consisting of an international community, an international value system and rudimentary structures for its enforcement' or indeed Klabbers' declaration that constitutionalism is 'an attitude, a frame of mind' all require interrogation.[1] Constitutionalism's plantation into the global legal order ought to be accompanied by a rigorous examination of its potential utility and operation, and this can only occur if the global constitutionalisation debate is rooted in, amongst other analysis, a normative constitutional frame.

Theories supporting global constitutionalisation propose that aspects of constitutionalism have or will become attributes of public international law. There is much to commend these theories and the additions they make to our understanding of the global legal order. Nonetheless, the importance of investigating whether these constitutionalisation theories are based upon the existing doctrine of constitutionalism or are an entirely new theoretical phenomenon should not be overlooked. Most global constitutionalisation theories, exemplified by Fassbender, De Wet or Klabbers, appear to be based within international law and seek to inculcate constitutional attributes to its operation. This book suggests that they would benefit greatly from a change in starting point and a footing within constitutionalism. Thus, this book queries whether global constitutionalisation theory may be improved by a more rigorous approach to constitutionalism itself. If, ultimately global constitutionalisation is adjudged to be a novel form of governance, sharing attributes with constitutionalism but distinguishable from it, it is then further suggested that an alternative moniker would prevent much confusion or renunciation.

Seeking constitutionalism's purchase within the global constitutionalisation debate emerges from a desire to understand its allure for international lawyers. Why has the international or global constitutionalisation gained such momentum? Why have academics reached for constitutionalism above alternative narratives of governance, including

[1] This is not to pick on Fassbender, De Wet or Klabbers but rather it is an indicator of a broader phenomenon; B. Fassbender, 'The United Nations Charter as Constitution of the International Community' (1998) 36 *Columbia Journal of Transnational Law* 529; E. De Wet, 'The International Constitutional Order' (2006) 55 *International and Comparative Law Quarterly* 51; J. Klabbers in J. Klabbers, A. Peters and G. Ulfstein, *The Constitutionalisation of International Law* (Oxford University Press, 2009), p. 10.

some that are more native to international law? Perhaps such a task is illusory, as it seems almost impossible to discover the attraction of a particular order, but perhaps in understanding its purchase, the rationales for the global constitutionalisation debate will emerge. In addition, this approach might also unpick troublesome aspects of the constitutionalisation debate; for example, whether the constitutional requirements for a governance order have been seriously deliberated upon or accommodated within these propositions. Further, whether constitutionalism's purchase has been considered, and if not, how should constitutionalism's requisite normative structure, the means of utilising its purchase and the benefits that should accrue to international law from its purchase be realised within global constitutionalisation? Thus, in light of the historical and present character of the global constitutionalisation debate, this work seeks to understand what constitutionalism may mean to global governance. It also attempts to ascertain whether constitutionalism and international law possess the wherewithal to become a mutually beneficial, interconnected form of global governance.

Constitutional language is frequently employed in the global constitutionalisation debate. But many of these terms are politically contingent, meaning that their use is not, of itself, evidence of convergence. Peters and Armingeon acknowledge, as do several others, that there is a lack of coherence in the use of the terminology surrounding constitutionalisation.[2] Rarely is there much agreement as to either its normative structure or the process of constitutionalisation itself. Thus, there are myriad definitions.[3] For those in favour of recognising an existing constitutional order, constitutionalisation is used to describe a process already completed, whereas for those who argue that constitutionalisation is currently taking place or may take place in the future, constitutionalisation is a contemporary development where the goal is a constitutional order that is, as yet, nascent.

In exploring the constitutionalisation debate this book understands that 'constitutionalism' and 'constitutionalisation' are used as legal terms of art, denoting a particular form of legal order and not simply to rename an entirely new process within global law. Klabbers argues that

[2] A. Peters and K. Armingeon, 'Introduction – Global Constitutionalism from an Interdisciplinary Perspective' (2009) 16 *Indiana Journal of Global Legal Studies* 385, 387; and K. Milewicz, 'Emerging Patterns of Global Constitutionalization: Towards a Conceptual Framework' (2009) 16 *Indiana Journal of Global Legal Studies* 413.

[3] Milewicz, 'Emerging Patterns', 415.

constitutionalism is something more than legalisation.[4] He claims that legalisation, juridification or other similar phenomena are related to issues of codification in discrete areas of trade or human rights. As Klabbers depicts it, changes in international law, such as the codification of particular rules like the Vienna Convention on the Law of Treaties, take place without greatly disrupting the Westphalian order. By this standard, constitutionalisation must be something more radical than simple law reform. In contrast to Klabbers, Peters argues that '[g]lobal constitutionalism is an academic and political agenda that identifies and advocates for the application of constitutionalist principles in the international legal sphere in order to improve the effectiveness and the fairness of the international legal order'.[5] Peters refers to this process as an 'academic artefact', a phrase borrowed from Weiler.[6] This seems to imply that the constitutionalisation debate is nothing more than an academic diversion that will not in reality affect the practice of international law. Yet, Peters' point could instead be viewed as an indictment of the lack of thoroughness within the constitutionalisation debate, a defect that could be rectified by a more methodical approach that ties the process to constitutionalism.

In this book, constitutional language is employed in specific fashions. First, in the case of global and international law, the former is used to describe international as well as other areas, such as regional, domestic or institutional law, which intersect within the world legal system. International law means the classical inter-state law that forms part of global law, though it is also, at times, used to refer to particular constitutionalisation theories. Constitutionalism describes a form of legal governance theory based upon particular norms, values and structures. Constitutionalisation is employed where a legal order is in a process, over a period of time, from a position not based upon constitutionalism to one taking upon itself its cloak. A constitutional order has already adopted the necessary elements of constitutionalism to make use of that title rightly.

'The earliest rules of international law can, I think, be attributed to the self-interest of states … and recognition that there are some mischiefs which can only be effectively addressed if addressed by more states than

[4] Klabbers in Klabbers, Peters and Ulfstein, *Constitutionalisation*, pp. 1–3.

[5] A. Peters, 'The Merits of Global Constitutionalism' (2009) 16 *Indiana Journal of Global Legal Studies* 397.

[6] Peters and Armingeon, 'Interdisciplinary Perspective', 385; A. Peters, 'Compensatory Constitutionalism: The Function and Potential of Fundamental International Norms and Structures' (2006) 19 *Leiden Journal of International Law* 579, 605; and A. Peters, 'Global Constitutionalism Revisited' (2005) 11 *International Legal Theory* 39.

one.'[7] The Westphalian legal order that sustained the international system over an extended period, is now, as Bingham recognises, giving way to a more differentiated legal system with goals beyond merely keeping states' interests in check. Habermas argues that '[a] world dominated by nation-states is … in transition toward the post-national constellation of global society. States are losing their autonomy, in part, because they have become increasingly enmeshed in the horizontal networks of a global society.'[8] The boundaries between international and domestic law are no longer easy to maintain.[9] This is not to suggest that, for example, all domestic courts will, without prejudice, follow international law, but rather that international law's influence is more pronounced than it was in the past.[10] At such a juncture for international law, where models of multilateralism and supra-nationalism, and the establishment of doctrines such as *jus cogens*, have already established a network of laws that cannot be accurately depicted as purely consensual, international legal theorists seek to clarify the nature of contemporary international law. Amidst this change, constitutionalism is but one of the theories that aspire to explain the current and future character of international law.

When governance moves from a non-centralised force and beyond a simplex order of apparent equal subjects towards a more complex structure, new understandings of its rationales to settle the transition become necessary. In the global legal order how to approach the evolution from a consensual to a more intricate order has become the subject of much debate. Without wishing to make a dramatic claim, which would exaggerate the current position of international law, there is now a need to choose how to advance its development. The theories developing alongside constitutionalisation present alternate visions of how international law ought to be understood. Attempts to understand the global governance order are not new, and these alternates signpost the difficulties lying ahead for constitutionalisation while also outlining the context within which these debates emerged. Some theories, including global legal pluralism, fragmentation,

7 T. Bingham, *The Rule of Law* (London: Allen Lane, 2010), p. 114; see also, for an earlier articulation of a similar account of moving beyond classical international law, Wolfgang Friedman, *The Changing Structure of International Law* (Columbia, OH: Columbia University Press, 1964).

8 J. Habermas, *The Divided West* (trans. C. Cronin) (Cambridge: Polity Press, 2006), pp. 115–16.

9 See, for example, the work within global administrative law, such as B. Kingsbury, 'The Concept of "Law" in Global Administrative Law' (2009) 20 *European Journal of International Law* 23.

10 Bingham, *Rule of Law*, chapter 10.

global administrative law and governance networks, present alternatives to constitutionalisation, while other accounts, such as New Haven and Verdross, capture international law's already snarled development.

Although not rejecting the significance of ascertaining whether constitutionalisation can truly be said to be occurring and the importance of the practical application of constitutionalism either to international law or global governance, this book focuses on the character of global constitutionalisation theories and their relationship with constitutionalism. As such, the various approaches to global constitutionalisation are compared and critiqued within a frame of constitutional norms to establish their present state and their relationship to constitutionalism, considering whether the purchase associated with constitutionalism has been absorbed into the global constitutionalisation debate.

This study begins by discussing the nature of constitutionalism itself, identifying its norms and assessing the rationales for seeking to transplant it beyond the state. Ensuring an understanding of constitutionalism before tackling global constitutionalisation allows us to approach the latter not from a base within public international law but rather from a constitutional footing. Such a method emphasises constitutionalism rather than public international law and in doing so captures the notion of constitutional purchase. Starting in constitutionalism eschews the partialities of the public international lawyer seeking to proselytise its worth or indeed its purchase. Peters points out that the constitutionalist approach helps to overcome 'the deniers of international law as law'.[11] Yet, arguing that constitutionalisation is the culmination of international law's evolution, thus proving it is, in fact, law, surely lacks credibility if the leap required is from a non-legal to a constitutionalised order. Taking a constitutional footing inevitably adopts the preconceptions of the constitutional lawyer. But in recognising it is constitutionalism at the centre of the debate, this book seeks to reorientate questions surrounding global constitutionalisation onto governance and the form it should take within the global legal order.

Arguing that constitutionalism operates in the global legal order suggests that it coalesces into a *constitutional* legal order. Munro identifies two different, though not conclusive, definitions of a constitution: the first, a collection of laws in a state, which are collectively identified as public law; the second, a single purposely written document establishing the

[11] Peters, 'Merits', 405.

basis of a legal order and known, since the French Revolution, as a constitution.[12] Tomuschat dismisses arguments, based on clarity and rationality, in favour of a written constitution, as peculiarities of an era of law in which they were created.[13] As several undocumented constitutions such as New Zealand or the UK prove, a written document is unnecessary for a system to be constitutional; yet, other aspects of constitutionalism, such as the rule of law or divisions of power, are not as easily dismissed. This book begins with a discussion of the shape in which these core norms appear if an order is to be described as constitutional. In examining these norms and their consistency it becomes possible to determine their potential presence within both the global constitutionalisation debate and broader international law.

Domestic orders possess some of the longest and most entrenched forms of constitutionalism. Further, with the exception of states in conflict and transition, domestic constitutions have completed the process of constitutionalisation and are thus a model on which to understand what the end of that process demands. Discussions on the transplantation of constitutionalism from the domestic to the global plane necessitate the detection of the norms that must be present to depict accurately a legal order as such. This will not entail an empirical study of these constitutional orders but rather a discussion of the common theoretical frameworks by which domestic constitutionalism is understood. In examining this literature, several different ever-present norms are discussed, and three (the rule of law, divisions of power and democratic legitimacy) are considered in detail, as each is closely connected to the exercise of constituent and constituted power. While the rule of law, divisions of power and democratic legitimacy are discussed as modes of constitutionalism and not as inevitably linked to domestic legal orders, it will largely be within the domestic realm that they are initially considered, as it is in this forum that they developed their basic constitutional meanings.

Starting here also enables a broader conversation on the development of constitutionalism as a legal order and the arguments against utilising it beyond the domestic realm. Opposition to the extension of constitutionalism and constitutional norms to the global legal order are based on the merits of the domestic monopoly over constitutionalism. Questions

[12] C. R. Munro, *Studies in Constitutional Law*, 2nd edn (London: Butterworths, 1999), p. 1.

[13] C. Tomuschat, 'Obligations Arising for States Without or Against Their Will' (1993–IV) 241 *Rec. Des Cours* 195, 217; the UK is a prime example of a state's ability to operate without one formal written document.

regarding the legitimacy and suitability of the global legal order becoming entrenched in constitutionalism, and whether the international legal order is of such a character that the norms of constitutionalism can never be successfully transposed, are considered in depth.

The perpetual link to a group or a body forms a core aspect of constitutionalism. Within states that body comprises the persons living within the constitutional jurisdiction. The constitution and ultimately constitutionalism itself serve the interests of such a body and, as mentioned earlier, this body is also the beneficiary of constitutional purchase. The implication that follows from such an assertion of linkage is that global constitutionalisation theories must consider what body its constitution serves. The identification of the subjects of constitutionalism sets the parameters within which the holders of both constituent and constituted power act, their relational structures and thus too the application of a constitutional governance order to that body.

Constituted power is the legal basis on which authority is exercised within a legal framework, whereas constituent power is the exercise of political power and the ultimate source of legitimate authority. Identifying constituent power holders aids in establishing the interests that an order should serve and thus ought to be an a priori action in considering the terms of a governance order. In order to understand to whom constitutional purchase will accrue within these developing governance orders, and the identification of constituent and constituted power holders, this book will focus upon community and constituency. The identification of constituent and constituted power holders forms part of the panoply of constitutional debate and substantiates the application of a normative order. Several theories are chosen that illustrate the historical development of community and constituency and their relationship with constitutionalism, and constituent and constituted power.

Having long been an aspect of political and legal debate, though perhaps not without controversy as to its exact parameters, community seems a ready-made solution to the identification of the body global constitutionalisation serves. This examination aims not to settle on an exact definition of community but rather to appreciate the implications of invoking community within global constitutionalisation and to understand the terms of its appeal. Naturally, this necessitates the consideration of theories of community's development domestically alongside constitutionalism as well as globally alongside international law. This book focuses on particular points of community's development to the exclusion of other potential halting points. In doing so a range of sources from Cicero to Jean-Luc Nancy will be invoked, not to depict them in their completeness but rather to comprehend further how constitutionalism ought to be understood as a particular form of governance order with a specific purchase accompanying its operation. In concentrating on the theories of community that exemplify some of the more generally understood implications of its use, this work aims to establish community's relationship with constituent and constituted power but does not intend to be an exhaustive critique, but rather a realisation of what a ready-made solution, international community, would mean for global constitutionalisation.

Set alongside community, constituency proffers an alternative body for understanding constitutional purchase and the body to which it is linked. Constituency is understood as a group of actors associated with the nexus between constituted and constituent power. Constituency vests authority or power elsewhere than with the group as a whole, but recognises that this power is exercised on its behalf or in its interest. In order to discuss constituency as a concept related to, and understood with regard to, constitutionalism as well as constituted and constituent power, inferences will be drawn from its potential use within constitutionalisation. The choices of constituency's advocates, at both the domestic and global points of constitutionalism, do not pretend to offer a complete analysis of constituency, but rather chart the potentiality for its invocation within a constitutionalisation process. An international constituency may act as an alternative basis for understanding constituent power within a constitutionalisation process.

While not exhaustive, the analysis of community and constituency attempts to understand how such bodies are identified and grouped together within the constitutional and global legal paradigm. Contrasting the use of constituency with community in a constitutional context will illuminate the role they could play in a global constitutionalisation process.

Fragmented and often partially conceptualised, the debates on global constitutionalisation come in many variants. In considering whether constitutionalism is implanted into global constitutionalisation, reviewing every distinction amongst the proposals is unnecessary. Rather, understanding how the debate has emerged, illustrating its nature and the forms into which it has developed establishes a basis for examining its relationship with constitutionalism. This does not suggest that omitted theories do not make valuable contributions to debate but rather that in attempting to make a coherent argument as to the place of constitutionalism within the constitutionalisation debate, certain positions are more illuminating than other, also credible, theories.

One variant of the debate in particular will be considered: the divide between world order and sectoral constitutionalisation.[14] The singling out of this partition above other categorisations (such as *jus cogens*, human rights or institutional constitutionalisation) arises from the notion that the form and structure of governance within a normative order varies with scale and content. Constitutionalisation encapsulates an entire legal order. Consequently, in the global arena, areas of law such as trade or human rights may come within constitutionalisation's scope. This necessarily opens up further debates as to how these areas of international law are balanced within the constitutionalisation theories, how they are prioritised and the nature of any hierarchical structure that emerges from a constitutionalisation process. As such, sectoral and world order constitutionalisation theories propose models of inculcation useful in teasing out the implications of normative constitutionalism that others, particularly those that focus upon institutional structures mirroring executives, legislatures or judiciaries, do not.

In choosing a wide range of constitutional, community, constituency and constitutionalisation models it is hoped that an ample understanding of the current place of these debates and how they interact with each other emerges. One obvious omission, but one that remains significant, is the debate on constitutionalisation taking place with regard to Europe, and more particularly within the European Union. The lack of attention paid to EU constitutionalism in the global debate may be owing to its institutionalised constitutional process. Constitutionalisation at the EU level has, particularly with the drafting of the EU Constitution and the referenda that accompanied its abortive launch, taken a more conscious political direction. This means that EU and global constitutionalisation debates are of a different character, though this is perhaps to the detriment of the latter. The EU model stands as an important example of how constitutionalisation evolves particularly in the frame of subsidiarity. Subsidiarity, a point of governance often absent from international law's deliberations, has had a central role in the development of the EU's legal order, which in many ways underpins its relationship with any global

[14] For example, those who argue for WTO or UN constitutionalisation, such as Fassbender or Petersmann, in contrast with those who are for world order constitutionalisation, such as De Wet or Peters; E. Petersmann, 'Human Rights, International Economic Law and "Constitutional Justice"' (2008) 19 *European Journal of International Law* 769.

variant.[15] These developments influence this study, particularly in how they have affected the theories of Walker and Weiler.[16] The various theories on European constitutionalisation broaden the global debate and offer some useful lessons on the nature or form that constitutionalisation may take beyond the state, but Europe itself does not form a central part of this book.[17] The EU relegation risks a false division of constitutionalisation theories, however; to focus on theories addressing a global process its absence is necessary.

The increasingly interdependent nature of the global system requires a growing cognisance of the inter-related aspects of both the particularised areas of global law and its overall scope. Global constitutionalisation provides a structure for understanding how these discrete areas of law relate to each other. This book depicts the inter-relationship between the global constitutionalisation debate and constitutionalism as a legal theory. In doing so, the work draws together a broad array of theorists from both constitutional and international legal theory to understand the contours of constitutionalism, demonstrating that constitutional norms are integral to the global constitutionalisation debate.

If global law was to be accepted as a constitutional system, or as being on the path to becoming such a system, this would be a pivotal moment for the order.[18] Global constitutionalisation theories differ on how to best understand such a process, but this book suggests that as a preliminary exercise all should be discussed within a normative constitutional framework. This will not lead to a conclusive answer on whether constitutionalisation is occurring in international law. Rather, it will consider whether constitutionalism as a doctrine is imbedded in global constitutionalisation theories, or whether the proposals within international law rest on an entirely separate basis, or even perhaps if the entire enterprise is

[15] Article 5 Maastricht Treaty, 24 December 2002 (2002) *Official Journal of the European Communities* C 325/5.

[16] J. H. H. Weiler, *The Constitution of Europe* (Cambridge University Press, 1999), p. 232.

[17] See, for example, J. A. Caparoso, 'The European Union and Forms of State: Westphalian, Regulatory or Post-Modern' (1996) 34 *Common Market Law Review* 29; J. H. H. Weiler, 'The Transformation of Europe' (1991) 100 *Yale Law Journal* 2403; J. H. H. Weiler 'Federalism and Constitutionalism: Europe's Sonderweg' (2000) *The Jean Monnet Working Paper* No. 10; J. H. H. Weiler, 'The Reformation of European Constitutionalism' (1997) 35 *Common Market Law Review* 97; N. Walker, 'European Constitutionalism in the State Constitutional Tradition' 58 *Current Legal Problems* 51; for a brief though succinct summary, see G. de Búrca, 'The Normativity of International Constitutionalism', in www.ejiltalk.org/author/gdeburca/, accessed 30 August 2013.

[18] Such moments of transformative change have been identified before; see F. Pollock, *The League of Nations* (London: Stevens & Sons, 1920).

worthwhile. The theories that underpin constitutionalisation potentially offer a good system for comprehending the operation of the global legal order. This discussion provides an understanding of constitutionalism's role within constitutionalisation and presents a basis for considering the preliminary questions necessary before contemplating constitutionalism within the global legal order.

2

Norms of constitutionalism

At times, constitutionalism's underlying rationale as a form of governance based upon normative values is sidestepped in favour of the employment of linguistic tropes without a rigorous interrogation of both their impact and suitability within a particular order. Such usage appears to be a particular issue in governance questions beyond the state. Within global constitutionalisation a shorthand form embracing a constitutional vernacular has emerged, which, on occasion, underestimates the necessity of questioning the constitutional elements of any proposed global governance narrative.[1] A lack of deliberative discussion on issues such as a global constitutional constituency exemplifies this concern, but it is also evident in the absence of debate on the aptness of constitutionalism as a form of governance within international law. Before considering the myriad possibilities for global constitutionalisation, this chapter examines constitutionalism itself, incorporating the identification of the aims of a constituted system, the nature of constitutional law itself, its functionality and ultimately whether it is worthwhile to pursue it as an idealised legal order.

Constitutionalism includes a broad array of concepts and doctrinal values. Perhaps constitutional law simply is superior to 'ordinary' law; yet, even this requires a substantive hierarchical system and particular governance structures. Even in long-established constitutional states, an ostensibly simple question such as 'what is a constitution?' is not readily answerable. Loughlin argues that 'the modern idea of the constitution results from a basic shift that took place in understanding the relationship between government and people: rejecting traditional orderings based upon status and hierarchy, it expressed the conviction that government,

[1] An exception to such criticism is the employment by Teubner of societal constitutionalism with very deliberate consequences, G. Teubner, *Constitutional Fragments. Societal Constitutionalism in the Globalization* (Oxford University Press, 2012); and for a further critique of its invocation see D. Kennedy, 'The Mystery of Global Governance' (2008) 34 *Ohio New University Law Review* 827.

being an office established by the people, must be based on their consent'.[2] Loughlin suggests that the purpose of constitutionalism's substantive and procedural requirements is to ensure the maintenance of a constitutional order founded upon legitimacy through consent. Accordingly, to be constitutionally apposite, an order must possess a combination of elements beyond becoming intricate or possessing aspects shared with constitutionalism. It must adopt a governance narrative that embraces both normative values and a particular bond between those governing and governed. Thus, a governance order needs to assume the value of constitutionalism's purchase in order to make the adoption of its tropes worthwhile.

This chapter questions whether constitutionalism's normative values, which up to recently had been confined to the domestic arena, can be employed effectively within global legal theory. Examining the rule of law, divisions of power and democratic legitimacy as three exemplifiers of constitutional norms, this section seeks to understand the rationale and substance of constitutionalism before delving into the globalised issues, questioning whether constitutional law, as an emanation of state law, is fit for purpose in the global realm.

2.1 Constitutionalism

In general terms constitutionalisation is the process by which a legal order goes from an ad hoc, decentralised and consent-based system to one where the remit of action of constituted power holders is curtailed by legal form and process; where law regulates the exercise of power and governance in line with substantive norms. Allott argues that a 'constitution is a structure-system which is shared by all societies; however, even such a shared ideal is difficult to pin down'.[3] While the meaning or consequence may vary depending on the roots of a constitutional culture, the ideal is not as ephemeral as Allott suggests. The variances within constitutionalism reflect the content and application of diverse state constitutions rather than the value of constitutionalism as a normative governance order. Constitutionalisation advances a pre-constitutional legal order, moving it away from a structure where the holders of power are entirely

[2] M. Loughlin, 'What Is Constitutionalisation?' in P. Dobner and M. Loughlin (eds.), *The Twilight of Constitutionalism* (Oxford University Press, 2010), pp. 47–8.

[3] P. Allott, *Eunomia*, 2nd edn (Oxford University Press, 2001), p. 167.

self-regulated and beyond review to a system encompassing scrutiny at its core.[4]

In contrast to constitutionalism, constitutionalisation represents both a legal and political process. The interaction between the political and the legal in the guise of community or constituency will be discussed in detail in Chapter 3, but for now it suffices to note that the nature of the polity to which a constitutional system is connected is an important consideration in understanding constitutionalism's operation. The polity served by constitutionalism becomes particularly important when attempting to transpose constitutionalism to the international realm. Inevitably, the holders of constituted and constituent power are political actors. This is not to suggest that the law will become politicised within a constitutionalised system, but rather, that as a result of constitutionalisation, the law is more likely to regulate political action and the holders of constituted power on a more consolidated basis than in a non-constitutionalised system.[5] Thus, constitutionalisation denotes the process by which political actors become regulated by constitutional norms as the governance order, often consciously, adapts to increasingly intricate power structures and systems.

A very broad concept of a constitutional order as a system of governance may be used, but, as has been pointed out elsewhere, this simply reduces constitutionalism to a mere set of organisational rules.[6] This book abandons such an approach, instead regarding constitutionalism as requiring a higher law binding both holders of constituted and constituent power within the demesne of the rule of law. The relationship that law maintains between the political aspects of a constitutional regime impacts upon constitutionalism, as later chapters will demonstrate.[7]

[4] For a broad discussion of constitutionalism, see D. Castiglione, 'The Political Theory of the Constitution' (1996) 44 *Political Studies* 417; and N. Walker, 'Taking Constitutionalism beyond the State' (2008) 56 *Political Studies* 519.

[5] For a general discussion of the historical relationship between power and international law, see R. H. Steinberg and J. M. Zasloff, 'Power and International Law' (2006) 100 *American Journal of International Law* 64; and T. M. Franck, 'Power of Legitimacy and the Legitimacy of Power: International Law in an Age of Power Disequilibrium' (2006) 100 *American Journal of International Law* 88.

[6] T. Cottier and M. Hertig, 'The Prospects of 21st Constitutionalism' (2003) 7 *Max Planck Yearbook of United Nations Law* 261, 280.

[7] See, for example, J. A. G. Griffith, 'The Political Constitution' (1979) 42 *Modern Law Review* 1; and A. Tomkins, 'In Defence of the Political Constitution' (2002) 22 *Oxford Journal of Legal Studies* 157.

Roth argues in positivist terms that a constitution serves simply to decide whether an enactment is valid law within a society, but he limits constitutionalism to a process of box ticking with miniscule normative content.[8] Such normative content includes core rules by which systems operate, such as delineating the holders of power, how they are chosen and further substantive details on particular laws, including duties and rights.[9] A more expansive or thicker view of constitutionalism's role also comprises the allocation of power and its control.[10] Habitually, alongside the orchestration of power, these duties and rights act as dampeners on the ability of power holders to take action. What the central tenets or basic understanding between the actors within the system are, at what point the wielders of power have strayed beyond the limits of the constitutional system and are thus acting *ultra vires,* and, ultimately, what the result of such a finding would be, are the concerns of constitutionalism.

An issue, infrequently raised, is the attractiveness of constitutionalism as an abstract ideal to both international lawyers and others engaged with governance. Often, constitutionalised systems are regarded as more coherent and perhaps, civilised, than their non-constitutionalised counterparts.[11] They are civilised to the extent that constitutionalism represents the epitome of efficient governance. For a legal system to function effectively, legal certainty is essential. While certainty can exist without constitutional law, arguably it brings an added element of assurance, not necessarily on content, but rather on the coherence of the legal system as a whole. Constitutionalised systems are ordinarily hierarchical and diverse in their power allocations, and delineate which aspects are 'constitutional' and therefore require additional procedures for their change or replacement. Within a constitutional order, power allocations are based upon divisions of constituted power, although the extent of partition and the form in which it comes vary between systems. Such power allocations provide constitutional systems with the legitimacy that Franck refers to as

[8] B. R. Roth, *Governmental Illegitimacy in International Law* (Oxford University Press, 2000), p. 52.

[9] For a general discussion see L. Alexander (ed.), *Constitutionalism: Philosophical Foundations* (Cambridge University Press, 1998).

[10] G. Maddox, 'A Note on the Meaning of "'Constitution"' (1982) 76 *American Political Science Review* 805.

[11] This may be particularly important for international law, which historically has relied upon notions of civilisation for legitimacy; Covenant of the League of Nations, Article 22; A. Orakhelashvili, 'The Idea of European International Law' (2006) 17 *European Journal of International Law* 315.

'right process',[12] which is not apparent in other systems of law. This legitimacy is perhaps the most desirable aspect of constitutionalism for those proposing its use within the global legal order.

Constitutionalism, theoretically at least, introduces continuity into a legal system.[13] Although constitutional regimes may change, such alterations remain rare, and the incidences under which they take place are circumscribed by the system itself. States may alter elements of their constitutional order through a collective and firm decision to bring about a substantial transformation of the constitutional regime. With the exception of the formation of an entirely new state, or incidences of change so fundamental that an order can be considered to be wholly new (for example, defeat in war, revolution or a radical political shift), such transformations often come in the guise of the settled constitutional arrangement. Thus, constitutions tend to be more steadfast than other forms of legal order, such as classical international law, which being consent-driven remain open to constant change and renegotiation.

Kumm makes a helpful distinction between constitutional theories and paradigms, which may be put to good use. He argues that constitutional theories are developed concepts that stand to examine the relative values within a system and how it works overall, whereas constitutional paradigms offer 'cognitive frameworks' that provide a 'conceptual structure' upon which to base an examination of the conduct of the law.[14] This differentiation is central to the position argued here, as it allows a delineation between the aims and structures of constitutionalism and, as such, different models to dislocate power, though the underlying rationale of doing so remains the same.

Walker argues that what is normally taken to be constitutional is 'a mature rule-based or legal order' but that this varies depending on the starting point.[15] Certain key mechanisms often are associated with constitutionalism; for example, the rule of law, divisions of power, and democratic legitimacy or human rights. But there remains a distinction between the underlying purpose of constitutional law and the functional structure

[12] T. Franck, *Fairness in International Law* (Oxford University Press, 1995), p. 477.

[13] See, as an example, the discussion by King regarding the continuity that constitutionalism has brought to the British Constitution, a decentralised constitution that is based upon a catalogue of documents and conventions. A. King, *The British Constitution* (Oxford University Press, 2007), p. 2.

[14] M. Kumm, 'The Cosmopolitan Turn in Constitutionalism' in J. L. Dunoff and J. P. Trachtman (eds.), *Ruling the World? Constitutionalism, International Law and Global Governance* (Cambridge University Press, 2009), p. 270.

[15] Walker, 'Taking Constitutionalism', 526.

that accompanies its operation. The aims are transposable to any constitutional configuration, whereas a particular structural system must adapt to the system of governance it serves. If the aim of constitutionalisation is to create a structure within which power is exercised and the rule of law prevails, then it becomes important to identify the appropriate 'governance point' at which such constitutionalisation should occur. One ramification of such a claim is the need to understand the relationship between such governance points, be they international, regional or domestic, and thus, the most appropriate allocation of constituted power amongst them. Further, such a standpoint suggests that constitutional structures rarely, if ever, mirror each other; nor is it an ambition to do so. Rather, the underlying rationale for constitutional orders is critical in discussing constitutionalism in the global context.

Constitutionalism must mean more than correlating systems employing tropes that can be transplanted into any system of governance; it must also embrace its core norms. A good case in point is the UK Constitution. Tomkins, while extolling the virtues of the unique nature of the UK Constitution, points to one core rule upon which he argues it rests, that 'the government of the day may continue in office for only as long as it continues to enjoy the majority support of the House of Commons'.[16] Whether or not this is an accurate description of the UK constitutional arrangement it suggests that domestic constitutional structures may vary according to circumstance. This form of parliamentary democracy, where the executive also forms part of the legislature, is certainly not replicated in all constitutional systems. So just as the US constitutional system, where the executive is entirely separate from the legislature, appears the closest fit, neither the UK nor US separation-of-power models is better or restrains power in a more 'constitutional manner'.[17] Both models share the aim of fettering and dividing power but they achieve this through different, though mutually constitutional, means. Admittedly what these two do share, which arguably may be lacking within the international realm, is the classic horizontal (and in the case of the United States also the vertical) separation of powers. The classic horizontal separation-of-power model rests on having a distinct executive, legislature and judiciary. The vertical separation of powers is contained within federal systems where

[16] A. Tomkins, *Our Republican Constitution* (Oxford: Hart, 2005), p. 1.

[17] For a description of the US and French separation-of-power doctrines, see M. J. C. Vile, *Constitutionalism and the Separation of Powers*, 2nd edn (Oxford University Press, 1967), pp. 131–232.

power is allocated at various points of distance from constituent power holders depending upon the perceived efficiency in decision-making. This point will be returned to later, but it is important to note that it is not useful to attempt to shoehorn or 'find' a legislature, executive and judiciary to satisfy a model that may not suit the global governance order. The aim of global constitutionalism may be to fetter power but this may be achieved through several means.

Dunoff suggests that normative values, including the rule of law, rules that constrain individual freedoms based upon tests of proportionality and necessity, horizontal and vertical separations of powers, rule-orientated settlement of disputes and inalienable human rights regimes are indicative of a constitutional system.[18] Such lists do not offer a checklist to test constitutionalisation processes against, but they may point towards the norms that are ordinarily indicative of constitutionalism. They establish an instructive narrative. Thus, whether a system is potentially open to the charge of constitutionalisation may be navigated through a consideration of whether such normative forms appear to be present within the governance order.

The approach taken in this chapter, focusing on the rule of law, divisions of power and democratic legitimacy is therefore not without its pitfalls. Most obviously in not considering the entirety of constitutionalism, and in concentrating on three elements, this approach could be accused of being too narrow. However, in also discussing the rule of law the broader questions relating to the place of law within a governance order will also be addressed. This analysis of the rule of law also pertains to the models of constituency discussed in the next chapter. Petersmann, in placing human rights at the core of international constitutionalisation, focuses upon the rule of law and the separation of powers. He argues that constitutional principles are required wherever power is exercised at the local, national and international level in a 'mutually complementary' manner. While Petersmann's focus is primarily upon economic law, it is his requirement of universal application that demands co-operation both horizontally and vertically, and stresses that constitutionalism be seen as elemental to all law.[19] The concentration of the rule of law, divisions of

[18] J. L. Dunoff, 'The Politics of International Constitutions' in Dunoff and Trachtman (eds.), *Ruling the World?*, p. 188.

[19] E. Petersmann, 'Human Rights and Economic Law in the 21st Century: The Need to Clarify Their Interrelationships' (2001) *Journal of International Economic Law* 3.

power and democratic legitimacy will focus on the broader constitutional questions that form part of the global constitutionalisation debate.

In assessing the role of constitutionalism within constitutionalisation, it is essential to build a coherent paradigm in which to examine constitutionalism's potential operation and to consider whether its rationale or its purchase has a place within the governance order. Examining some of the fiats of constitutionalism such as the rule of law, divisions of power or democratic legitimacy outside of their contextual application within a particular legal system may neglect important features of constitutionalism's implementation. Further, the differentiation between the rule of law, division of power and democratic legitimacy is not always clear. For example, the rule of law could encompass the division of power and its operation; yet the rationales of each norm and their impact upon constituent and constituted power holders differ and thus are worthy of separate contemplation. The division of power and the exercise of governance form an important aspect of seeking answers concerning why and how power is exercised in a particular fashion within a legal order and thus its potential worth beyond the system in which it originated.

Three omitted norms – tying individual freedoms to tests of proportionality and necessity, human rights regimes and rule-orientated settlements of disputes – deserve more deliberation than will be granted within this book. The first two deal with the individual and are essential in understanding the necessity of regulating individual action and guaranteeing individual protection from constituted power holders.[20] The latter instils a system of dispute settlement that takes the function out of the individual's hands and places it within the governmental order.[21] Their omission here does not suggest that those omitted constitutional norms are insignificant or unimportant; rather their exclusion results from the focus of this book on global constitutionalism, and the identification of potential constituent and constituted power holders.[22] These omitted norms do not form part of the process connected to the identification of constituent and constituted power and the relationship each has with constitutionalism.

20 C. Gearty, *Principles of Human Rights Adjudication* (Oxford University Press, 2005), p. 122.

21 Tomkins, *Republican*; E. Petersmann, 'Constitutionalism and International Adjudication: How to Constitutionalize the UN Dispute Settlement System?' (1999) 31 *New York University Journal of International Law & Policy* 753.

22 See, for example, S. Gardbaum, 'Human Rights as International Constitutional Rights' (2008) 19 *European Journal of International Law* 749; Petersmann, 'Constitutional Justice', 769.

But, as these absent norms regulate others within the system, although they remain unconsidered here, they are inherent to any order claiming a constitutional moniker.

The identification of the nexus between the holders of power and those on whose behalf it is exercised provides the focus of debate on the process of global constitutionalisation. Working in combination as the legal fulcrum about which the exercise of constituent and constituted power is exercised, the rule of law, division of power and democratic legitimacy must form a substantive part of any discussion of the potential of constitutionalism beyond a state. The exercise of constituted power is checked by both the division of power and the rule of law. Constituent power is exercised, to an extent, through the persistence of democratic legitimacy within a constitutionalised regime. While other constitutional norms remain vital, the link between constituent and constituted power finds its axis here as the rule of law, division of power and democratic legitimacy are intrinsically linked to the suitability and potential presence of constitutionalism for the operation of a governance order that locates the body it serves at the centre of its operation.

It is important to note that there is no settled content for the rule of law, or indeed any other norm. Generally, although most believe they know the content of the rule of law, this has not aided in its exact delineation. While discussing the subject, Lord Bingham, a former Lord Chief Justice of the House of Lords, stated that 'I chose as my subject "The Rule of Law". I did so because the expression was constantly on people's lips, I was not quite sure what it meant, and I was not sure that all those who used the expression knew what they meant either, or meant the same thing.'[23] While this is not to suggest that the concept of rule of law in domestic legal systems is so vague as to be obtuse, it does suggest that constitutionalism does not have a set pattern to simply replicate within global constitutionalisation theories. If a core constitutional norm such as the rule of law remains open to discussion as to its exact content, there remains a margin for adaptation when transposed into a different legal order.

Further, running apart from any notion of constitutionalism, the debate on the rule by law must also be addressed as an alternate explanation of international law's current development. Rule by law, in which the holders of constituted power exercise their warrant through the law but are not regulated by it, or, to put it bluntly, are above the law, has most

[23] Bingham, *Rule of Law*, p. i.

recently come to prominence regarding discussions on Chinese domestic law.[24] Yet, given China's incremental expansion of activity within international law, the potential for describing global governance's development within the terms of the rule by law and its impact upon any constitutionalisation process, particularly regarding divisions of power and democratic legitimacy, must form part of this chapter's discussion.[25]

A constitutional system should include a configuration of the power relations between actors as well as clear and reviewable paths of law-making. In doing so, the constitutional order delineates the relationship between constituent and constituted power holders. Existing constitutional regimes accomplish such configurations by adopting norms that encompass an overall objective of maintaining the rule of law. Indeed, Cottier and Hertig are clear in their assertion that both the rule of law and the separation of powers are core concepts of liberal constitutionalism.[26] A global constitutional system would also maintain these characteristics, but these elements are nearly always opaque in their features and therefore cataloguing their content would probably not serve much purpose. Care must therefore be taken before embarking upon identifying what is and what is not constitutional. There are certain elements, such as the rule of law, that are easily called upon but are difficult to identify in their detail. There are other elements, particularly within administrative law, where the dividing line between what is rightly called constitutional and what is left to administrative law is not as clear.[27] It is not possible to give full scope to constitutional theory here, but in focusing on the rule of law, divisions of power and democratic legitimacy it is hoped to give a fuller context to the broader global constitutional debate and the recognition of the norms of constitutionalism.

Within constitutionalism, law restrains the political frame of action. In a process of constitutionalisation the legal framework resides somewhere along a spectrum, from where political action is undertaken unfettered by the law to a position where restraint is placed on the pursuit of constituent and constituted power. This does not necessarily mean that

[24] See, for example, D. Guo, 'The State and the Society of Rule by Law, and the Society by Citizens' (2007) 5 *Journal of Political Science and Law* 3; T. Ginsburg and T. Moustafa, *Rule by Law: The Politics of Courts in Authoritarian Regimes* (Cambridge University Press, 2008).

[25] A. L. Goodhart, 'Rule of Law and Absolute Sovereignty' (1957) 106 *University of Pennsylvania Law Review* 943, 494–8.

[26] Cottier and Hertig, '21st Constitutionalism', 266.

[27] A. W. Bradley and K. D. Ewing, *Constitutional Law and Administration Law*, 14th edn (Harlow: Pearson, 2007), pp. 657–8.

the final evolutionary destination must inevitably be a constitutionalised system. Rather this book asserts that, in claiming constitutionalism as a terminus, proponents of global constitutionalisation need to identify the features of a constitutionalised system. Further, at the core of any claims to an on-going global constitutionalisation process must be the accurate employment of the norms inherent in any constitutional order.

2.2 The norms of constitutionalism: the rule of law, divisions of power and democratic legitimacy

2.2.1 Rule of law

The rule of law, both as an instrument enabling a modicum of certainty within a legal order and as a tool to prevent the entrenchment of power, possesses normative functions that are instrumental in establishing law at the centre of a political unit.[28] This section considers how the rule of law operates within constitutionalism and thus, ultimately, what it may mean for global constitutionalisation. Singling out the rule of law, alongside the divisions of power and democratic legitimacy, as intrinsic links to constituent and constituted power immediately sets it as central to governance, even beyond constitutionalism. Accordingly, it becomes essential to acknowledge that while the domestic and international rules of law debates are fundamentally linked and thus are of great import to each other, its mere presence does not foreshadow an automatic constitutionalisation process.[29] Rather, the rule of law's increasing importance to debate within international law signifies a further legalisation as institutions, particularly courts, together with several self-contained regimes centred upon particular areas of law, rise in number. In such scenarios, the rule of law points towards legalisation. In contrast, in circumstances where the entrenchment of the rule of law forms part of a broader normative project centred upon constitutionalism it becomes an indicator of a potential constitutionalisation process.

The intention behind this analysis is to grasp the importance of the rule of law to the constitutionalisation debate, and doing so aids in establishing its role in the global context. Koskenniemi contends

[28] Though as Griffith warns, 'The Rule of Law is an invaluable concept for those who wish not to change the present set-up.' Griffith, 'The Political Constitution', 15.

[29] See A. Nollkaemper, 'The Internationalized Rule of Law' (2009) 1 *Hague Journal on the Rule of Law* 74.

that 'the rule of law hopes to fix the universal in a particular, positive space (a law, a moral or procedural principle or institution)'.[30] He also warns against judging questions such as sovereignty upon such tenets as civilisation, democracy or indeed the rule of law itself. This warning forms part of a broader argument against confusing the rule of law with broader questions regarding international law's evolution. This is a point of great import for international law's historical development, as too often the rule of law's employment masks apparent inadequacies in global governance.[31]

The rule of law can mean little beyond political rhetoric without some specific content behind its employment.[32] Raz cautions against assuming too much will about the importance of the rule of law. He argues that to assume too much will often result in nothing more than a reaffirming slogan.[33] As Waldron asserts, in the context of domestic law, it can easily mean nothing more than our side is great.[34] Although this does not give full credence to the actual importance of the rule of law, it does characterise why, as a notion within constitutionalism, it is vital to understand its role as a norm forming part of the constitutionalisation process and not simply as a rallying cry or part of a vague argument on governance; even if in the latter circumstance, the mere invocation of the rule of law, even a flawed one, shows its significance.[35]

Raz quotes Hayek, stressing that 'stripped of all technicalities' the rule of law 'means that government in all its actions is bound by rules fixed and announced beforehand – rules which make it possible to foresee with fair certainty how the authority will use its coercive powers in

[30] M. Koskenniemi, *The Gentle Civilizer of Nations: The Rise and Fall of International Law 1870–1960* (Cambridge University Press, 2001), p. 507.

[31] *Ibid.*, p. 178. [32] Bingham, *Rule of Law*, p. 171.

[33] J. Raz, *The Authority of Law* (Oxford University Press, 1979), p. 210; there are many other important discourses regarding the rule of law, which will not be considered in detail here, such as R. Dworkin, 'Political Judges and the Rule of Law' in A. Kavanagh and J. Oberdiek (eds.), *Arguing about the Law* (London: Routledge, 2009), pp. 191–211.

[34] J. Waldron, 'Is the Rule of Law an Essentially Contested Concept (in Florida)' in R. Bellamy (ed.), *The Rule of Law and the Separation of Powers* (London: Ashgate, 2005), p. 119.

[35] This is not to suggest that currently there is no rule of law within international law. The Universal Declaration of Human Rights asserts that 'it is essential, if man is not to be compelled to have recourse, as a last resort, to rebellion against tyranny and oppression, that human rights should be protected by the rule of law' *Universal Declaration of Human Rights* General Assembly Resolution, 217A (III) UN Doc. A/810 (1948) or indeed 2005 World Summit Outcome Document, UN Doc. A/RES/60/1 (16 September 2005), available at www.un.org/womenwatch/ods/A-RES-60-1-E.pdf, para. 134, accessed 9 December 2013.

given circumstances, and to plan one's individual affairs on the basis of knowledge'.[36] This definition is neither fully procedural nor substantive in character, instead focusing on the restraint of government, and as such, constituted power holders. The debate on substantive versus procedural rule of law remains significant particularly as global law seeks to establish itself as fully compliant with its core tenets.

Describing the rule of law as an all-encompassing doctrine that includes all laws and the systems to which these pertain is all too easy and should be avoided.[37] Such claims become tangled in attempting to identify the rule of law as an embodiment of an entire legal system and ultimately are unsuccessful in establishing its role within constitutionalism. Raz correctly argues against using the rule of law to merely describe all the positive attributes of a particular legal system, an error that is readily replicated beyond domestic orders.[38] Such uses undermine the rule of law's value beyond mere legalisation. For example, it is argued in the international context that '[t]he symbolic value of the ideal of the rule of law makes it worth preserving. The ideal itself cannot bring about international order but without it the concept of international order loses its attractive force.'[39]

This claim underscores the difficulties for constitutionalisation. The assumption that constitutionalism requires not simply symbolism but substantive action reflecting the necessary attributes of the rule of law must form part of constitutionalisation in any legal order. Such symbolic invocation for political intention pertains towards rule by law rather than then submission of constituted power to law. It is not enough to claim that the presence of the rule of law creates a constitutional legal order; the rule of law cannot be merely symbolic but must have some role to play within the legal system. Otherwise it will become, as Waldron cautions, nothing more than an affirmation that our side is better.[40]

[36] Raz, *Authority*, p. 210; F. A. Hayek, *The Road to Serfdom*, 2nd edn (London: Routledge, 2001).

[37] Raz, *Authority*, p. 210.

[38] See, for a further discussion, M. Kumm, 'The Legitimacy of International Law: A Constitutionalist Framework of Analysis' (2004) 15 *European Journal of International Law* 907.

[39] D. Georgiev, 'Politics or Rule of Law: Deconstruction and Legitimacy in International Law' (1993) 4 *European Journal of International Law* 1, 3.

[40] Waldron, 'Contested Concept' in Bellamy *The Rule of Law*, p. 119.

Tomkins is wary of approaching the rule of law from the 'politics bad, law good' perspective.[41] Evangelisation of the law can very easily occur if the rule of law is accorded a place that replaces political and authoritative power. This arguably is the case when advocates, in their attempt to prove that international law is more than politics, sometimes overemphasise the rule of law instead of understanding the elemental role it can play in establishing the remit of action of authoritative power.[42] The rule of law maintains that law not power prevails and underpins other values that follow in the constitutional order, including divisions of power and democratic legitimacy. Loughlin argues, while discussing the nature of politics with regard to the state, statecraft and constitutional law, that

> many of the ideals associated with law, especially those of the rule of law and the assimilation of law to justice, help to create intimacy, shape identity, generate trust, and strengthen direct manipulation by power-wielders remove certain disputes from partisan political politics and this too bolsters faith in the system. Belief in the law-governed nature of the state can be a means of generating political power and a powerful aspect of state-building.[43]

This he links with the idea of seeing constitutional law as a 'third order of the political' (the first being politics as conflict and the second being politics as statecraft), a system of law that is protected from the manipulation of power. He argues that the rule of law, within constitutionalism, is an aspect of a 'political right', where the 'sovereign authority of the state can be recognised'.[44] This link with the political directly connects the exercise of constituted power to a constitutional order and thus also to the exercise of constituent power, and further recognises the importance of the political to the rule of law's operation.[45]

Generally, it is not disputed that the rule of law is desirable for a legal order; rather it is in the particulars where disagreement occurs. A quite narrow and very much common-law version of the rule of law, identified by Dicey, necessitates 'the equal subjection of all classes to the ordinary law of the land administered by the ordinary Law courts'.[46] Here, the

41 Tomkins, *Republican*, 13.
42 For a discussion of this position see Georgiev, 'Politics or Rule of Law', 4–7.
43 M. Loughlin, *The Idea of Public Law* (Oxford University Press, 2003), p. 42.
44 *Ibid.*, p. 43.
45 Loughlin, *Idea of Public Law*, pp. 99–113; and S. Tierney 'Sovereignty and the Idea of Public Law' in E. A. Christodoulidis and S. Tierney (eds.), *Public Law and Politics: The Scope and Limits of Constitutionalism* (London: Ashgate, 2008), p. 15.
46 A. V. Dicey, *Introduction to the Study of the Law of the Constitution*, 8th edn (London: Macmillan, 1915), pp. 198–9.

judiciary acts to uphold the checks-and-balances system linking the rule of law to the separation of powers, and reflecting the political climate at Dicey's time of writing his seminal overview of UK public law. When he was writing in 1915, in the confines of the UK system, such a narrow definition of the rule of law, reliant on political actors in Parliament, may well have held sway. Yet, beyond the particular importance of parliamentary sovereignty in the UK system, such a restricted vision of the rule of law holds limited resonance. For instance, both Loughlin's and Raz's perspectives as to the components of the rule of law are far broader and recognise the importance of both constituent and constituted power in its operation.[47]

As Goodhart points out 'there is no distinction in theory between the absolutism of Parliament and that of the most despotic monarchs', a point of critique of not only Dicey's rule of law but also incidences when its presence is claimed; however, in reality, it is a governance order with an instrumental use of law.[48] The critical nature of this distinction becomes evident in discussions of Chinese constitutionalism, which openly uses a rule-by-law paradigm on the basis of a transition towards an eventual rule-of-law structure.[49] The combination of the lack of supervision by constituent power holders in a context in which legitimacy centres on the common operation of a governance order, it is not the absence of law but rather its instrumental use that distinguishes rule by law from its counterpart.[50] A question arises as to whether a system may be described as constitutionalised if it, as yet, contains only a rule-by-law order. Arguably, it cannot, and this opens the question for global constitutionalisation as to whether it is on a trajectory towards the rule of law as a fully operational element of its governance order if traces of rule by law remain.

Dicey's emphasis on the judiciary wielding the power to enforce the rule of law arguably reduces the ability of other constituted or indeed constituent power holders to act to ensure its operation. Such reliance on one constituted power holder, here the judiciary, also concentrates the ability to tailor its operation to one point of governance, an argument that will be later discussed in relation to democratic legitimacy. Scepticism of Dicey's position does not deny the place of the judiciary, as often they are the actors who place the rule of law beyond formal legality, but rather

[47] Loughlin, *Idea of Public Law*, p. 43. [48] Goodhart, 'Rule of Law', 950.

[49] R. Peerenboom, *China's Long March towards the Rule of Law* (Cambridge University Press, 2002).

[50] S. Chesterman, 'An International Rule of Law?' (2008) 56 *American Journal of Comparative Law* 331, 336.

requires us also to emphasise the place of democratic actors within the rule of law. To insist that the operation of the rule of law is left to the judiciary compromises the democratic nature of constitutionalism, as it takes an important factor of its structure and places it beyond the holders of constituent power. In a constitutionalisation process that is underdeveloped or ill-defined in its governance structures, such reliance on the judiciary becomes ever more attenuated, the danger of which may be observed within global governance where the role of courts has yet to be settled firmly.[51]

The rule of law does not require that all actions of power should be prescribed or described by law; no legal system achieves or would arguably want to achieve this aim, as such curtailment of politics would restrain reform and progression, introducing an entirely conservative model of constitutionalism.[52] Fuller's famous list of essential elements of the rule of law: general, public, prospective, clear, compatible with one another, possible to obey, stable and consistently applied, have been influential in understanding its operation.[53] Yet, as Dworkin has alluded to, this procedural vision of the rule of law may buttress an evil system.[54] The procedural rule of law, as proposed here by Fuller, certainly leads to urgent questions as to its potential use. The procedural rule of law's advocates concentrate on its proposed democratic nature as a bar put on Dworkin's evil system.[55] The relative importance of procedural rules versus moral or substantive rules remains unsettled, yet this list does present what the law should at the least at a minimum entail.[56] Yet, keeping Raz's warning in mind, the conception of a rule of law, procedural or substantive, is central to a constitutionalised legal system, and the ambiguities should not be used to enable an otherwise questionable constitutionalisation process to pass muster.[57] The procedural rule of law appears to be neutral as to content. It does not require there to be one ideological system or another,

[51] For a discussion of the place of the judiciary and legality, see Gearty, *Human Rights*, p. 60.

[52] Though see Bianchi on ad hocism, which will be discussed later. A. Bianchi, 'Ad-hocism and the Rule of Law' (2002) 13 *European Journal of International Law* 263.

[53] L. Fuller, *The Morality of Law* (New Haven, CT: Yale University Press, 1964).

[54] R. Dworkin, 'Political Judges' in Kavanagh and Oberdiek (eds.), '*Arguing about the Law*', pp. 191–211.

[55] For an argument in favour of a pure procedural rule of law, see Gearty, *Human Rights*, p. 60.

[56] D. Dyzenhaus, *Hard Cases in Wicked Legal Systems: South African Law in the Perspective of Legal Philosophy* (Oxford: Clarendon Press, 1981).

[57] Guo, 'Society by Citizens', 3.

but what procedural rule of law, at the very least, does seem to necessitate is a system where law cannot be exercised, created or acted upon in an arbitrary fashion. It thus maintains a sphere within which the law must operate, though in this characterisation without any particular substantive element to this law.

Allan argues that respect for the rule of law by citizens and the judiciary does not require absolute obedience to the legislature but rather what he describes as a 'more discriminating response, respectful of the constitution as a source of moral constraints on those in power'.[58] This perspective acknowledges the importance of the democratic or constituent elements of the rule of law while also placing constitutionalism alongside it and emphasises the relationship between the two in ensuring against majoritarianism. Thus, it is argued, the rule of law is central to constitutionalism and vice versa.[59]

Arguably, within a differentiated system with a weak judicial arm it would be inadvisable to simply rely upon those with the lawmaking authority to both establish and maintain the rule of law. This is the case for a number of reasons that will be reoccurring themes throughout this piece – the position of constituted and constituent power, the presence or absence of a constituency or community, as well as the disparity in representation or democratic gaps in constituencies. An assurance of democratic legitimacy within the global legal structure would militate towards accepting Fuller's procedural rule of law as appropriate for that order. However, even if this were the case, a basic substantive structure would have to set the parameters of both legal and political action to prevent the potential development of an 'evil system', which Fuller suggests is not at issue, but as Allan argues with regard to majoritarianism, remains a possibility. This necessarily leads to the question of what would constitute the substantive elements of the rule of law. Bingham proposes that (amongst other elements) the rule of law requires 'that the laws of the land should apply equally to all, save to the extent that objective differences justify differentiation', but more than that it requires normative content.[60]

[58] T. R. S. Allan, 'Fairness, Equality, Rationality: Constitutional Theory and Judicial Review' in C. F. Forsyth and I. Hare (eds.), *The Golden Metwand and the Crooked Cord* (Oxford University Press, 1998), p. 17.

[59] However, Gearty is critical of this approach and favours a rule of law that does not focus upon content but rather relies on the constructed system of lawmaking; Gearty, *Human Rights*, p. 64.

[60] T. Bingham, 'The Rule of Law' (2007) 66 *Cambridge Law Journal* 67, 73.

The rule of law directly interconnects constitutionalism and politics. From the perspective of international law, sovereignty traditionally (in the Westphalia mode) tends to play a very particular role and that is to establish the absolute authority of the state.[61] This could be set against Loughlin's consideration of sovereignty where authority is identified in a governance order.[62] Nonetheless, outside of limited sovereignty there is a need to understand how the exercise of authority or sovereignty internally within law works and what impact, if any, global constitutionalisation would have upon domestic understandings of the rule of law. An important element in Bingham's approach to domestic constitutionalism is compliance by states with their international legal obligations.[63] Presently, this is more relevant to domestic rule of law per se; nevertheless, within the system of law that may emerge from constitutionalisation, respect for legal obligations both horizontally at the international and domestic level and vertically between the systems would be relevant. If the rule of law in the domestic sphere maintains the exercise of authority within the realms of the law then it must necessarily have the same purpose within the global sphere. Thus, the rule of law becomes elemental to any constitutionalisation process within the global legal order. Therefore, characterising the relationship between the two as entirely separate becomes impossible. Should the global legal order become constitutional, then the interaction between domestic and global constitutional rules of law would require some commonality with regard to their mutual understanding of its meaning.

The rule of law at the basic level requires the law to be applied equally, created openly and administered fairly. As a minimum requirement, this, when incorporated into constitutionalism, ensures a system that restrains the exercise of constituted power. The rule of law can subsist without constitutionalism but it is essential to a constitutional order and therefore is a must for any process of constitutionalisation or theories that underpin the debate. Later chapters will discuss what this would mean for a global constitutionalisation process, but presently it is important to state that constitutionalisation necessitates a substantive rule of law.

61 D. Krasner, *Sovereignty: Organised Hypocrisy* (Princeton University Press, 1999), pp. 20–5.

62 See, for instance, O. Schachter, 'International Law in Theory and Practice', 178 *Recueil des Cours* 2, 674; and H. Charlesworth and C. Chinkin, *The Boundaries of International Law: A Feminist Analysis* (Manchester University Press, 2000), pp. 124–70.

63 Bingham, 'The Rule of Law', 81; and Bingham, *Rule of Law*, p. 129.

2.2.2 Divisions of power

Investigating divisions of power within constitutional paradigms, this section considers the forms in which such divisions operate. If constituted power is to satisfy constitutionalism, it must be divided; however, the nature of such divisions, and their importance to constitutionalism within a constitutionalisation process, are contestable. An examination of the functional rationale of division of constituted power, its basis as a norm of constitutionalism and its relationship with other norms are considered herein to illuminate the justification for its inclusion. Several domestic constitutional models, centred on a separation-of-powers model, are considered. Rather than suggesting that global constitutionalisation should follow one or other domestic models, a point that will be returned to in later chapters, this discussion considers the varied forms in which divisions occur within domestic orders.

Loughlin argues that the separation of powers is an Enlightenment construct and, as such, there is no inevitability about its presence in constitutional orders.[64] In contrast, Petersmann traces the separation of powers from Plato, through the Enlightenment, to modern states, maintaining that restraint of power was often regarded as a necessity through the history of debate over governance orders.[65] Loughlin's perspective clearly links divisions of power to sovereignty and the Enlightenment move from the sovereign as monarch to other agents of constituted (e.g. Parliament in the UK) or constituent (e.g. US or Irish constitutionalism) power. Indeed, possessing sovereignty remains a feature of contemporary governance associated with the monopoly of power within a state.[66] Questioning the utility of present divisions of power and regarding their presence as an anachronism that resulted from a theory that historically achieved most of its original aims raises important issues. The utility of ensuring separate power structures in a shift from a monarchic to a democratic system, while no longer a present concern, was during a period of domestic constitutionalisation. The question is whether similar structures are required during transformation at the global level. Global constitutionalisation presents an ideal opportunity to either abandon an

[64] Loughlin, *Idea of Public Law*, pp. 32–53, 48. Indeed Loughlin credits Montesquieu and Locke as the founders of the doctrine. Though he also states that they both recognised the essential role of the government.

[65] Petersmann, '21st Century', 12.

[66] Krasner, *Sovereignty*.

outmoded function, or, at the very least, question its purpose as a tool of governance during a period of transitional governance to nascent constitutionalism.

Loughlin remarks that '[t]he error of constitutional legalism is of a most basic kind, that of mistaking a part for the whole'; as such, it could be argued that often constitutional analysis is unreflective of the fleeting nature of governance and constitutional frameworks.[67] As the historical context changes, so too must the accompanying constitutional structures, and Loughlin suggests that the theoretical elements that underpin constitutionalism are of paramount importance. This critique is connected to the domestic exercise of power mirrored in the debates surrounding the 'crisis of territoriality' and its implications for the state and the extent of the state's remit within international law.[68] This approach questions the division of constituted power at the domestic level, querying whether a further orientation upwards to the international level or downwards to a more local level is underway.

In concert with other tenets such as democratic legitimacy, whose full operation sits as part of the divisional structure, divisions of power form a core constitutional norm. Divisions of power restrain constituted power holders from making despotic use of their monopoly within states. Sovereignty remains central to governance both within and beyond the state during a process of global constitutionalisation, requiring a restraint of constituted power. During the process that led sovereignty to move from the individual to the state, the division of power was necessary. Potentially then, as its constituted power holders first begin to exercise their warrant, a nascent constitutionalism requires division as a precaution to maintain other constitutional norms, such as the rule of law. From Loughlin's perspective the division of the traditional separation of powers into a triumvirate of carefully identifiable sectors of power does not need emulation. Certainly, the executive, legislative and judiciary separation-of-powers model does not need replication within global constitutionalisation. Instead, funnelling power into different avenues to prevent the over-grasping nature of power's character is of central import and underlies the division required.

For Loughlin it is not the doctrine of separation of powers as originally envisaged by Locke that is the focus of current debate but rather the

[67] Loughlin, *Idea of Public Law*, p. 49.

[68] S. Benhabib, 'Borders, Boundaries, and Citizenship' (2005) 38 *Political Science and Politics* 673.

centrality of law and legalism to the exercise of power.[69] If the notion of a check on unfettered governing by one group of actors is at the core of the divisions of power, and replication is essential within global constitutionalism, this opens up a space broader than what, at first, seems plausible in governance beyond the state. While some form of division, based upon functions between points of governance is required, a pure division between the executive, legislature and judiciary is unnecessary. As such, in evaluating the variant functionality of models of division such as vertical, horizontal or mixed systems of division, the underlying rationale of the entrenchment of legalism in governance is what the division brings into the realms of constitutional normativity. Thus, while the historical rationale for the division of constituted power may not be present within global constitutionalism, the need to prescribe the exercise of sovereignty once it shifts from one core point (the state in international law) to other points, requires regulation and to be present during a process of constitutionalisation.

Shifting the focus from the executive, legislative and judicial separation to what is described as the geographical or vertical separation of powers may produce a useful basis for analysis of global constitutionalisation as part of the inter-related multiplicity of constitutional orders. The geographical separation of powers focuses on the vertical distribution of power. Different functions of constituted power are performed at the local, federal, national, regional and international levels. An example of this at work would be those EU federal states that have strong local governance within the federal system, regional commitments at the EU level and global commitments in the guise of the operation of Chapter VII Security Council resolutions. As such, this is not a new doctrine, having already found a place within the context of federalist states, a state having undergone devolution or in a process of integration, as within the EU in the form of subsidiarity.[70] As developed by Loveland, geographical division of power could be as pertinent to global constitutionalism as it has been in portraying the federal state or the EU.[71]

[69] See, for example, I. Ward, *The English Constitution, Myths and Realities* (Oxford: Hart, 2004), pp. 78–81; J. Locke, *Two Treatises of Government*, 3rd edn (Cambridge University Press, 1988).

[70] See, for example, I. Pernice, 'Multilevel Constitutionalism and the Treaty of Amsterdam, European Constitution Making Revisited' (1999) 36 *Common Market Law Review* 703.

[71] I. Loveland, *Constitutional Law, Administrative Law and Human Rights: A Critical Introduction*, 5th edn (Oxford University Press, 2009), p. 14.

Geographical division of power describes different territorial centres operating at separate levels of governance. In other words, it regards power as divided into geographical locations or spaces as well as across one geographical/state space in the traditional sense, thus a combination of vertical and horizontal divisions. For example, within the federalised state this means that power may be located centrally, as well as at the federal state level. In terms of the connection between the exercise of constituted power and legalism, the geographical separation of powers in distributing power vertically, and also by inculcating a regulatory element of supervision into each layer of power, provides for a limitation on the exercise of constituted power to be fused into the system.[72] While the horizontal divisions of power remain weak, the vertical separation of powers provides for balance to be established in the system.

Explaining US constitutional history and federalism, Loveland describes the geographical separation of powers as 'creating a multiplicity of powerful political societies within a single nation-state, each wielding significant political powers within precisely defined geographical boundaries' and further that the geographical separation of powers was a 'fundamental political principle underpinning the constitutional settlement'.[73] While admittedly this is within a specific constitutional context it potentially does offer a wider application where the complexities and differentiations between the political societies require a settlement that recognises and incorporates these into the constitutional structure. In a legal system that has multiple layers of constituted power and where the exercise of constituent power may take place simultaneously at different points, a vertical separation of powers is appropriate to regulating the exercise of power. Within global constitutionalisation the issue then becomes whether there is a move towards a unitary system with one horizontal separation of powers or one based upon a vertical geographical separation of powers (or a combination of both vertical and horizontal layers).

What makes the US system particularly important and arguably relevant for our purpose is that it provides for a 'legally constituent basis for the *simultaneous* co-existence of alternative governmental programmes'.[74]

[72] G. J. Craven, 'A Few Fragments of State Constitutional Law' (1990) 20 *University of Western Australia Law Review* 353, 355.

[73] Loveland, *Constitutional Law*, p. 311; Loveland also notes that Canada has a similar federal arrangement along the geographical line. For another discussion of US constitutional history, see M. Tushnet, *The Constitution of the United States of America: A Contextual Analysis* (Oxford: Hart, 2009), pp. 9–39.

[74] Loveland, *Constitutional Law*, p. 311.

Such a basis is not available to those states that have unitary or single separation of powers (that is non-federal states such as Ireland). Though, importantly, states that are neither devolved nor federal and thus only possess the horizontal model generally remain constitutionally viable. This is most often because of the lack of remoteness between constituent and constituted power holders, either due to geographically compactness or active and direct democratic structures. Arguably, both the USA and Australia possess two separation of powers structures (or three if those that exist within the states themselves are included). The legislative, executive and judicial order at the federal or horizontal level (together with the horizontal at state level) as well as a vertical separation of powers recognisable in the federal and state government structure. This combined vertical and horizontal model provides a system that is pluralist but also ensures that constituent power is not distanced from governance.[75] This notion of constituency will be discussed in some detail later, but presently it is important to note that this geographical separation of powers would, at least, give room for the acknowledgement of pluralist legal systems both domestically and internationally, though it does seem to give more space to the former than to the latter.

A related, though not identical, model is suggested by Cottier and Hertig, a division of power described as a '[f]ive story house'.[76] Levels of governance include the local, through a federal system, to the state, to the EU and finally at the global governance level. According to the authors, each of these has constitutional governance elements, though their interaction with other constitutional norms is not prominent in their consideration of this governance structure beyond the descriptive. While not all current state systems are federal, the proposal calls for two levels at the very least; the domestic and international. Significantly, it does not require that each system mirror others as regards to structure or content. While the authors do not directly address the issue of division of power as such, this is very much linked to the idea of the allocation of powers and is akin to geographical models of division. These present a reasoned basis for understanding how a division of power may be understood beyond the horizontal model, where the state is no longer taking centre stage as an ultimate authoritarian base.

[75] South Africa also provides another version of the geographic separation of powers; A. Johnston, 'South Africa: The Election and the Transition Process – Five Contradictions in Search of a Resolution' (1994) 15 *Third World Quarterly* 187.

[76] Cottier and Hertig, '21st Constitutionalism', 299–304.

Loveland argues that particularly within UK constitutionalism, the lack of a geographical division of power (until devolution, though he argues with the added complication of parliamentary supremacy that this is not geographical separation of powers as such; however, he does acknowledge the place of local government)[77] meant that the UK lacks constituent status and therefore could only have a moral basis of governance. While there is not enough space here to enter into the debate as to the status of UK public law, it raises some issues as to the possible form and value of vertical division of power. The nature of constituted power and questions of democratic legitimacy find some prominence in questions relating to the distance between constituent and constituted power holders and the potential limit of remoteness.[78] The nexus between constituency, constituted and constituent power is also pertinent when considering the impact of value- or moral-laden power structures, which aim to resolve questions of remoteness and whether the existence of a horizontal or vertical division of power or both can ensure that this is not at issue.[79]

An order may be horizontal, horizontal and vertical, or, potentially, vertical only; there is no 'perfect' system. Divisions of power aim to divest sole holders of constituted power of a portion of their authority. This divestment may be achieved through a number of structures, but division remains central and must exist for a governance system to be described as constitutional, particularly in the nascent period of its operation. Divisions of power maintain the closeness between constituent and constituted power holders ensuring that both remoteness and democratic legitimacy are not at issue within the governance structure. They also enable constituted power holders to ensure their co-actors exercise their warrants within the realm of the rule of law, making them a requisite constitutional norm.

Cottier and Hertig present a model where the importance lies with the vertical divide, Loveland argues that separation of powers may intertwine both forms, while Loughlin regards the separation of powers as a relic of an earlier era. The models suggested by geographic separation of powers, as well as by Cottier and Hertig, imply that there is no specific minimum required to establish a 'true' division of power, but arguably questions of remoteness suggest otherwise. Ultimately, a division of

[77] Loveland, *Constitutional Law*, pp. 312–46.

[78] Craven, 'A Few Fragments', 355.

[79] Presenting clearly the more traditional account of the preference for this unity over federalism, see Ward's description of Bagehot in Ward, *The English Constitution*, pp. 20–2.

power allocates constituted power between governance structures. While the geographic model incorporates two forms of division of power, one horizontal and the other vertical, the question is whether a functioning system may have but one axis of division and still rightly be called constitutional. Arguably, states that are neither devolved nor federal possess the horizontal model only and, yet, function constitutionally. Hitherto, there are no sole vertical divisions of power in operation that satisfy the necessary attributes of constitutionalism within the international or domestic order. Such a conclusion implies that to ensure the fettering of constituted power within a constitutionalisation process, a strong divisions system that excludes remoteness yet ensures that each point of governance possesses some restraint over another with at least a horizontal and, in some orders, a necessary vertical system to accompany it, is indispensable for constitutionalism.

2.2.3 *Democratic legitimacy*

The entrenchment of democracy as an ideal and valid governance system within states has been protracted; however, it has all but succeeded in establishing, where constituent power is recognised as essential, the notion of equitable group decision-making as the standard of legitimate authority. While at times its implementation leaves a lot to be desired, democracy's claim to hold constituted power holders to account by the exercise of constituent power holders' warrant is broadly accepted as a necessary element in establishing legitimate democratic authority. The question of whether this third norm, democratic legitimacy, is indispensable and sits as a core element of constitutionalism, or whether the rule of law and division of powers together sustain legitimacy in a constitutional governance order, lies at the centre of this investigation. This section focuses on the concept and normative value of democratic legitimacy in constitutionalism rather than debating the bases of democracy's many and myriad forms.[80] Just as with the rule of law and division of powers, the section asks whether democratic legitimacy needs to be present to invoke the term 'constitutional' and, further, to what extent and form it must be ensconced.

Democracy is not a monolithic notion. Within domestic governance, democracy habitually comes in two forms: direct democracies, where

[80] For a worldwide view of the instances of democracy, see www.freedomhouse.org/reports, accessed 30 August 2013.

constituent power holders are engaged in governance, and representative democracy, where government is appointed by those elected in the exercise of constituent power holders' warrant. Democratic legitimacy is bound to the recognition of constituent power holders, as without their identification, even outside of constitutionalism, it is almost impossible to adjudge whether democracy is even operational. In establishing a route towards legitimate decision-making, democracy links constituent and constituted power holders. In this book it is democracy's function as informed by its place in establishing legitimate authority and its operation in connection with other norms from which it garners some of its legitimacy that marks its place as fundamental to constitutional purchase. Although democracy may be participative or representative or both, in order to establish legitimacy, arguably, it must have some substantive form linking constituent and constituted power holders together and from whence to garner who will benefit from constitutionalism's operation.

Whether other forms of political authority may claim legitimacy to the extent necessary to embody constitutionalism and claim that moniker is a necessary query. Albeit that such questions remains unconsidered here beyond understanding that constituent power's necessary force in a system relying on the rule of law would largely be absent from a governance order devoid of democracy.[81] Grumm argues emphatically that the democratic legitimacy and the rule of law cannot be separated without diminishing the achievements of constitutionalism itself.[82] He argues that politics must be submitted to law but also that other sources of legitimacy, in democracy's stead, would undermine the function of a constitution. The question then is whether a democratic constitutional order is a *sine qua non* of constitutionalism or rather whether constitutional purchase can subsist by relying on the rule of law and divisions of power in combination with other constitutional norms but absent democracy.

Historically, certainly there were states, such as the UK, that were constitutional without being simultaneously fully democratic, a process that remained unfulfilled in the UK and other states until women were finally given the vote in parity with men.[83] This implies that from a

[81] J. Dunn, *Setting the People Free: The Story of Democracy* (London: Atlantic Books, 2005), pp. 13–15.

[82] D. Grumm, 'The Achievement of Constitutionalism and Its Prospects in a Changed World' in Dobner and Loughlin (eds.), *Twilight*, p. 10.

[83] Though children's rights advocates may claim for a further enfranchisement, this is a question of degree rather than class of person; A. Nolan, 'The Child as "Democratic Citizen": Challenging the "Participation Gap"' (2010) *Public Law* 767.

certain perspective it is possible to regard constitutionalism as independent of democracy in achieving legitimacy or alternatively its presence is necessary to regard constitutionalism as fully inculcated into a governance order. Justice Breyer of the US Supreme Court argues that 'constitutions create a framework for a certain kind of government … [whose] general objective can be described … as … democratic self-government'. This suggests that within constitutionalism, as it is currently understood, democratic legitimacy is an essential aspect of its operation. Further, while the UK may have been on a trajectory towards constitutionalism, as with transitional governance orders, the absence of a fully operational democratic structure suggests incomplete implementation or at the very least a historically primitive understanding of constitutionalism.[84] It is a charge that may also be made against the constitutional structures of states that still do not allow women to exercise the vote or indeed South Africa during the time of apartheid.[85]

Gould links democracy with an individual right to self-government, which also establishes a right to democratic participation.[86] While this right of participation is rudimentary in establishing legitimacy of action by the constituted power holders, it is the ultimate base of governance. Whether substantive as well as procedural equality between constituent power holders is necessary is not without controversy, as are questions related to the recognition of an elite polity, and this necessarily ties with Gould's argument. Such debates hold resonance in critiques of the acclaimed sovereign equality of states, a point that will be returned to in the discussion of global constitutionalisation. Democratic legitimacy overcomes claims of absolute truth based in religion or theory, or the idea that elites are best placed to decide the common good, by its operation within the broader normative regime.[87]

Although democratic legitimacy may be equated with the popular opinion that governments should carry out the wishes of those who elected them, in common with Rehfeld, for the purposes of

[84] C. Turner, 'Delivering Lasting Peace, Democracy and Human Rights in Times of Transition: The Role of International Law' (2008) 2 *International Journal of Transitional Justice* 126.

[85] Only two states completely restrict women's suffrage, Saudi Arabia and the Holy See, while others, such as Lebanon, have restrictive qualifications exclusively for women.

[86] C. Gould, *Rethinking Democracy: Freedom and Social Co-operation in Politics, Economy, and Society* (Cambridge University Press, 1990), p. 45.

[87] Grumm, 'The Achievement of Constitutionalism' in Dobner and Loughlin (eds.), *Twilight*, p. 10.

constitutionalism as a normative doctrine, this is rejected as insufficient for full legitimacy, as public opinion must also be bound by the rule of law.[88] Critiques of participative democracy centre upon the limitations of public opinion if democracy is not understood to mean majoritarianism. Thus, although the preference may be for participative democracy, as this seems to be the most relevant in ensuring that constituents are embedded in the system, in conjunction with the other essential elements of constitutionalism, such democratic action is not synonymous with majoritarianism. Constitutional democracy ought not to operate so as to disenfranchise some holders of constituent power, but rather democracy must be tempered by other norms, establishing a more complex understanding of constitutional democracy focused upon forms of governance. As Sunstein argues, majority rule should not be identified with democracy, as constitutionalism itself curtails the majority from actions that would repress the minority.[89] Democracy's restraint is provided by the rule of law, divisions of power as well as the rights and duties that are central to constitutionalism and necessary to assert the equality between constituent power holders, themselves fundamental to democracy. As such, constitutionalism's own legitimacy emanates from the observance of its core norms.

Wheatley argues that 'the principle of equality between human persons and need for justification for the exercise of political authority leads to a recognition that democratic laws can only be legitimated through discursive procedures of opinion – and will-formation that result in a consensus among participants'.[90]

Rehfeld obliges some justification for the holders of constituent power to accept the legitimacy of governmental action, including a requirement for transparency. The opinion of the constituent power holders and the justification for and transparency of action all contribute to establishing the legitimacy necessary for a democratic system to function. According to Mouffe democratic participation is ineradicably antagonistic in the sense that debate is always occurring.[91] While the nature of this antagonism can be curtailed by associating with deliberative or majority democracies, the

[88] A. Rehfeld, *The Concept of Constituency* (Cambridge University Press, 2005), pp. 15–16.

[89] C. R. Sunstein, *Designing Democracy: What Constitutions Do* (Oxford University Press, 2001), p. 97; for an interesting discussion of the various theories that discuss democracy and judicial review, see J. Goldsworthy, 'Structural Judicial Review and the Objection from Democracy' (2010) 60 *University of Toronto Law Journal* 137.

[90] S. Wheatley, *The Democratic Legitimacy of International Law* (Oxford: Hart, 2010), p. 1.

[91] C. Mouffe, *The Democratic Paradox* (London: Verso, 2000), p. 117.

essential idea of equal participation and responsibility remains. In a deliberative democracy, reasoned discussion to reach consensus on some form of compromise results in law being accepted and coming into operation. This does not necessarily result in wide agreement, but rather a debate on what decision ought to be made.[92] Thus, deliberative and participatory democracy requires a substantive rule of law as well as a rights-based commitment to expression and debate and, while the latter is not comprehensively discussed here, it illustrates that constitutionalism requires the presence of a network of interdependent norms.

Pitkin argues that constitutions carry out two functions. The first deals with 'something we are', while the second to something we do, consciously and deliberatively.[93] Democratic legitimacy arguably fulfils the latter function. Such an assertion indicates a need for some form of participatory democracy. Sunstein argues that democracy has an 'internal morality'.[94] According to Sunstein this, echoing Lord Bingham on the rule of law, includes equality and protection of other rights as well as a form of participative democracy that does not simply rely upon majoritarianism. Without these elements there is a violation of this internal morality.[95] This indicates that democratic legitimacy depends on the rule of law and the division of power to make certain that the structures subsist to ensure the morality is maintained within the system and the exercise of democratic rights actually occurs.

Therefore, if a constitution is to be regarded as democratic, the other essential elements of constitutionalism, such as the rule of law and divisions of power, must also function on a legitimate basis. That is, they must operate on a transparent and justifiable foundation. According to Llanque '[d]emocracy is the dynamic element in constitutional democracies, whereas the constitution is the static element'.[96] Further, he argues that once a constitution is established it is static unless changed by the people or otherwise and, as such, constitutionalism and democracy may be at odds until this change takes place. But constitutionalism is reliant on democracy to change legitimately the content of its own order.[97] Such an active role for democracy within constitutionalism goes some way to

[92] S. Wheatley, *Democratic Legitimacy*, pp. 102–5.

[93] H. F. Pitkin, 'The Idea of Constitution' (1987) 37 *Journal of Legal Education* 167, 167–8.

[94] Sunstein, '*Designing Democracy*', p. 242. [95] *Ibid.*, p. 10.

[96] M. Llanque, 'On Constitutional Membership' in Dobner and Loughlin (eds.), *Twilight*, p. 175.

[97] Constitutions may also change through revolution.

temper constituted power holders from changing a constitutional order without the intervention of constituent power holders. Thus constituent actors provide a supervisory role similar to that operating amongst constituted power holders within divisions of power.

However, counter to that, while the rights and duties of constitutional subjects can be debated, they are by their nature bound by the constitution until the democratic decision to change the nature of the rights and duties is taken. Notwithstanding that these changes must remain within a particular normative frame. Therefore constitutionalism and democratic legitimacy are bound together, as any legitimate change to the constitution, besides revolution, can only take place through a democratic process. Although the ideals of representative or direct democratic legitimacy may be pitted against each other, the pull of democracy and constitutionalism arguably settles opposing views to an extent necessary to establish democratic legitimacy within the system.[98] The notion that a constitution serves to actively underpin a form of participation is more attractive than Llanque's stark account of a static constitution. The role of constituent power holders thus becomes essential to a normative constitutional order served by democratic legitimacy, which remains open to change but within a normative framework.

Besides the rule of law and divisions of power, democratic legitimacy arguably is of paramount importance in identifying those entitled to participate in the process that ensures constitutionalism is maintained. One method of going about this is to identify the holders of constituent power. This is discussed in the next chapter; however at this point, it is important that the relationship between constitutionalism and democratic legitimacy is guaranteed. Democratic legitimacy maintains the link between the holders of constituent power and those who exercise constituted power, it ensures that power is exercised in a transparent and justifiable basis, and inculcates a process for the removal of constituted power in situations where such actors no longer have the support of the constituent power holders. This is indispensable to a constitutional order and, thus also, to the content of constitutionalisation debates. Democratic legitimacy ensures that both aspects of the operation of constitutional purchase, the form of governance order it establishes alongside the benefits accrued by those making use of its form, are functional within the governance order.

[98] Llanque, 'On Constitutional Membership' in Dobner and Loughlin (eds.), *Twilight*, pp. 175–7.

2.3 The relationship between domestic and global constitutionalism

Paulus queries whether 'domestic constitutionalism can fulfil similar functions at the international level'.[99] This section focuses on this question as well as the relationship between governance at the global and domestic levels. Considering their commonalities and differences and whether a governance order may be shared between them, the section discusses what are essential functions for one realm but not necessarily for another, and, more critically, what is indispensable to constitutionalisation in both orders. Although not seeking to shoehorn international law into domestic governance structures, this chapter aims to understand if constitutional law is fit for purpose in the global realm and considers what may be expropriated from domestic constitutionalism and what is better left behind and reimagined.

According to Klabbers,

> the ordinary meaning of constitution or constitutionalisation ... suggests not only a system constituted by a certain norm or set of norms, but also has a normative dimension; when people think of constitutionalisation, or constitutionalism, or any suchlike conjunction, the association is not only with something that is constituted in a technical sense, but also, and predominately, with something that is constituted in a politically legitimate sense; a constitutional order is a legitimate order, deriving its legitimacy (in part at least) precisely from its constitutional nature.[100]

Klabbers suggests commonality in all constitutional orders; nevertheless, the differing historical rationales for domestic and global governance intimates why some norms are not yet commonly present in each system. Both domestic constitutionalism and modern international law date from the same period, the end of the Thirty Years War.[101] As such, the bases for both are rooted in the same governance theories.[102] Yet, constituted power holders in each are different and thus the form of power division is also dissimilar. As such, attempting to locate exact replicas of domestic

[99] A. L. Paulus, 'The International Legal System as a Constitution' in Dunoff and Trachtman (eds.), *Ruling the World?*, p. 72.

[100] Klabbers in Klabbers, Peters and Ulfstein, *Constitutionalisation*, p. 8.

[101] The Thirty Years War (1618–1648) concluded with the Treaty of Westphalia amongst other agreements. See, for example, the discussion of Krasner on Westphalian Sovereignty in Krasner, *Sovereignty*, pp. 20–5.

[102] Cottier and Hertig, '21st Constitutionalism', 262.

structures will not succeed. Questioning whether the underlying rationales of domestic and global constitutionalism are meaningfully similar to the degree necessary to be identified as being constitutional or if they are found to be so dissimilar as to warrant an alternative governance order in the latter must be a central part of the global constitutionalisation debate. Peters argues that there 'is no distortion of norms which are "objectively" something else, but a legitimate form of interpretation' to reconstruct some areas of international law as constitutional.[103] Arguably, this is correct: there is no cessation of core constitutionalism if it was or if it is used within the global context.

International constitutional theory is far from new. It may be traced back to Holtzendorff, in 1877, or Bridgeman in 1911, or even Schmitt and Verdross in the pre-war period. Nonetheless, as Opsahl observed in 1961, many early uses of international constitutional law should not be considered as serious attempts at describing a particular theory or approach.[104] Instead, this extended use of constitutionalism, over a long period, indicates a wish to describe international law in a familiar context. Claims regarding the inconsistent use of constitutionalism in international law are not baseless; yet the growth of the debate over recent years has led to a clearer understanding of what is meant by global constitutionalisation. Lauterpacht wrote in 1936 that 'while the Covenant of the League is no more "law-making" than any other treaty, the substance of its law differs so radically from other international conventions in its scope and significance as a purposeful instrument in the process of political integration of mankind as to deserve the designation of a "higher law"'.[105] As such, the idea of a move towards a deeper understanding of the nature of constitutional law is just an aspect of global governance's evolution, however, the familiarity and legitimacy that constitutionalism offers are clearly also attractive in describing governance systems. This may also explain its descriptive use regarding the increasingly multi-level and complex structure in the relationships between international, regional and domestic legal orders.

The global debate often attracts a strident defence of constitutional law as a solely domestic legal affair whose aims and purpose can only be realised in this sphere.[106] Yet, Walter argues that

103 Peters, 'Revisited', 40.

104 See the discussion of T. Opsahl, 'An "International Constitutional Law"?' (1961) 10 *International and Comparative Law Quarterly* 760, 761; in this article Opsahl analyses some of the earlier doctrines that invoked a constitutional order.

105 H. Lauterpacht, 'The Covenant as the "Higher Law"' (1936) 17 *British Yearbook of International Law* 54, 64–5.

106 Walker, 'Taking Constitutionalism', 519.

> it is quite possible to separate State and constitution and to transfer the notion of constitution into non-State contexts. The point is, that the concept of constitution changes its meaning when it is transferred and this change of meaning is reinforced by the current structural changes of the international system: the disaggregation of the state on the one hand, and the process of sectoralization within international law.[107]

In furtherance of the global agenda, Fassbender asserts that the doctrine of subsidiarity regulates how a multi-level system of governance may operate.[108] Thus, he argues an international constitution does not have to replicate a domestic variant, as the tasks and responsibilities of each order will be slightly different. Nonetheless, this potentially misses the thrust of the arguments against using constitutionalism beyond the state. Some of the structures and functions must be similar; if there are no similarities in the global variant then the global governance order cannot rightly be called constitutional and, as such, theorists must reach for another nomenclature.

Walker identifies four concerns in taking constitutionalism beyond the state: inappropriateness, inconceivability, improbability and illegitimacy.[109] These four rightly portray the difficulty as more conceptual than empirical but nonetheless keep normative constitutionalism to the fore.[110] Inappropriateness is associated with the idea that constitutional principles in domestic law relate to 'good governance' structures developed to suit domestic systems and thus are only apt here. Inappropriateness implies that constitutionalism is unsuitable for international law. Further, the basis for the separation of powers and the independence of the judiciary as bulwarks against tyranny are not, as yet, associated with global governance, thus making their transplantation to the global arena inappropriate.[111]

[107] C. Walter, 'International Law in a Process of Constitutionalization' in J. E. Nijman and A. Nollkaemper (eds.), *New Perspectives on the Divide between National and International Law* (Oxford University Press, 2007). De Wet also argues that there is no reason for not using constitutional law in the international context, explaining that, for instance, Germany and the United States make use of it in their federal systems and also the EU makes use of it in its constitutional language. De Wet, 'The International Constitutional Order', 52.

[108] Fassbender's perspective comes from seeing the UN as the constitutional structure, and as such it is perhaps more necessary to divide the functions between the state and the non-state. See B. Fassbender, *Security Council Reform and the Right of Veto: A Constitutional Perspective* (The Hague: Kluwer International Press, 1998).

[109] Walker, 'Taking Constitutionalism', 520.

[110] *Ibid.*, 522. For another discussion of the core arguments against using constitutionalism domestically, see Cottier and Hertig, '21st Constitutionalism', 282–96.

[111] Walker, 'Taking Constitutionalism', 520–1.

But this argument limits the scope of constitutional norms and the reality of the global legal order. Good governance must be a requirement wherever power is exercised. As Sarooshi argues, the complexity of claims regarding sovereignty makes it directly conceivable that within international institutional arrangements power is exercised.[112] Therefore, good governance measures are needed to regulate the exercise of power in the global legal order. Some arguments against appropriateness link to questions of international law as law. Constitutionalism cannot be a basis for international law simply because it would grant to it what the domestic system has always possessed; acceptance as law.[113] If the aim of the promoters of global constitutionalisation is to gain an acceptance of its place as law, then it is a project that would rightfully not succeed. As the global order does indeed possess law then there must be an exercise of power in its application, formation and invocation, involving some political decisions that ought to be regulated by norms associated with good governance. Exclusivity is arguably a difficult case to make within law, and constitutional principles have matured in the domestic context, but this in itself does not mean they cannot have application elsewhere where similar governance concerns occur.

Inconceivability, or implausibility, is interlinked with inappropriateness. Walker states that '[t]he invocation of the ideas and practices of constitutionalism involves a distinctive way of thinking about the world – an *epistemic horizon* and political imaginary that presupposes and refers to the particular form of the state'.[114] Accordingly, for each sovereign body there is a *demos* that is linked to constitutionalism, which it is argued is non-existent in international law. Closely connected to constituency and community, the question of whether there is a constituent body in the global legal order is significant and shall hereafter be dealt with in some detail. However, one preliminary issue is the difficulty in framing the nature of a global *demos*, be it community or constituency.[115] To restrict this concept to a people and nothing beyond creates difficulties for the application of constitutionalism beyond the state that ought not to

112 D. Sarooshi, *International Organizations and their Exercise of Sovereign Power* (Oxford University Press, 2007), p. 1.

113 For a good summation of these kinds of arguments, see F. Megret, 'International Law as Law' (6 September 2010). Available at SSRN: http://ssrn.com/abstract=1672824, accessed 9 December 2013.

114 Walker, 'Taking Constitutionalism', 521.

115 For a discussion of the difficulties associated with constituency and democracy in international law, see T. Macdonald and K. Macdonald, 'Non-Electoral Accountability

be underestimated. If there is no identifiable world polity of any kind, it would almost suggest that there is not only no global constitutional law, but no international law which clearly is erroneous.

Improbability relates to the exercise of political power. The dubious character of grafting a legal form onto naked politics makes the global legal order an improbable site for constitutionalism. The configuration of the Westphalian state at the centre of authoritative decision hermetically seals power within states, making international law the sole interaction between these entities. This structure maintains the state at the centre of a constitutional order.[116] Yet, the shift away from the state as the sole subject of international law has become evident in a number of areas. For example, Joerge and Petersmann, amongst others, cogently argue that sovereignty is invested in international institutions.[117] Further, the state is no longer the sole holder of constituted power in other areas of international law; which is apparent in the law of state responsibility[118] or the competences of the ICC,[119] and has long since given way to supra-nationalism in the form of the EU,[120] suggesting that the simple Westphalian analysis no longer suffices.

Walker describes illegitimacy as the symbolic ideological claim made for arguments focused on the constitutionality or otherwise of acts.[121] The main thrust of this claim is that it would be dishonest to claim that international law is constitutional. If global constitutionalism could be characterised as inappropriate, inconceivable or improbable then it could not be legitimate, and its claims would remain unsubstantiated by law.[122] Thus, illegitimacy is bound to the other challenges to constitutionalisation, and thus it would be easy to claim that if these three were unsubstantiated, then legitimacy would surely follow. Nonetheless, legitimacy's central

in Global Politics: Strengthening Democratic Control within the Global Garment Industry' (2006) 17 *European Journal of International Law* 89.

116 Walker, 'Taking Constitutionalism', 521–2.

117 Sarooshi, *International Organizations*. See also C. Joerge and E. Petersmann (eds.), *Constitutionalism, Multilevel Trade Governance and Social Regulation'* (Oxford: Hart, 2006); Fassbender, 'The United Nations Charter'; H. H. Koh, 'Why do Nations Obey International Law?' (1996–1997) 106 *Yale Law Journal* 2599.

118 J. Crawford and S. Olleson, 'The Continuing Debate on a UN Convention on State Responsibility' (2005) 54 *International and Comparative Law Quarterly* 95.

119 De Wet, 'The International Constitutional Order', 55.

120 E. Stein, 'Lawyers, Judges and the Making of a Transnational Constitution' (1981) 75 *American Journal of International Law* 1; Peters, 'Revisited', 39.

121 Walker, 'Taking Constitutionalism', 522.

122 *Ibid.*, 522.

place in any legal order makes its presence critical to any claim towards constitutionalisation. Potentially, the adoption of constitutionalism may lead to a stronger, not weaker, claim of legitimacy within the global legal order as its governance becomes tested against the constitutional norms outlined earlier in this chapter.

Some claims of incompatibility appear dualistic as they ignore the ever-growing interaction between international and domestic law.[123] International and domestic law, as two systems of governance, are not alien to each other. A gradual move towards multilateralism accompanies a progression of decision-making upwards, requiring a need for a broader understanding of international law beyond the state.[124] As Bingham argues, the displacement of this monopoly of constituted power requires domestic public law to reassess its approach to law beyond the state.[125] The centrality and importance of domestic public law requires there to be a law at the international level, which, at the very least, has a similar depth of normativity and structure. Arguably, this may be found best within global constitutionalism.

If Bingham is correct, and states should now take full account of their international responsibilities in the same manner as they do their domestic obligations, then arguments against global constitutionalism also undermine governance within the domestic realm.[126] If governments must follow international law as they do domestic law then good governance is as much a consideration for international law as it is domestic law. It is essential then that domestic constitutionalism is considered as indispensable to understanding the nature of the core principles relating to global constitutionalism. The utility of learning from the domestic order, though not being bound by its structures, becomes clear. Political power is exercised by states; however, the emergence of actors such as the UN Secretary General, suggests activity in the political realm beyond the state.[127] The exercise of political power should not be without some restraint, and that moderation should be provided by the law.[128] This does not mean that it must be constitutional law, but it does make it improbable that a legitimate exercise of power can exist outside of some overarching moderating

[123] J. P. Trachtman, *The Future of International Law* (Cambridge University Press, 2013), p. 41.

[124] Sarooshi, *International Organizations*.

[125] Bingham, *Rule of Law*. [126] *Ibid*., p. 128.

[127] See, for example, the description of the office in L. Gordenker, *The UN Secretary General and the Secretariat* (London: Routledge, 2005).

[128] E. De Wet, 'Conflicts between International Paradigms: Hierarchy versus Systemic Integration' (2013) 2 *Global Constitutionalism* 196.

structure, and thus monopoly of constitutional norms by domestic law is unsustainable.

Fassbender argues that 'we are searching for a sub-discipline of public international law, namely *the constitutional law of the international community*, a law which may be influenced by constitutional ideas and practices developed in a national context, but which "stands on its own feet"'.[129] Allott argues that 'a constitution is a structure system which is shared by all societies'.[130] What both of these authors are in agreement on is that there is a shared common understanding of a system of governance that is constitutional. Global constitutionalisation is a process by which international law moves beyond its sovereign foundations as well as its vertical and Western bias, to a system of law founded on a process that is hierarchal, normative and structured. Constitutional and public law structures are not exclusive to the domestic sphere.[131] While constitutional law has only become truly entrenched in the majority of domestic systems since the end of the Second World War and the period of decolonisation, such developments are not uniform.[132] Certainly, in countries such as North Korea, where the semblance of a constitutional democracy could not be said to exist, there is still a constitution.[133] Thus, even domestic constitutionalism is not infallible.

The push towards constitutionalism emerges from the notion that a simplex, consent-based understanding of international law is no longer sufficient or, in practice, relevant. This is most closely recognised by those who argue for a constitutionalisation within either the UN[134] or the WTO.[135] The root of domestic constitutionalism was the move away from monarchy to a liberal society. While this process is not immediately

[129] B. Fassbender, 'We the Peoples of the United Nations, Constituent Power and Constitutional Form in International Law' in M. Loughlin and N. Walker (eds.), *The Paradox of Constitutionalism* (Oxford University Press, 2008), p. 269.

[130] Allott, *Eunomia*, p. 167.

[131] Peters, 'Revisited', 39.

[132] J. Tully, 'The Imperialism of Modern Constitutional Democracy', in Loughlin and Walker (eds.), *The Paradox*, pp. 315–38.

[133] See, for example, a report in *The Economist* that states that apparently a recent constitutional change in North Korea places the military at the heart of the Constitution making them a priority in all questions of law. 'Banyan: The Mother of All Dictatorships', *The Economist* (print edn), 25 February 2010.

[134] See B. Fassbender, 'Rediscovering a Forgotten Constitution: Notes on the Place of the UN Charter in the International Legal Order' in Dunoff and Trachtman (eds.), *Ruling the World?*, pp. 113–47; E. De Wet, 'The Emergence of International and Regional Value Systems as a Manifestation of the Emerging International Constitutional Order' (2006) 19 *Leiden Journal of International Law* 611.

[135] D. Z. Cass, *The Constitutionalization of the World Trade Organization* (Oxford University Press, 2005); J. P. Trachtman, 'The Constitutions of the WTO' (2006) 17 *European Journal of International Law* 623.

mirrored in international law, the movement away from state-centric into both vertical and horizontal global governance structures indicates a similar shift in constituted power. Burgeoning maturity and sophistication in political life in the seventeenth and eighteenth centuries is mirrored in the present global legal order that potentially is not just a new era in international law but also a force of change in all governance structures. De Wet describes a constant movement and a 'shift of public decision making away from the nation State towards international actors of a regional and functional (sectoral) nature'[136] and points to the adoption of the UN Charter as the 'constitutional moment' in international law, which increased the speed of change.[137]

International law should not, and certainly does not, and possibly should never, entirely resemble domestic law. Therefore, to gain legitimacy through an attempt to 'bootleg' domestic constitutionalism and call it global constitutionalisation would fail, as the underlying purpose of the systems are dissimilar. If global constitutionalisation is the ultimate aim, then constitutional law must be a good in itself, and therefore a global constitutional system should have some 'added value' to the global legal order presently operating. The possibility of constitutional purchase being available at the global governance level is there, and the question is whether the narratives accompanying the constitutionalisation debate have adopted constitutionalism's normative content to the extent necessary to make their claims wholly plausible.

2.4 Conclusion

Constitutionalism is a governance system operating around a series of interacting legal norms that is available to any governance order both wishing and willing to adopt its content and thus gain constitutional purchase. All domestic legal orders make claims towards possessing constitutions and generally aver to hold to constitutional norms; yet, even here this is not necessarily always true.[138] Whereas national constitutions as documents of governance rarely cease to exist in situations where constitutional norms are either absent in the first place or cease to operate, constitutionalism as a governance order is not present. Thus,

[136] De Wet, 'The International Constitutional Order', 53. [137] *Ibid.*, 54.

[138] For example, Goodhart considers the impact that the domestic rule by law has for international law, arguing that if a differentiation is made between those states that employ rule by law and those that use rule of law, then this also has an impact on international law. Goodhart, 'Rule of Law', 943.

constitutionalism possesses ascertainable content that is readily identifiable. At times this content is observable as an operational aim, a reality, or in other instances deemed inoperative but with such a status considered deficient in a functioning constitutional order. Thus, while the execution of constitutionalism may vary from order to order, core underlying norms remain present. Similar to the possession of statehood in international law, once a state possesses a constitutional order it remains rare for that state to lose that claim, but as with statehood, on occasion, it does happen or at the very least its status becomes questionable. A governance order seeking to adopt normative constitutionalism, as opposed to merely being constituted, must adopt norms either immediately in a 'constitutional moment' or over time in a process of constitutionalisation.

Constitutionalism regulates the allocation of constituted power and its exercise as well as the process in which constituent power holders exercise their warrant through their interaction with these norms. The rule of law, divisions of power and democratic legitimacy serve to regulate domestic legal orders and invariably are turned to when a new constitutional arrangement is created or an old one revamped.[139] The importance of the content of these three norms is particularly relevant where a liberal or, at least, democratic notion of constitutionalism prevails and is also vital to the operation of constituent and constituted power. Their content or relative form as they develop remains unsettled and, as such, attempts to fit exact models of domestic constitutionalism onto other governance orders, in this instance the global legal order, ultimately fail to form a convincing argument. Yet, this is not to suggest that other governance orders may not adopt constitutionalism; for example, it is possible to argue that these norms of constitutionalism may be individually present in the global legal order.[140] Nonetheless, their interactions both with each other and with constituted and constituent power, alongside other constitutional norms, make the moniker 'constitutional' relevant and correct, and it is this point that must be addressed in the global constitutionalisation debate.

This discussion on the nature of constitutionalism, the rule of law, divisions of power and democratic legitimacy is intended to make way for a discussion of the schools of global constitutionalisation. The chapter

[139] See. for example. H. C. Lockwood, *Constitutional History of France* (Charleston, SC: BiblioBazaar, LLC, [1889] 2009); R. C. Van Caenegm, *An Historical Introduction to Western Constitutional Law* (Cambridge University Press, 1995).

[140] See, for example, Fassbender, *Security Council Reform*; R. St. J. MacDonald, 'The Charter of the United Nations in Constitutional Perspective' (1999) 20 *Australian Yearbook of International Law* 205; Cass, *World Trade Organization*.

does not aim to be an exhaustive overview of constitutionalism but rather seeks to decipher the norms that ought to be present. Further, these norms are considered in the context of a normative constitutionalism seeking to regulate constituent and constituted power, and not understanding constitutionalism itself as a constitutive force within a legal order. Indeed, deciphering between constituting a legal order and constitutionalism as a form of governance is central, in some ways, to understanding the global constitutionalisation debate. If the argument is that constitutionalism is as relevant to the global realm as it is the domestic, then the underlying doctrines of either system cannot be sealed off from one another, as the former must be able to adapt constitutional norms into its operation, though not to a degree that they cease to possess their original normative value. The rule of law, divisions of power and democratic legitimacy must be present to rightly describe a system as constitutionalised, and it is from this perspective that the following discussions on both constituent and constituted power as well as the global constitutionalisation debate continue in the following chapters.

3

Who benefits? Constituent and constituted power

In the abstract, constituent power holders choose the form and substantive character of the governance system under which they wish to be governed and live co-operatively. As a product of constituent power holders' choice of governance order, constituted power holders are selected and granted their licence to exercise their power within the remit of that particular system. Yet, the evolution of governance orders tends towards the chaotic, in that they are not often the result of consensual or linear development, for example, the dissolution and emergence of states in the pre- and post-colonial eras. Nonetheless, the identification of constituent and constituted power holders ought to form a necessary aspect of any emergent governance order, particularly in circumstances where constitutionalisation is identified as the process of emergent governance. Indeed, choosing constitutionalism requires that any resultant intermediate structures ought to remain transitionary, pending the completion of a constitutionalisation process and the full exercise of both constituent and constituted power holders' warrants.

The recognition of constituent power holders transcends constitutionalism, as their presence represents the basis of any governance order, no matter how their warrant is exercised, ignored or tied to constituted power. Constitutional governance, in its ideal form, guarantees processes that ensure the perpetual identification of constituent power holders and enables the exercise of their warrant. Yet, as this chapter reflects, in the majority of constitutionalisation processes, such tasks are either ignored or put into modes of classification, which repeatedly have been shown to be detrimental to the very task of constitutional governance. In this chapter, community is used as an example of such a classification of constituent power holders. For constitutionalism, the identification of constituent and constituted power holders underpins the legitimate governance order that it seeks to inculcate. Yet, remarkably within global constitutionalism, such a core issue remains a largely peripheral debate. Attempts to identify non-traditional constituent power holders as part of the global constitutionalisation debate have proved problematic, generating a need for a process of continual re-recognition operating alongside any proposed constitutionalisation process.[1]

This chapter questions the collective identification of constituent power holders within constitutionalism. Aiming to develop an understanding of their importance and operation, this chapter discusses how constituent power holders have come to be defined, their relationship with constitutionalism, their impact upon governance and, finally, the collectivisation of constituent power through community and constituency. While such considerations are discussed against the backdrop of global constitutionalisation, this chapter understands constitutionalism as a governance order that is capable of identifying both its constituent and, as such, its constituted power holders beyond any particular site of practice.

The dearth of discussion on constituent power within global constitutionalisation seems extraordinary. The centrality to legitimate governance of those who hold constituted power and those on whose behalf such power is exercised ought to mean that other questions remain largely moot while their identification remains unattainable. Arguably, if the holders of constituent power remain unidentified and thus cannot exercise their warrant, the exercise of constituted power is inevitably constitutionally illegitimate. However, it may be possible to exercise power legitimately under a different governance regime, based upon, for example, the natural law or moral authority. Constituted power is the legitimate basis on which authority is exercised within a legal framework, whereas constituent power is the exercise of political power and the ultimate source of legitimate authority. Divestment of constituted power's potential for autocracy is maintained by the operation of norms established in constitutionalism, but this authority must be initially granted by constituent power holders to be legitimate. Identifying the holders of constituent power establishes the remit of a legal order, as it aids in differentiating between what is and what is not a constitutional order's jurisdiction. Global constitutionalisation remains abstract, while serious consideration of the operation of constituent power remains absent, for without its consideration global constitutionalisation remains unsettled.

[1] G. Teubner, 'Societal Constitutionalism: Alternatives to State-centred Constitutional Theory' Storrs Lectures, Yale Law School 2003/2004, available at SSRN: http://ssrn.com/abstract=876941, 3, accessed 9 December 2013.

3.1 Constituent and constituted power holders and their relationship with constitutional governance

The pivot of constituent and constituted powers underpins constitutional orders. Their operation buttresses the operation of every constitutional norm. From democratic deficits to human rights violations and other distortions of its exercise, the absence of an identifiable constituent power often leads to constitutional crises. According to Loughlin, constituent power enables lawyers to identify the holders of political authority, and it is from this basis that legal authority is exercised as delegated power.[2] Constituent power is bound to representation or democratic legitimacy and, as such, is connected to those who grant constituted power to the governance structures as the ultimate source of governmental authority.[3] Schmitt defines constituent power as 'the political will, whose power and authority is capable of making the concrete, comprehensible decision over the type and form of its own political existence'.[4] This is bound to Schmitt's idea of the nation and very much associated with the commonality of community, which has, at times, been conflated with constituent power. Nonetheless, the connection with will-formation and democratic legitimacy clearly remains instrumental to constituent power.[5]

Contrariwise, constituted power is the exercise of political and legal authority granted by constituent power holders through a legitimate process. Often bound up with constitutional legal norms, such as the rule of law and divisions of power, constituted power consequently links to the governance structures established by these norms. Lawyers are generally much more content to work with the notion of constituted power, as constitutional lawyers understand this to be the traditional arena of politics.[6] Constitutional subjects, in the exercise of their constituent power, grant legitimacy to the governance order or the holders of constituted power.

Underscoring the inter-relationship between constituent power and constitutionalism, Chalmers argues that constituent power is essential to any constitutional settlement owing to its centrality in identifying the

[2] Loughlin, *Idea of Public Law*, p. 99.

[3] See, for example, R. A. Dahl, *After the Revolution?* (New Haven, CT: Yale University Press, 1970), pp. 64–7, on the principle of affected interest, which approaches the nature of constituent power from a top-down basis.

[4] C. Schmitt, *Constitutional Theory* (Durham, NC: Duke University Press, 2008), p. 125.

[5] A. Negri, *Insurgencies: Constituent Power and the Modern State* (trans. Maurizia Boscalgi) (Minneapolis: University of Minnesota Press, 1999), sections 2.2–2.3.

[6] Loughlin, *Idea of Public Law*, p. 99.

subjects of constitutional law. Indeed, he argues that, 'constituent power mediates the relationship between the political system and society. It is part of a broader panorama which locates the political and legal system within a way of life in which law and politics play a limited role and in which there is a conception of the human condition to which they must orient themselves.'[7]

Tierney, describing the relationship between these two forms of power in domestic paradigms suggests that '[c]onstituent power – the unbridled, democratic power of the sovereign people, every moment reinvented anew – and the constituted power of the state, wherein fundamental constitutional norms consecrated in the constitutional foundational moment are elevated beyond the reach of the temporal majorities'.[8]

Two features of both Chalmers' and Tierney's approaches should be acknowledged: first, both are inescapably domestic in their approach and, second, their constituent power holders are inevitably individuals. This first trait intrinsically sets constituent power, alongside constitutionalism, as embedded in a state-level governance order. But, while it is important to acknowledge some reticence in straying too far from constitutionalism's domestic attributions, its discourse remains relevant to any governance system. Tierney understands constituent power as relating to the people and constituted power to the state establishing the outer edges of constitutionalism's concern in domestic fora. Such characterisations are readily understood wherever constituent power holders choose a governance order and, as a product of the system, identify and pass to constituted power holders their collective licence to govern. Yet, here also lies the problem for global constitutionalisation: when constituent power holders are not individuals their identification becomes additionally problematic. This goes some way to explaining the reliance on categorisations of community, which has become a significant and, at times unhelpful, trope of governance and constituent power beyond the state.

7 D. Chalmers, 'Constituent Power and the Pluralist Ethic' in Loughlin and Walker (eds.), *The Paradox*, pp. 293–4. For a further discussion of constituent power, with particular regard to sovereignty, see A. Kalyvas, 'Popular Sovereignty, Democracy, and the Constituent Power' (2005) 12 *Constellations* 223; and A. Arato, 'Carl Schmitt and the Revival of the Doctrine of the Constituent Power in the United States' (1999–2000) 21 *Cardozo Law Review* 1739; Schmitt, *Constitutional Theory*; C. Schmitt, *Political Theology – Four Chapters on the Concept of Sovereignty* (University of Chicago Press, 2005).

8 Tierney, discussing Loughlin's approach: Tierney, 'Sovereignty' in Christodoulidis and Tierney (eds.), *Public Law and Politics*, p. 15.

The unsystematic development of domestic constitutionalism has led to the identification of constituent power holders as an a priori group.[9] As such, constituent power viewed through a governance lens became intrinsically linked to particular actors as the vassals of power. While these individuals have changed their character over time – class-based orthodoxies as constitutionalism, characterisations of nationalism or the identification of constituent power holders as intrinsically linked to democratisation in modern constitutional structures – the distinction between constituent power holders and individuals has become less apparent. This evolution necessitates a consideration of both constituent and constituted power manifestly different from categorisations of persons, particularly if constitutionalism is to be reimagined for a global order.

Significant debates on the primacy of either constituent or constituted power and their places as sources of constitutional authority cannot be disassociated from their identification.[10] Walker argues that within the relationship between constituent power and constitutionalism there is often discord between the identification of the people or states as possessing constituent power, and the relationship between them and the supranational order, in that case the EU.[11] This is true in any scenario that goes beyond particular actors as the holders of constituent power and is at the core of what global constitutionalisation faces in becoming a legitimate form of governance. Thus, who the holders of constituent power are within a global order must be addressed if global constitutionalisation is to gain traction as a theory.

Often the fall-back in identifying actors in a governance order community becomes transposed, generally without regard for the agenda that accompanies it, to the global legal order. Yet, this should not be surprising; after all, community has played a significant role in domestic constitutionalism and, in particular, the identification of constituent and constituted power holders. Ascertaining the holders of constituent power is a necessary task. Constituent and constituted power maintains the link between the operation of constitutional norms, such as the rule of law, divisions

[9] This could also be referred to as classes in the Hartian sense, 'the law must predominantly … refer to *classes* of person'; H. L. A. Hart *The Concept of Law*, 2nd edn (Oxford: Clarendon, 1994), p. 124.

[10] See, for example, a description of Schmitt and Kelsen's discussions in H. Londahl, 'Constituent Power and Reflexive Identity: Towards an Ontology of Collective Selfhood' in Loughlin and Walker (eds.), *The Paradox*, p. 9.

[11] N. Walker, 'Post-Constituent Constitutionalism? The Case of the European Union' in Loughlin and Walker (eds.), *The Paradox*, p. 265.

of power and the establishment of democratic legitimacy, as well as those subject to authority and on whose behalf such power is exercised.

Constituent power holders do not maintain identical interests in either to whom constituted power should be granted or in the operation of the constitutional order. Constitutionalism aims to mediate such competing interests; for example, democratic legitimacy curtails majoritarian absolutism as it reconciles the interests of the holders of constituent power. In ascertaining who the holders of constituent power are, it becomes imperative to establish a categorisation that facilitates differentiated interests, while also maintaining a legal order as an element of democratic legitimacy. The question is then about how to identify this group while preserving such characteristics. To consider which supports better the workings of constituent and consequently constituted power, as well as constitutionalism more broadly, two potential models are examined: community and constituency. Within the historic development of constitutionalism, the former reoccurs as a means of identification, while the latter could potentially be an alternative model for understanding constituent power.

3.2 Community

Governance and community have long been intertwined. Marcus Aurelius linked law's function and citizenship, arguing, '[i]f reason is common, so too is law; and if this is common, then we are fellow citizens. If this is so, we share in a kind of organized polity. And if that is so, the world is as it were a city-state.'[12] Marcus Aurelius argues that this common reason makes us part of the polity, a polity based in a particular form of governance. This section rests upon asking whether such a link is appropriate and further whether constituent power, as associated with community, serves constitutionalism.

Abi-Saab contends that the community debate should focus on the degree to which a legal rule is based upon its presumed existence. In focusing on the nexus between the governance order and community, he opens up questions on whether some degree of community is present at all times, on all topics in a governance order, and, as such, whether it is necessary for constitutionalism.[13] 'The often unthinkingly liberal use of community

[12] Marcus Aurelius, *The Meditations* (trans. M. Hammond) (London: Penguin Classics, 2006), Book VI, Part I, 4.4; arguably, this is a natural-law perspective on the role of community.

[13] G. Abi-Saab, 'Whither the International Community?' (1998) 9 *European Journal of International Law* 248, 249.

in legal contexts may be a result of its rather nebulous character.[14] Within constitutionalism the existence and nature of a community, its establishment and links to law, and its use, particularly in delineating the holders of constituted power, bears upon the entirety of that legal order. The binding of community to the development of constitutionalism and, as such, the identification of the constituent power holders requires serious consideration. The aim of this section is to understand how community is understood and utilised in identifying the holders of constituent power within constitutionalism. The question is whether the connotations associated with community are apposite with constitutionalism.

Anderson argues that communities are imagined by their members, and it is this perception of belonging to the community that is vital in discourse on constituent power.[15] Basing constituent power holders within community makes it imperative to understand constitutionalism's interaction with its delineation. The perception and employment of community draws the governance context within its parameters. As such, rather than leading to a definition, the theories of community discussed herein are exemplars of its relationship with governance. Identification and consideration of widely held perceptions of community, and the relationship between these perceptions and the constitutional governance order, should lead to an appreciation of the effect of its transposition into global constitutionalisation. Further, the recognition of constituent power holders as well as the potential for differentiated interests within community requires examination. An alternative analysis of community would perhaps not raise such acute effects as will be discussed in this chapter; yet the reliance on community's rhetoric, without consideration of the consequences, requires that its perception and its invocation, rather than a definitive account of its meaning, are necessary.

This is not to imbue community with a mystical ability justifying theories of constitutionalisation in all contexts, or suggesting that each time it is utilised an author must defend its applicability. Simply, this discussion acknowledges that when invoking community as part of

[14] For a good examination of the broad use of 'international community', see B. Simma and A. L. Paulus, 'The "International Community": Facing the Challenge of Globalization' (1998) 9 *European Journal of International Law* 266.

[15] B. Anderson, *Imagined Communities*, 2nd rev. edn (London: Verso, 1991). Though, as Buchanan and Pahja point out, '[w]hat Anderson failed to take sufficient notice of ... is the extent to which the very boundaries of the imaginable for "most of the world" are already determined by a particular form of the nation-state prescribed by the West'. See R. Buchanan and S. Pahuja, 'Law, Nation and (Imagined) International Communities' (2004) 8 *Law, Text, Culture* 137, 138.

constitutional governance, the importance of its meaning must, at a minimum, be acknowledged, and cognisance of its implications recollected. To do otherwise allows fixed conceptions of community, some of which will be dealt with in this section, to inculcate themselves into a governance framework without consideration of their potential consequences. Considering the link between constitutionalism and community aids in understanding whether community is a reliable basis for ascertaining who the subjects and, as such, the holders of constituent and constituted power are within constitutionalism. Further, if entrenching a constitutional legal order within a community paradigm is shown to be incompatible with constitutionalism then it may be argued that an alternative to community should be utilised.

3.2.1 *Characteristics of community: binarity and commonality*

Two characteristics of community's operation, commonality and binarity, illustrate its use within constitutionalism. Community, as it is commonly used, establishes a framework that is innately binary.[16] It is binary in the sense that it establishes a group that share characteristics or principles that those not in the community either do not share or are not considered by the community to possess. This characterisation is based upon an understanding of community centred upon notions of commonality, solidarity, compatibility or shared norms, creating division between those within the community, who are perceived to have compatibility, and those outside who do not. This binarity may not necessarily be problematic; in some instances it may even be positive or benign, but when matched with governance can become problematic.[17]

Commonality makes community a coherent whole, it grants a motivation or an essential reasoning behind the coming together of a group and is one of the main posits of binaries. Two aspects of binarity's operation demonstrate, in combination with commonality, the difficulties with its invocation. First, the impact upon those outside the community and, second, the effect upon those within the community including their

16 Though some authors, particularly Nancy, have sought to move away from the binary nature of community; see J. Nancy, *The Inoperative Community* (Minneapolis: University of Minnesota Press, 1991), p. 1. It is contended that community in the majority of its usages does maintain it. See, for example, T. Franck, 'Clan and Superclan: Loyalty, Identity and Community in Law and Practice' (1996) 90 *American Journal of International Law* 359.

17 D. Kostakopoulou, 'Thick, Thin and Thinner Patriotisms: Is This All There Is?' (2006) 26 *Oxford Journal of Legal Studies* 73, 83–4.

considerations of the community's instilled ethos or notions of commonality.[18] Most importantly, the impact of these community characteristics upon the operation of governance structures, particularly in identifying constituent power holders, needs consideration. Outlining each aspect aids in understanding the use of community in the context of constitutionalism and the complications associated with use of a dichotomy to identify a definitive group of actors within law. Commonality, as an essential attribute of predominant community rhetoric, forms the core of the binary community. Though some, particularly Nancy, sought to move away from the binary nature of community, it is contended that community's majority use maintains this value as definitional.[19]

Beginning with Aristotle and following with Hegel, Burke and Nancy this section offers several variations of commonality. These theorists illustrate the broad spectrum and historical development of community in the context of governance. While admittedly not comprehensive in its analysis of commonality within community this section identifies its associated tropes, which potentially may be transposed into global constitutionalisation. Two aspects of community are particularly problematic. First, suggestions that those within the community who wish to challenge the content of commonality would in some manner harm the underlying rationale for the association's origin. Second, the common use of commonality stifles both those within and without the community, and creates a hegemony of ideas that may perpetuate some of the more negative attributes of law and potentially constitutionalism. Negative notions derive from the implication that those not counted within the community do not share an essential (generally positive) commonality. Arguably the inclusion of commonality in the most widely held definitions of community potentially creates an elitist and exclusionary vision that not only limits internal variations, but also automatically denigrates those that do not maintain this commonality and are thus, by definition, excluded from the community.

Commonality and binarity are not necessarily negative, inevitably wrong or deconstructive, indeed, they may create consensus amongst competing interests. However, questioning whether community inculcates the notion that existing outside of the community is a negative and that questioning this consensus places a participant beyond a community's

[18] I. R. Wall, *Human Rights and Constituent Power: Without Model or Warranty* (Abingdon: Routledge, 2011), p. 12.

[19] Nancy, *Inoperative*, p. 1 and Franck, 'Clan and Superclan', 359.

interests is vital when it is attached to governance. If the result of such exclusion results in a misidentification of constituent power holders as only members of a particular community, this infects constitutionalism with unnecessary connotations, an outcome that if it can be avoided by global constitutionalisation, must be attempted.

3.2.2 Aristotle and community

> The members of every state must of necessity have all things in common, or some things common, and not others, or nothing at all common. To have nothing in common is evidently impossible, for society itself is one species of community; and the first thing necessary thereunto is a common place of habitation, namely the city, which must be one, and this every citizen must have a share in.[20]

Commonality resides at the core of Aristotle's community, fundamentally binding this iteration with constitutionalism.[21] For Aristotle, change in both the community and the constitution occurs tangentially. A community order can only operate if there is authority, and this authority is established within a constitutional framework. In Aristotle's vision commonality is essential to this idea of community and constitution, though the degree of commonality required is somewhat unclear.[22]

The meaning behind Aristotle's all things in common or some things that are in common remains nebulous, and this ambiguity has become inherent in community's usage. Aristotle does not appear to be striving for absolute unity or homogeneity, though from first glance such a prerequisite suggests that plurality would be harmful, internal homogeneity thus becoming an essential. Aristotle seeks to accommodate some plurality and deliberation but yet still requires a measure of commonality to a degree that may result in the exclusion of internal reflection on the community's own character. Thus questioning whether a redefinition of commonality may be proposed or is impermissible, which may result in a de-legitimisation of the structures that serve a community, is often not queried. As such, the association created by Aristotle is based upon fixed notions of commonality. At its core, Aristotle's community is defined by

20 Aristotle, *A Treatise on Government* (trans. W. Ellis) (London: J. M. Dent & Sons, 1928), Book II, chapter 1.

21 See Aristotle, *A Treatise*; Aristotle, *Politics* (trans. R. Kraut), rev. edn (London: Penguin Classics, 1981); Franck, 'Clan and Superclan', 359.

22 Aristotle, *Nicomachean Ethics* (University of Chicago Press, 2011), p. 186.

those within or outside of the community who do or do not share a specific commonality no matter what its content is, and without this commonality the community itself lacks a foundational attribute.

At a minimum, Aristotle's commonality suggests a common place of habitation. While this, at first glance, appears inclusive it may also be interpreted as a basis for segregation. For those outside of the community, even if simple habitation as an objective standard is the reason, it is not always a clear guide; it suggests a permanent marker of residence that is not always present. Within state-bound constitutionalism the borders of the state establish a partially objective test. Aristotle's habitation requirement pushes the stateless, who in any case were possibly slaves or those not worthy of citizenship (such as women), out of the constitutional community and removes the possibility of being or becoming a legal actor, yet slaves and women remain objects of the law. Since the Westphalian era, the entirety of the globe has been covered by states, or areas made claim to by states; thus a territorial link gives an impression of a neat solution.[23] Nonetheless, the inclusion of the stateless, international organisations, individuals, corporate bodies and non-governmental organisations to the pantheon of actors in law calls Aristotle's habitation requirement into question as a tool for deciphering the space that community operates within. Therefore commonality and habitation must be understood in the Aristotelian community from the perspective that the entire populace of the city or community are not in fact citizens and so, by community's definition, are not holders of constituent power; they are the objects but not the subjects of law and governance.

Beyond territoriality, legal personality, if based on shared characteristics, remains linked to commonality and may be an alternative, if subjective, test for membership of the community. As it is broader than territoriality, legal personality may encompass a more adequate test for constitutionalism; yet even this remains problematic as a basis for the identification of constituent power holders. Such alternate tests depend upon the extent of constitutionalism's remit, including whether membership of the community and, as such, sharing a commonality, is contiguous with constituent power. In conflating commonality with citizenship, either on subjective or objective grounds, commonality allies constitutionalism with nationalism.[24] Nationalism often bases itself upon setting

[23] The high seas, while not state based, are regulated through state-based regulatory frameworks, from state flags and piracy to fishing quotas.

[24] For a discussion of nationalism and some of the uses it is put to in this regard, see Franck, 'Clan and Superclan', 359.

a seemingly objective notion of commonality or character that is then relied upon to defend an identity or nationalism as statehood.[25] To be a subject of constitutionalism one must be in the community and to be in the community one must share this commonality. This form of community potentially excludes, out of hand, those who are in fact subject to constitutionalism but not necessarily, in accordance with this definition of law, subjects of it or possessors of constituent power.

For Aristotle, the highest achievement of humanity lies in creating a state.[26] Yet, curbing eligibility for citizenship to narrow categorisations of commonality, and thus curtailing the possession of constituent power, sustains established governance orders. Such an approach limits Aristotelian governance to an elite who, in possessing constituent power, can be trusted to reason and make decisions for the rest of the community and, as such, set the content of constitutionalism. When members define the rules of community's membership around commonality then it is forced upon those who wish to join the community, if it is even possible to possess the attribute. Thus the commonality is necessary to possess constituent power. Aristotle's community inherently establishes a tiered system, with those who share a commonality, habitation or otherwise deciding its content. It is this group that ultimately decides what the defining commonality is and so too dictates who the holders of constituent power are within that governance order. This top-down approach is not uncommon.[27] Such communities grant the holders of constituted power or, within the community ideal, those that determine the commonality the right to dictate who grants to them their ultimate legitimacy to do so.[28]

There has been criticism of Aristotle's interpretation of constitutionalism with community and his communitarianism as romanticism, leading to hegemony of one set of ideals, race or interests and thus identification of the community with certain historic conceptions of nationalism that appears to be borne out in analysis.[29] While reading Aristotle's

[25] See, for example, N. Berman, '"But the Alternative Is Despair": European Nationalism and the Modernist Renewal of International Law' (1993) 106 *Harvard Law Review* 1792.

[26] 'By nature man is a political animal. Men have a natural desire for life in society, even when they have no need to seek each other's help', Aristotle, *Politics*, Book I, chapter 2.

[27] See, for example, Dahl, *After the Revolution?*, pp. 64–7.

[28] For a discussion of the vested interests of elected representatives in deciding their electorate, see J. Hart Ely, *On Democracy and Distrust: A Theory of Judicial Review* (Cambridge, MA: Harvard University Press, 1980), p. 117.

[29] C. J. Nederman, 'Freedom, Community and Function: Communitarian Lessons of Medieval Political Theory' (1992) 86 *American Political Science Review* 977.

community leads to an interpretation of commonality in a manner that puts hegemony at its fore, this is not a foregone conclusion. Commonality does not lead intrinsically to an exclusionary definition or an assembled basis of ideals that lends itself to marginalisation. Yet, if commonality is the method on which community membership is established, and, as such, is at the heart of community's meaning, as Aristotle seems to suggest, and it is not exclusionary, it would have to be a very broad commonality. In fact, it would have to be so broad that arguably it would no longer serve a purpose beyond the preconceptions that would accompany its use. Aristotle's conglomeration of community and commonality sets the basis of binarity that becomes the recognised hallmark of community-based delineations of the possessors of constituent power within domestic constitutional governance orders.

3.2.3 Burke and shared purpose

Burke's and Aristotle's understandings of the commonality necessary for community share several attributes, although with Burke's addition of a substantial constitutional theory beyond the classical discussion.[30] Community, commonality and constitution interlinking was an important marker in the development of both a basis for legal transformation and to ascertain constituent power within a communitarian basis.[31] While governance and, as a result, constitutionalism were implicit in other derivations, Burke's explicit association of community with constituent power entrenched its usage in modern constitutional terminology.

Burke saw community as a continually developing polity and constitutions as an 'organism something like the human body, constituted as a community of senses with distinct powers and privileges, a mixed being of natural and conventional behaviour, a creature of biology and habitat'.[32] This essentially conservative view of both constitution and community, while suggesting possibilities of progression, in fact tends towards

[30] See E. Burke, *A Philosophical Enquiry into the Origins of the Sublime and the Beautiful* (ed. J. T. Boulton) (University of Notre Dame Press, 1958); E. Burke, *Reflections on the Revolution in France* (London: Hackett, 1987).

[31] Grumm, 'The Achievement of Constitutionalism' in Dobner and Loughlin (eds.), *Twilight*, p. 3.

[32] E. Burke, *Appeal from the New to the Old Whigs* (Whitefish, MT: Kessinger Publishing, LLC, 2007). See further, C. Douzinas, *The End of Human Rights: Critical Legal Thought at the Turn of the Century* (Oxford: Hart, 2000), p. 151.

maintaining the status quo. The human body, evolutionary necessities aside, is an enduring unchanging entity. There is no possibility of a radical change or reimagining of a community, which does not, by its very nature, change in some perceptible way. According to Burke, while constitutions are living and breathing they cannot radically change, thus making any modifications, either to the community or the constitutional, infinitesimal. This is also bound to Burke's idea of empire, particularly in its British variant, as well as the role of the sovereign, here Parliament, that was an aggregate of many states.[33]

Burke wrote during a period of revolution, and this clearly influenced his somewhat reactionary response to the changes in constitutionalism that he saw emerging during this time.[34] Tradition and a strong sense of community based around this notion can be significant in forming the basis on which constituent power is attributed, particularly when this combines with the formation of a constitutional narrative. This is particularly the case in Burke's recognition of constitutionalism as including liberty, as the French Revolution supposed, but also including a particular structure, which should be founded on command not equality to ensure order.[35] In Burke's case community becomes interlinked with order and its maintenance, which narrows any possibility of competing or rival interests.

Burke is regarded as one of the founders of communitarianism and, as such, the community is central to his views on constitutional structures. Burke's community ensconces the traditional values of one shared purpose or one commonality that maintains strands of community that change only over extended periods of time. Burke's commonality centres upon a shared basis in constitutionalism and the state but not one that is egalitarian but rather where, through the constitution, the elite serves those not capable of such office. Further, for him while '[l]aw, being only made for the benefit of the community, cannot in any of one of its parts resist a demand which may comprehend the total of public interest', this does not necessarily lead to the protection of those whose interests are not bound to it, nor does it appear to be open to contestation.[36] This interest is very much based on a communitarian understanding that was wrapped

[33] E. Burke, 'Conciliation with America' in P. Langford (ed.), *Writings and Speeches of Edmund Burke* (Oxford: Clarendon Press, 1981), p. 193.

[34] E. Burke, *Reflections*, p. 160. [35] *Ibid.*, pp. 161, 187.

[36] E. Burke, *Speech on Presenting to the House a Plan for the Better Security of Independence to Parliament* (London: Dodsley, 1780), p. 49.

in Burke's idea of constitutionalism based on the interests of that society, in this instance the British system.

Yet, it is a form of community and constitutionalism that conjures allegiance and affection from the subjects of the legal order, and the constituent power holders maintain the association between order, allegiance and community, and so support the state. This commonality maintains the status quo to the extent that any change can only occur over a lengthy period of time. The significance of Burke's link of communitarianism with the state lies in its maintenance of a constant connection between community and constitutionalism, where one supports the other and thus must always be in line with the other's values, curtailing the role of constituent power to the preservation of both the community and the state.

3.2.4 *Hegel and common character*

Centring on the individual, Hegel takes a different, though no less significant position on commonality than Aristotle.[37] Hegel argues that the individual is independent of the community but at the same time remains dependent upon it for survival. The individual cannot exist without the external world; there is no room for atomisation. The other is necessitated; without the other there can be no recognition. Hegel argues that this custom presupposes the community of subjects and minds. According to Douzinas, within Hegel's broader theory this means that '[s]urvival depends on overcoming this radical split from the not-I, while maintaining a sense of uniqueness of self'.[38] Unlike Aristotle, for Hegel, the relational value with others becomes part of a community's paradigm.

First of all, communities contain the family, then civil society and lastly the state.[39] To function coherently, the family unit relies on other families, thus compelling the formation of a community. This creates the community and the community necessitates the state. For the community to function, and the family and civil society to be of utility, the state must be interlinked to the community; it is the method by which conflicting social

[37] See G. W. F. Hegel, *Philosophy of Right* (New York: Cosimo Press, 2008); S. Houlgate, *Freedom, Truth and History: An Introduction to Hegel's Philosophy* (New York: Taylor & Francis, 1991); Anon., 'Hegel's Political Philosophy of the State' (1917–1918) 31 *Harvard Law Review* 78; C. Douzinas, *Human Rights and Empire: The Political Philosophy of Cosmopolitanism* (New York: Routledge Cavendish, 2007).

[38] Douzinas, *Human Rights and Empire*, p. 37.

[39] Hegel, *Philosophy of Right*, p. 193.

forces can be transcended. This interlinks community, and as such its constitutional order, with the state. This suggests that rather than allowing debate to flourish as a priority, in becoming part of the constitutional function competing interests need to be submerged. Marx believed that this need to transcend conflicting forces was one of the main faults with Hegel's view of the state because it ignored the social context of human relationships.[40] Yet, the split between the self and the not-I remains significant at this point, as it confirms the existence of another that possesses a different valued identity.

Hegel argued that what gives communities their individual identity is the existence of an identifiable common character that informs beliefs and differentiates it from others. This discernible common character, shared and recognised by all in the community, leads to a unified society.[41] This common character mixes the concept of the legal community, in the guise of the state, with the societal community, as identified in beliefs and a common character, marrying the two in governance. The legal and the societal community are one in the same; both share a common character and establish the state community. All members of the state community share this common character and, if not, they are excluded from the legal, societal and state community to the extent of exercising constituent power.

National identities do not necessarily correspond with existent states but rather establish that which is considered necessary, a common character, to create a community and, as such, a state. Character relates not simply to language or culture but beyond such features to how a legally constituted community understands itself and operates in the world. The self and, so too, the not-I appear evident in this description. The recognition of others, that is, the other communities as states, remains important as the image of self is not always the correct one.[42] This, in turn, requires the recognition of specific character traits as part of the common character or as part of other communities but absent from yet others. Naturally, identifying such characteristics is problematic, which feeds into the difficulties in recognising communities and, as such, states, leading to disorder rather than unity. Attributes change, requiring communities to evolve and making development an imperative, while also leading to problems when a common character changes to an extent that the community loses

[40] K. Marx, *Critique of Hegel's Philosophy of Right* (ed. Joseph O'Malley) (Cambridge University Press, 1970), p. 82; Douzinas, *Human Rights and Empire*.

[41] Houlgate, *Freedom, Truth and History*, p. 15.

[42] Hegel, *Philosophy of Right*.

its unifying dynamic. Without change in the nature of character there can arguably be no progression but a static snapshot of the group as it was at a particular moment. Such stagnancy feeds into states, making constituent power holders reliant on a past moment that no longer suffices to explain their presence. Such issues are present where constitutions fail to evolve, with states becoming relics of historical significance and present irrelevance.

Aristotle's theory that commonality equals membership of a community shares much of its functionality with common character; certainly there are similarities regarding the identification of what are virtuous character traits that are the basis of common character or commonality and those that are undesired. If an atomised individual does not share character traits with any other, this infers that they will not be admitted to the community of which others may be members.[43] The earlier discussion of the binary underpinnings of community becomes evident in identifying specific common traits. If a character trait of a specific community is regarded differently by members, both positively and negatively, potentially those unimpressed by its inclusion may be subsumed by the idea that this common character is of such a fundamental nature that it cannot be changed or discarded without critically harming the community.

Thus Hegel's common character community operates in a similar fashion to Aristotle's commonality community. Both displace those who differ from or disagree with characteristics or simply do not and cannot possess them, preventing such individuals from actively taking part, including holding constituent power, as members of a community. Both concepts dampen the discussion even amongst those who, while sharing such characteristics, do not necessarily consider them to be an underlying good of the community. This emphasises harmony within the community as opposed to discord or debate on the underlying nature or the identified common character, stultifying growth. Both commonality and common character produce a binary system, which for those on the outside of the community may have intrinsically negative implications. Hegel's community reinforces the idea of the original members establishing the required character traits, which ensures that to gain recognition as a member of the community aping of these characteristics is necessary. When this form of community becomes intertwined with a legal order and the basis of membership, the commonality is determinative of constituted power, thus

[43] Anon., 'Hegel's Political Philosophy', 80.

leading to differentiation based upon subjective understandings within a group of what is a necessary common character.

3.2.5 *Alternative communities: Marxism, Nancy and the community of being*

Marxism recognises two forms of community: the community as communion and the community of being. The community as communion recognises the individual only as far as they remain part of the broader group; the individual partakes in community only to the degree that they are subsumed into a larger whole. In contrast, the community of being is 'what takes place always through others and for others. It is not the space of the egos – subjects and substance that are at bottom immortal – but of Is who are always *others* ... community therefore occupies a singular state: it assumes the impossibility of its own immanence.'[44] This depiction of community is the very opposite of commonality. Nancy's community relies upon characteristics held by others in the community, an external identification of the possession of a commonality that has been branded as essential to join the multitudes and possess constituent power rather than the personal possession of a commonality.

This distinction between being in community with others and belonging to the more commonly conceived community acts as an essential differentiation to the operation of constituent power.[45] Marxism regards the development of society to be the change from one socio-economic function to another. Marx argued that both religion and the state have created communities that are false and that it is only when a genuine community of social and economic equals is created that community will fulfil its proper purpose.[46] In each of these, Marx identifies a defining aspect of the community, which its members believe or follow in the guise of religion, the state, or social and economic equality. A community of individuals of equal standing sharing in common beliefs and goals operate a form of ideal governance. Yet, even if solidarity and reciprocity are central, such a community will not necessarily result in a basis for legal development that

[44] Nancy, *Inoperative*, p. 15.

[45] V. Kartashkin, 'The Marxist-Leninist Approach: The Theory of Class Struggle and Contemporary International Law' in R. St. J. MacDonald and D. M. Johnston (eds.), *The Structure and Process of International Law* (Leiden: Martinus Nijhoff, 1983), p. 78.

[46] K. Marx, *Capital: A Critique of Political Economy – The Process of Capitalist Production as a Whole*, Vol. III, Part 2 (ed. F. Engels) (New York: Cosimo, 2007), p. 967.

accommodates dissent from those within the community who disagree on the process of identifying such common beliefs or goals.[47] Arguably, identifying subjects of constitutionalism within this community almost becomes unnecessary as the ideal that operates regulates the governance order making constituent power of less value.

For Nancy, community as generally represented is negative.[48] Nancy states that 'the gravest and most painful testimony of the modern world, the one that possibly involves all other testimonies to which the epoch must answer … is the testimony of the dissolution, the dislocation, or the conflagration of community'.[49] Here Nancy identifies a community narrative that establishes a hierarchy of ideals, which is ultimately binary and exclusionary, as that which has impacted upon how community is now conceived and utilised. In contrast, Nancy argues that community should be conceived of as a group of 'beings in common', and using this he attempts to draw away from the issues presented in the work of Hegel and Aristotle in establishing community as a form of hegemony.[50] Being in common with others is the opposite of common beings or of belonging to an essential community, as the individual must always be facing others, never themselves, and so is part of the community and the community is also part of them.[51] On the other hand, common beings are what are identifiable in the more general community discourse. This is an attempt to divert away from the identification of common character or commonality as the essential element of community.

Nancy suggests a difference between a common being and a being in common, as demonstrated in Burke, as communitarianism, since it

> assigns to community a common being, whereas community is a matter of something quite different, namely, of existence inasmuch as it is in common, but without letting itself be absorbed into a common substance. Being in common has nothing to do with communion, with fusion into a body, into a unique and ultimate identity that would no longer be exposed.[52]

[47] E. Frazer, *The Problems of Communitarian Politics, Unity and Conflict* (Oxford University Press, 1999), p. 52.

[48] Nancy has entirely moved away from the use of community, preferring to substitute it with 'being together', 'being in common' and 'being-with'; further, his abandonment of this term underlies the difficulties that he emphasised in his earlier work; see J. Nancy, 'The Confronted Community' (2003) 6 *Postcolonial Studies* 23, 31.

[49] Nancy, *Inoperative*, p. 1. [50] *Ibid.*, p. 52.

[51] Douzinas, *The End of Human Rights*, p. 215.

[52] Nancy, *Inoperative*, p. xxxviii.

The common substance alongside Aristotle's commonality have within them the tools to create both an elitist and exclusionary community. In contrast, Nancy identifies a community that is not allied with communion and where individuals or Is are not subsumed into the greater whole, but also recognises the other within the community. Though he acknowledges that community has been a dominant feature of philosophical thought and that these other conceptions of community have negatively impacted upon social and political growth, Nancy's community does not emerge from the historical resonances of empire that are the foundations of Aristotle, Hegel and Burke, a point recognised in his later abandonment of the term.[53]

The significance of Nancy's community lies in its attempts to reverse Aristotle's idea of commonality and the essentialism that its binary nature creates. The idea of a whole or community based upon allegiances as the basis for the community is far removed from Nancy's idea of being in common, where the creation of community does not involve subjugation or being subsumed into the greater whole. Yet, as Nancy admits, community largely operates around what he characterises as common beings; thus it remains difficult to imagine community emerging from the more prevalent descriptions in a manner that would completely transform the general conception of its meaning.

Even under this alternative identification the customary configurations in which commonality or common character are necessary for communities to operate as a basis for governance remain operative. If the identification of community is generally as common beings and as such it subsumes the members into it, even if Nancy was successful in escaping the more common implications, it is hard to foresee a general use of community that would not have this association. While Nancy's definition of commonality certainly eschews some of the issues that the other connotations of commonality present, it does not do enough to prescribe its more general invocations. Community's appeal within constitutional governance is rarely with Nancy in mind.

3.2.6 *Commonality and community*

Frazer argues that '"community" is a concept with open frontiers and vague contours … which conveys a wealth of meaning … it is shot through with value judgements, it conjures up associations and images

[53] Nancy 'Confronted Community', 34.

from a wide, wide range of discourses and contexts'.[54] This summation distils the difficulties in extracting a meaning for community within governance, while also setting out why a discussion of its by-products remains important. As Frazer asserts, community comes with a vast set of meanings that, while not always employed by those who use it, nonetheless makes it an inefficient tool for devising a basis for a legal order. In these four iterations of community commonality appears as an essential trope within its operations. These four examples, while not intended as a comprehensive survey, point to the effects on constituent power when commonality is an essential characteristic of community membership that in turn stands for a governance order. Even when rejecting commonality, as in Nancy's case, it still forms a central element of community debate. Consequently, even in instances where distance is sought between community and commonality the latter remains a definitional feature of community theories. Authors such as Nancy identify the negative ramifications of commonality and seek to avoid its implications; yet these are too well entrenched in community's common use to evade completely its underlying assumptions.

Framing commonality as common habitation or purpose could be understood to be a shared perception of interest in the common good. While conceptions of the common good vary, an interest in its achievement could be utilised as a basis for commonality. Yet, such a common civic virtue exists only in the abstract. In addition to the difficulty of identifying commonality, as Douzinas argues 'an exclusionary construction of culture as immanent to belonging and the interpretation of majority values as the absolute truth; these traits mimic, at the local level, state distain and oppression of all minorities'.[55] Commonality also stands in stark contrast to Nancy's 'beings in common', which rejects the idea that any form of commonality is required within community. Ultimately, as Douzinas articulates, Aristotelian commonality establishes hegemony of one set of principles, which is historically Eurocentric and colonial. Thus, as a basis for community in any sphere it would be difficult to extract objective parameters from the holders of constituted power that would not be self-serving; as such, it is more likely to be defined as their interest rather than the interests of those holding constituent power. Even such a suggestion presupposes that commonality has enabled an identification

[54] Frazer, *The Problems of Communitarian Politics*, p. 60.

[55] Douzinas, *The End of Human Rights*, p. 138.

of the subjects of constitutionalism, which is not exclusionary in the first place.

Nancy's theory seems appealing. It illustrates how community can be used in a positive sense to bring about equality of participation and membership; however, the predominance of commonality in most incidences calls into question its use as a basis for identifying the subjects of constitutionalism and constituent power. It is unlikely that commonality's elitism married with the binary community can be dismissed to an extent that would legitimate community's use in order to establish constitutional governance. Commonality, common character or compatibility may not necessarily be negative attributes and, as long as they draw members together, they remain important. The difficulty lies when commonality is used to define the group that holds constituent and, thus, constituted power. If the members of the community are ultimately the holders of constituent power this bases constitutionalism on exclusionary grounds.

Aristotelian commonality creates an elitist and exclusionary community, visible in many of the theories that followed his theories. As Nancy suggests, if the basis of constitutionalism is to rely on commonality, it will, as shared traits are identified as necessary for the community, create a hierarchy of ideals where the individual actor is subsumed into a greater whole. Even if Nancy's own form of community was utilised as a basis for constitutionalism, arguably the more entrenched perception would remain. None of the alternative versions of commonality, including Hegel's common character or Burke's common purpose, addresses this underlying difficulty of perception. While Nancy's vision is attractive, it is unlikely that it will become the majority view, and thus commonality remains a central characteristic of community.

Those who do not share the commonality, even if they were to gain membership at a later date, will only be assessed as part of the community when they have adopted its commonality. The space created by commonality, if it were to be adopted into constitutionalism, would therefore be negative. Naturally, not every subject of the myriad individual governance regimes holds constituent power or is involved in its development, but basing the group on commonality establishes an order that, like Aristotle's or Burke's, will be restricted to elite citizens and unreflective of actual subjects and objects of governance. Commonality subsumes those who question its nature within community, even assuming that the commonality identified by community is a positive attribute, silencing or at least dampening dissent. By focusing on beings in common, Nancy seeks to avoid these damaging definitions of community; yet the generally purveyed version is what is foremost in mind when it is used in establishing constituent power.

Certainly, community binarity is not unique amongst forms of association; however, its inculcation of and implications for constitutionalism are critical to its use as a paradigm to establish constituent power. Three elements characterise its negative binary nature. First, there are those who come within the community and those who do not, and to be without generally carries adverse associations. Second, communities silence those who fall within the community but who do not support, or who come to doubt, the entirety of the community's ethos; dissent is thus not an aspect of the community narrative. Third, these two elements combined make community an exclusionary space. Thus, community in the guise of commonality emphasises harmony or at least a common interest and vision of what is best for the community. While harmony may indeed subsist in certain moments, it is often fleeting. Arguably, any commonly conceived positive attributes of community are outweighed by the perception created within its innately binary nature, which establishes an exclusionary space and dampens discourse. Beyond the limits set by the generally conceived notions of commonality the implication for constituent and constituted power is detrimental to constitutionalism.

Community is unsuited to constitutionalism as it prejudges the suitability of constituent power holders prior to any grant of power on the basis of a preordained characteristic. In turn, in circumstances where constituent power has been granted, it prevents its holders from discussing the basis for that community's foundation, as to do so would question their possession of legitimate power.

Aristotle wrote that

> [s]ince we see that every city-state is a sort of community and that every community is established for the sake of some good (for everyone does everything for the sake of what they believe to be good), it is clear that every community aims at some good, and the community which has the most authority of all and includes all the others aims highest, that is, at the good with the most authority. This is what is called the city-state or political community.[56]

Community's operation is not necessarily always negative. There are positive attributes that often bind a legal order together; however, in the context of constitutionalism, its binary nature, its reliance on commonality and the overarching descriptions of the existing state community carry

[56] Aristotle, *Politics*.

with them unnecessary associations. Community inculcates a top-down approach, where the elite institutes the commonality necessary to hold constituent power. Commonality excludes room for competing interests and debate of conflicting mores, as to do otherwise would undermine the foundational value of community. Since it is reliant upon the legitimate possession of constituent power to confer constituted power, such communities undermine democratic legitimacy. Thus, it is suggested that an alternative to community is required to sustain constitutionalism and constituent power.

3.3 Constituency

Constituency consists of a group of actors associated with the nexus between constituted and constituent power.[57] Alternatively, it could be defined as the context where power is exercised and vested outside of a distinct group but on its behalf and in its interest. While such characterisations may be linked to any legal governance order, as it provides parameters for the exercise of constituted and constituent power, it is most closely associated with constitutionalism. These definitions root constituency in an understanding of process rather than as a static snapshot of a group attached to a legal order. Rehfeld suggests that most political theorists rarely give the concept of constituency much thought, resulting in only passing references.[58] Yet, importantly, he also argues that constituency is not indelibly linked to voting or electorates, broadening constituency beyond an indication of a right to participate to a much wider political concept linked with the legal order that it substantiates.[59]

Questions as to constituency's role in the identification of constituent power include whether it is compatible with elements of constitutionalism, such as the rule of law, divisions of power and democratic legitimacy, and whether any of its underlying concepts, such as binarity, could prevent it from being a sustainable choice to identify the group associated with constituent power. Further, constituency's potential drawbacks, such as binarity, vagueness and lack of predictability, need some consideration, as such attributes may place it beyond any useful invocation as a basis for constituent power. Ultimately, this analysis leads to an inquiry as to the

57 For an alternative view, see I. R. Wall 'A Different Constituent Power: Agamben and Tunisia', in I. R. Wall, C. Douzinas and M. Stone (eds.), *New Critical Legal Thinking: Law and the Political* (London: Birkbeck Law Press, 2012).

58 Rehfeld, *The Concept of Constituency*, pp. 30–3.

59 *Ibid.*, pp. 4–5; this would be in relation to electoral constituency.

viability of constituency as an alternative to community and whether, by itself, it is a potentially superior basis to understand how constitutionalism transforms, and, in addition, its practicable future within global constitutionalisation.

3.3.1 Constituency and process

Process plays a key role in defining the parameters of constituency. Here, process is understood as a series of interconnected actions or functions interacting to establish an ever-evolving definition of a group associated with the operation of governance.[60] Within constituency, process functions as a series of interconnected activities in combination with actors that collectively establish the parameters of a constituency. This role of process within a legal order establishes the boundaries within which law is interpreted and applied. How these processes interact defines the remit in which a constituency operates. This recognises constituency beyond a strict positivist or static construction and opens it to development and change.

Constituency is not predicated upon the existence or requirement that some form of constitutionalism be present; therefore, while the contextual discussion here is constitutionalism, constituency may exist alongside alternate governance processes. Utilising process establishes a constituency within a constitutional process that is not, in Kingsbury's words, '*statu nascendi*' or inert in either the domestic or other realm.[61] This definition of process links to law as it functions and operates independently of constitutional moments. As such, constituency functions in any legal order and enables that order to change and evolve as the functions that the legal order serves to advance. Admittedly, constitutional process makes understanding constituency easier and accusations of vagueness less conceivable; yet this does not discount its operation in other governance orders.

The norms that have already been discussed – the rule of law, divisions of power and democratic legitimacy – are combined in examining the parameters of constituency, and it is their operation that ensures that constituent power may be identified within constituency. The processes within constitutionalism that create constituency's parameters

[60] See R. Higgins, *Problems and Process: International Law and How We Use It* (Oxford University Press, 1994).

[61] Kingsbury, 'Concept of "Law"', 36.

are cumulative and do not give way to debates on their relative content; instead their operation and application identify the strictures of law and constituency. The underlying rationales for the norms of constitutionalism's existence are linked to an identifiable group whose relations are moderated by these norms. Those who are entitled to engage in a democratic process, the holders of constituent power are, as has already been described, connected with the holders of constituted power, who are checked by the rule of law and the division of power. It is this connection between the holders of constituent and constituted power with the rule of law, divisions of power and democratic legitimacy that also moderates their action and establishes the process, and thus also identifies a constituency and its members.

One criticism that could be levelled at process is that it will lead to uncertainty in identifying the law and thus to ambiguity in identifying the subjects of a constituency. Higgins, as a proponent of legal process, admits that it may make it more difficult to identify norms and sources but that this in itself does not preclude predictability, an essential element of law.[62] Predictability is necessary for establishing the parameters of constituency, particularly with regard to its associations. Process does not necessarily result in vagueness; simply it is an understanding of constitutionalism that encompasses all the interactions involved. The extent of these processes, as identified in the operation of the rule of law, divisions of power and democratic legitimacy, and the complexity of their operation, function as to define constituency. The rule of law and divisions of power are fundamentally linked to constituted power, while democratic legitimacy is reliant upon constituent power; as such the process involved in these norms locates the subjects of the constituency.

To eliminate the charge of uncertainty, the parameters of constituency must be made clear; if the subjects of constituency remain ambiguous, then the charge of vagueness will be vindicated. Constituency is reliant on the core elements of constitutionalism itself and the operation of its related norms. In the absence of democratic legitimacy arguably there are no constituent power holders, or at the very least they are unable to exercise their authority. Therefore, the process that would define a constitutional constituency is also absent. Other forms of constituency may still be present, but the constitutional constituency would not endure. Process functions as the hinge around which the identification of constituent

[62] Higgins, *Problems and Process*, p. 8.

power holders rests, as such constitutional norms are objective factors, establishing the certainty necessary for its operation.

3.3.2 *Constituency as binary*

Constituency, like community, is binary, though, as it operates as a continual process of redefinition, perhaps not in the temporal completeness of the latter. In similar terms to community, the subjects of constituency's legal order may both possess or lack constituent power. As already discussed, community's binary nature creates a negative imputation upon those who are not contained within it. Further, community does not enable constituent power holders to exercise fully their warrant thus undermining its use in constitutionalism. Community's negative imputations of exclusion emerge from its association with exclusionary or ascendancy roots combined with its abnegation of internal critique based upon the non-recognition of others. In such contexts community has a dampening effect on law's development. Binarity remains an essential element of constituency but unlike its association with community's operation, concerns regarding exclusion based upon negative imputations are largely absent.

Constituency excludes subjects of constitutionalism from constituent power, but it is the method by which the assemblage is created that rules out the negative elements associated with omission from community. If the relevant constituency is indelibly linked to constitutionalism, then it is the processes associated with it that outline the parameters for this constituency. As the constitution evolves, the constituency linked to it also develops. The divide between rule and process acts as the delineation of those within and without, and the combination of both creates a constituency. As an example, the prerequisites of democratic legitimacy require that the holders of constituent power exercise their warrant. If an actor has a democratic right to participate in a constitutional regime, then they are part of the constitutional process and therefore are also part of the process that establishes the constituency, coupled with also being members of that constituency. The holders of constituted power are curtailed by the rule of law and divisions of power; they are therefore part of the constitutional process and are also members of the constituency linked to its operation.

This delineation of constituency requires that those absorbed into the system become part of the constitutional process as is it functions and thus establishes membership, but it also permits members to contribute to its change as constitutionalism evolves. Enabling new participants to engage with the process of evolution and not forcing their adoption of the entirety of what has already been settled, with little impact of their admission upon content, is what differentiates community from constituency. Admission would not be based upon the subjective decision of existing subjects of the constituency founded upon the possession of characteristics but rather by their engagement with a process that necessitates their presence within the constituency.

The potential power of current members of a constituency to exclude others undermines its use within constitutionalism. Constituency's operation becomes problematic if the established constituent power holders can redesign the constitutional process to exclude those who wish to have influence upon the content of constitutionalism, but are excluded from the process by the holders of constituted power. Those within the constituency, if they wish constitutional law to be applicable to those outside the constituency have no choice but to include these outsiders in the process. For the constitution to be applicable, all must form part of the constituency. It is the operation of constituent and constituted power as tempered by the rule of law, divisions of power and democratic legitimacy that sets the operation of the constitution and its associated processes.

Thus, the assemblage creates a constituency not based upon negative connotations of external association. Unlike Aristotle's commonality, a subject does not have to satisfy a test as to its possession to become a constituent power holder. Rather, the processes involved in constitutionalism set the parameters of constituency's remit. Being outside of a given constituency does not imply any lack of compatibility, commonality or otherwise; indeed, these factors are irrelevant to constituency. This is because constituency's borders are not based upon any value, but upon participation in the constitutional process and the creation of space in which an understanding of constitutionalism operates. Participation may become problematic in circumstances where the process itself hampers or fails to enable all to engage. In such circumstances constituency relies on constitutionalism to ensure that all who should participate hold the necessary tools to do so and take their place.

In domestic law, the alliance of nation with constituency often creates a negative component, disrupting the political balance or structure of a state.[63] The omission of common interest, such as a national identity, as the

[63] This may be particularly problematic within states with multiple national identities and can lead to continual subdivision of the state when the state or constituency itself is

basis of a legal relationship enables global constitutionalisation or any other non-state constitutionalism to avoid such consequences. Participation stands as the basis of membership, and not the sharing of a commonality with other participants. As such, being in a constituency is not necessarily good or bad, and entry requires no change in personal identification. Absence from the constituency does not institute pariah status, nor is it a value-based judgement. Constitutional constituencies potentially ignore nationalistic boundaries, which have evolved to become states and been used as rationales for smaller and smaller entities of commonality conditioning participation on a sense of common mores. Constituency introduces the notion of constituted and constituent power allocations to the stakeholders within the space established by process. This is a broader and a more fluid understanding than that connected to community.

As it is reliant upon a constitutional system to operate according to the rule of law, divisions of power and democratic legitimacy, process may be exclusionary to the extent that these elements of constitutionalism do not always function successfully. The exclusion of women from the vote for such a long period is an example of a constitutional process excluding actors that should have been considered members of the constituency. This is a weakness in constituency. Yet, as states rely on constitutionalism to ensure the legitimacy of a governance order, this reliance would also have to be maintained at the global level to ensure the legitimacy of the constituency and constitutionalism, both of which must be operating at their optimum levels.

Constituency brings together into an identifiable assemblage a broad array of participants possessing competing interests; yet constituent power allows for discussion and debate between these interests. Constituency creates an on-going space for debate. The use of constituency does not suggest harmony. A constituency can reflect a broad spectrum of ideas and interests, which may be in competition but are balanced within a constitutional process. The nature of constituent power is such that its holders do not necessarily share the same mores or interests. Thus, constituency creates an arena within which dissent and disagreement is part of the process and indeed integral to its operation. Consequently, being outside of the constituency is not in itself a negative, nor is holding characteristics or interests that the majority does not share. Constituency does

defined by a collective national identify that does not serve all its citizens. The break-up of Yugoslavia or, indeed, devolution within the UK are two examples of states divided along nationalistic lines.

not suggest anything about outside parties and does not create a space restricted by morality.

3.3.3 *Constituency in the development of constitutional governance*

A good comparator, from the perspective of vagueness and potential claims of lack of predictability, is the operation of the UK's constitutional order and the creation of its constituency.[64] King argues that it is continuity rather than discontinuity that has been the hallmark of UK constitutionalism, and establishing this continuity in constituency aids in countering charges of vagueness.[65] Certainly, the UK public law system is *sui generis*, but its modern constitutional history has been a process that has proved the steadfastness of constitutionalism.[66] The UK Constitution has, without reliance on the identifiable structures of other domestic constitutional configurations, functioned successfully over a long period of time, arguably operating just as effectively as codified constitutions. For that reason, some consideration needs to be given as to how these processes operate in the UK context and their relative importance to constituency's functionality.[67]

Munro states that the distinction between the UK constitutional structure and most others is that in the vast majority of states a document or a set of associated documents are definable as the constitution. This is not necessarily as straightforward as drawing a line between written or unwritten constitutions, but rather written constitutions and documentary constitutions. In the case of the UK, where the constitutional structure is based upon many sources, there is no single set of documents that can be singled out as containing the entirety of its constitutional arrangements. Within the UK's constitutionalisation process, although there could be what are identified as 'constitutional moments', such as after the Civil War and Restoration, much has been preserved since before this period, while other elements are still being identified and developed.

Constituency in UK public law is linked to the operating governance structure and as such is concurrent with its constitutional structure. Although there is opacity, this does not prevent the functioning of the

64 Though some reject the British Constitution as a true constitutional entity, see, for example, D. Grimm, 'The Achievement of Constitutionalism' in Dobner and Loughlin (eds.), *Twilight*, p. 11.

65 King, *The British Constitution*, p. 2.

66 Other documentary constitutions include Israel, Saudi Arabia and New Zealand.

67 King, *The British Constitution*, pp. 2–4.

system. As Lord Bingham stated in *Watkins* v. *Secretary of State for the Home Department*, it is possible to

> open the door to arguments whether other rights less obviously fundamental, basic or constitutional than the right to vote and the right to preserve the confidentiality of legal correspondence, were sufficiently close to or analogous with those rights to be treated ... in the same way. Since, in the absence of a codified constitution, these terms are incapable of precise definition, the outcome of such argument in other than clear cases would necessarily be uncertain.[68]

Every element of the constitutional structure does not need to be catalogued. This murkiness is not only the preserve of the UK Constitution or indeed documentary constitutions. The system of unenumerated rights in Ireland, rights not listed in the Irish Constitution but that can be derived from it and are thus constitutional, is yet another example.[69]

As a purely statist system, UK constitutionalism does not share the same issues as non-state constituencies, and therefore some comparisons are difficult to maintain. Nevertheless, the creation and establishment of a constitutional system linked to an identifiable constituency is certainly relevant to non-state constitutional regimes. The parameters of the constituency are more readily identifiable within the confines of the state; however, it is through the process of constitutionalism and its nexus with constituency that the parameters become distinct and the operation of constitutional norms becomes evident. Importantly, the vagueness of some aspects of UK constitutionalism does not lead to unworkability; the process of constitutional law allows it to operate successfully. Process can therefore be the basis for a functioning constitutional order, even in systems with dispersed constitutional sources. The holders of constituent and constituted power, together with norms of constitutionalism, can be readily identified. While certainly there maybe underlying arguments regarding vagueness and process, it remains possible for constitutionalism to operate and, as such, for a constitutional constituency to emerge.

3.4 Conclusion: community or constituency?

The assertion that constituency is preferable to community centres upon defining constituency as an assemblage whose attributes are defined by

[68] *Watkins* v. *Secretary of State for the Home Department* [2006] UKHL 17 at para. 26.

[69] These are contained in Article 40.3, as interpreted by the Irish Supreme Court in *Ryan* v. *The Attorney General* [1965] Irish Reports 294.

the processes that take place within its operation. In contrast, community by and large defines its membership by the commonality that they purport to share. This inversion is fundamental in understanding why constituency better advances constitutionalism. Constituency's link to constitutional norms establishes its borders and binds the identification of constituent power holders to these norms. Community, in contrast, in its most common invocation is bound by commonality.

Redefining a constituency to include or exclude participants does not require the constituent power holders to reconceptualise the constituency, as there is no value judgement attached to its parameters. In contrast to community, which requires reconceptualisation if the participants in community are to change, a constituency can gain or lose participants, depending upon contingencies beyond previously established parameters. The borders of constituency are fluid enough to incorporate various elements but not so permeable as to be consequently vague and unworkable as a result of opacity.

While the parameters of constituency are as debatable as constitutionalism itself, this does not take away from the utility of a process centred on constituent and constituted power. Proposing constituency as a viable alternative to community relies on a process dependent upon the operation of constitutional norms, which are open to manipulation. Critics might argue that this is a mere rebranding exercise, that constituency is community by any other name, but this is not the case. Instead, constituency establishes an arena within which constitutionalism and the entirety of its interactions may be understood. Constituency's characteristics are associated with the legal order it serves, in this case constitutionalism, and as such constituency is compatible with constitutionalism. Its binary nature leads to exclusion, but exclusion based upon process and not upon value judgements. Its binary nature does not dampen debate. The parameters set are entirely decipherable and essentially positive. Therefore, constituency serves constitutionalism and, in particular, the functioning of the rule of law, divisions of power and democratic legitimacy.

In characterising the subjects of constitutionalism as linked to constituent and constituted power it is necessary to ensure such a grouping bases its operation upon processes that do not subsume or dictate interests amongst subjects. In the case of constituency, this is ensured by the operation of constitutionalism itself and not by an unconnected sense of commonality. This core rationale is the prime reason for preferring constituency above community in identifying the holders of constituent power within a constitutional order. Constituency brings the discussion back to one of the core aims of this book, whether participants, such as states, can be considered constitutional actors.[70] If the global constitutional process establishes the borders of the global constituency, the question is no longer whether states and other non-state actors in global law can be considered constitutional actors. Rather, the question is whether there is a global constitutional process and, if this is answered positively, who the legal actors engaged in this process, are. This analysis will lead to the identification of the constituent power holders within a global constituency.

[70] Teubner, 'Societal Constitutionalism', 3.

4

The global constitutionalisation debate in context

A plethora of perspectives clamour for attention within current global legal theory, with three particular modes of debate readily identifiable: first, purely theoretical discussions that aim to give a philosophical foundation to international law; second, theories that combine the philosophical approach with descriptive proposals on the contemporary operation of international law as well as incorporating proposals for the future; and, third, purely descriptive discussions of present international law sitting alongside the other two. While the first will not be a central focus, the second and third are intertwined with any understanding of global constitutionalisation, with it sitting, most accurately, in the second category. These categorisations should be regarded as on a spectrum. It must also be acknowledged that they are not hermetically sealed, with each influencing the other's development as well as relying on broader on-going legal theoretical debates. Therefore each proposition stretches the parameters of these classifications and ought not to be understood as inferring a judgement as to their relative worth.

Some current debates, such as global legal pluralism, have antecedents whose current characterisations advance prior theories, whereas others, such as fragmentation or global administrative law, represent a response and attempt to depict the variegated system emergent within international law. The global constitutionalisation debate sits amongst these propositions, at times borrowing elements and at others regarding it as entirely apart from these propositions. This chapter aims to contextualise these debates in the landscape of contemporary international law and to question how global constitutionalisation interacts with and uses these other approaches to global legal theory and, further, what these debates tell us about the global legal order.

In the first forty years following the Charter, long-established state-based iterations combined with theories disputing the classical visions' very existence have forged the core debates within international law.[1] Though unfolding events would stretch traditional accounts to a point of absurdum, with the exception of those such as Verdross, Jenks, Scelle and Friedmann, international legal theory moved apparently little beyond the classical law of nations.[2] The New Haven School forging a process-based approach, the critical approaches of Kennedy, the rise of the feminist debate and TWAIL (third-world approaches to international law), amongst others, fashioned alternative narratives that undermined some of the accepted tropes of previous decades.[3] Their work was followed by the neo-colonial, queer, CLS (critical legal studies) and other critiques adding to the clamour for a reorientating and re-examining of both the historical and cultural foundations of international law's operation. Alongside these debates, considerations of Kant, Kelsen, Marx, Grotius, Suarez, Vitoria and Vattel, and their respective legacies, continues apace. Such historical approaches, buffeted somewhat by Koskenniemi's evaluation of international legal history, tend towards an understanding of how we have arrived at our present position as a tool to comprehend where the global legal order may venture.[4] This ensures that the older philosophical approaches continue to have purchase, and it is in this guise that towards the end of the chapter both the New Haven School and Verdross are considered.[5]

As international law continues to expand and becomes ever more intricate, the requirement for a more fully realised conceptual basis for the global legal order has become a focal point of current debate. The diversity in debates that emerged, particularly since the end of the Cold War, presents an important opportunity to assess the perceived urgency to develop a core to the international legal order's structure. An assortment of approaches, within the three categories outlined, with varying success, seek to fulfil this role.

[1] R. Domingo, *The New Global Law* (Cambridge University Press, 2011), pp. 53–77; S. Marks, *The Riddle of All Constitutions: International Law, Democracy, and the Critique of Ideology* (Oxford University Press, 2003), pp. 30–1.

[2] C. W. Jenks, *Law, Freedom and Welfare* (London: Stevens & Sons, 1963); G. Scelle, *Droit international public: manuel élémentaire avec les textes essentiels* (Paris: Domat-Montchrestien, 1944); Friedman, *Structure*; A. Verdross, 'Forbidden Treaties in International Law, Comments on Professor Garner's Report on "The Law of Treaties"' 31 (1937) *American Journal of International Law* 571.

[3] D. Kennedy, *International Legal Structures* (Berlin: Nomos, 1987); Charlesworth and Chinkin, *A Feminist Analysis*.

[4] Koskenniemi, *The Gentle Civilizer*.

[5] A. Anghie, *Imperialism, Sovereignty and the Making of International Law* (Cambridge University Press, 2004); Douzinas, *The End of Human Rights*, p. 215.

These theories, amongst an array of proposals, sponsor alternatives to understanding, developing and challenging the international legal order's content and structure. Such variety suggests that, at present, no single method sets out global law's composition. This presents an opportunity to evaluate how it is that global governance proffers such oscillating depictions. There have been a number of worthwhile and appealing attempts to give foundations to these developments, including global legal pluralism, fragmentation, global governance networks and global administrative law. Each of these approaches has in common, while attempting to decipher both the positive and negative potentialities presently before global governance, the desire to understand how international law actually works.

The third category of approaches, rather than seeking a more theoretical understanding of the global legal order, is both more descriptive and perspective. This approach sees both the possibilities for reform within international law, particularly in the fragmentation debate, but also potential future difficulties. Through understanding past developments and critiquing whether international law has successfully fulfilled its role to date, these theories most often present an alternative descriptive basis that seeks to illustrate the global legal order's true nature. Such discussions require more than an analysis of international law for law's sake alone, but rather an attempt to conceptualise a system of global governance. Both fragmentation and global administrative law form part of this category, with each pushing the limits of traditional representations of international law.

Global constitutionalisation falls within the second category. This group attempts to combine both a descriptive analysis with a more theoretical underpinning and is evidenced not only in constitutionalisation but also within global legal pluralism and global governance.[6] These theories stand on a spectrum between the first and third categories with various proponents offering differing quantities of description and theory, but all generally contributing a basis to understand both present and future global governance.

The question this chapter asks is not why constitutionalisation is the preferred choice over these alternatives but rather what the broader context can tell us about the rationales for a constitutional approach. This chapter requires a perspective that considers the wide spectrum of present

[6] For an interesting discussion of how such discussions proceed, see A. von Bogdandy, 'General Principles of International Public Authority: Sketching a Research Field' (2008) 11 *German Law Journal* 1909, 1910–11.

global legal theory, but at the same time this inquiry should not become muddled in the finer points of difference between these approaches. The four approaches of global legal pluralism, fragmentation, global governance and global administrative law will each be considered as alternative and complementary understandings of global governance. The core rationale, content and impact of each of these theories are discussed, followed by a consideration of their impact upon the constitutionalisation debate. Similarly, the two historical approaches of New Haven and Verdross both constitute accounts of governance within the global order that have heavily influenced present depictions.

This chapter considers why constitutionalisation and the debates surrounding it are worth analysing as a basis for discussion of international law's future and thus what has instigated or prompted this current proliferation of approaches. Global constitutionalisation offers a platform for debate, enabling a cogent and deliberative discussion of global governance but within a constitutional paradigm that funnels its approach into a particular form. Thus before dealing with global constitutionalisation it is important to consider what alternative approaches to the global legal order offer and what this tells of its state.

4.1 Context of debate

4.1.1 Global legal pluralism

Global legal pluralism focuses on international law as a non-hierarchal system of autonomous pluralist legal systems based upon democratic institutional orders.[7] Global legal pluralism centres on international law and human rights, and aims to evoke a legal system based upon recognising the multiple normative communities of practice that have emerged. As such it does not aim to replicate the traditional debate between sovereign principles and universalist systems. Law emerges from normative communities that are not arranged nor compete in a hierarchal order. As

[7] S. Wheatley, 'Indigenous Peoples and the Right of Political Autonomy in an Age of Global Legal Pluralism' in M. Freeman and D. Napier (eds.), *Law and Anthropology: Current Legal Issues* (Oxford University Press, 2009), p. 351; P. S. Berman, 'A Pluralist Approach to International Law' (2007) 32 *Yale Journal of International Law* 301; P. S. Berman, 'Global Legal Pluralism' (2006–2007) 80 *Southern California Law Review* 1155; A. Fischer-Lescano and G. Teubner, 'Regime Collisions: The Vain Search for Legal Unity in the Fragmentation of International Law' (2005) *Michigan Journal of International Law* 99; P. S. Berman, *Global Legal Pluralism: A Jurisprudence of Law Beyond Borders* (Cambridge University Press, 2012).

law is rarely the purview of one system alone, hybridity becomes essential. It is in the hybrid arena between these normative communities where law interacts and develops into the system of global law we understand today.

Global legal pluralism usually eschews the debates on polycentric legal pluralism that take place with regard to domestic systems. Legal pluralism focuses upon one geographic area, centring on the relationship between law and society. Thus, the focal point is on understanding domestic legal orders in the context of the multiple interactions and relationships of various forms of law within that order or alternatively considering the ideological diversity within legal orders.[8] In itself this has resulted in a multitude of approaches making an important contribution to socio-legal studies. Legal pluralism's roots in legal anthropology have long been influential in domestic debates on multiculturalism, colonialism and human rights, and while the vestiges of this may be observed amongst the global legal pluralists, the latter tend towards a different form of debate though with firm roots in this polycentric idea.

Two elements are central to understanding global legal pluralism. The first is its non-hierarchal nature and the second, the importance of non-state actors to the operation of the doctrine.[9] The non-hierarchal approach seems difficult, though not impossible, to reconcile with a working system of law, particularly when the Westphalian state is not prefigured as paramount. Within pluralism, hierarchies are replaced either by 'mutual observation between network nodes' or by a 'sequence of decisions within a variety of observational positions … which never leads to one final collective decision on substantive norms'.[10] Hybridity also operates to replace normative hierarchal orders.[11] Global legal pluralism challenges the Westphalian state-centric focus of classical international law and concentrates upon examples such as *lex mercatoria*, the role of multinationals in establishing normative orders or the operation of religious institutions. Thus, it combines a theoretical approach, which shuns hierarchy, while also taking a descriptive line to understanding current

8 Fuller, *The Morality of Law*; L. Bernstein, 'Opting Out of the Legal System: Extralegal Contractual Relations in the Diamond Industry' (1992) 21 *Journal of Legal Studies* 115; J. Griffiths 'What Is Legal Pluralism' (1986) 24 *Journal of Legal Pluralism and Unofficial Law* 1; A. S. Hofri-Winogradow 'A Plurality of Discontent: Legal Pluralism, Religious Adjudication and the State' (2010) 26 *Journal of Law and Religion* 101.

9 S. Wheatley, 'Democratic Governance Beyond the State: The Legitimacy of Non-state Actors as Standard Setters' in A. Peters, L. Koechlin and T. Förster (eds.), *The Role of Non-state Actors in Standard Setting* (Cambridge University Press, 2009).

10 Fischer-Lescano and Teubner, 'Regime Collisions', 1018 and 1039.

11 Berman, *A Jurisprudence of Law Beyond Borders*, p. 139.

and future international law, its recognised formal aspects and other normative points.

Within global constitutionalisation, global legal pluralism is an extremely useful tool in explaining the variant legal regimes that appear to coexist particularly in a post-state formulation. For example, within EU trade or human rights, global legal pluralism may regard each as its own regime or process of constitutionalisation alongside state-based constitutional structures, fitting together in a pluralist order that also recognises the multitude of actors, or indeed constituent power holders, within the global pluralist order. Such a formulation would also recognise variety amongst the points of constitutionalisation, or in the instance of one single constitutional structure, its potential operation with other non-constitutional elements.

One of the biggest difficulties for global pluralism is the lack of claim settlement structures. This is probably most obvious in the varied questions of jurisdiction. Competing claims and a system of balance between them are central to a legal order. Law and the claims associated with it will inevitably overlap. If individual laws or legal orders are not considered to take place within a vacuum, then they will inevitably clash and therefore require a system to regulate these conflicts. If, at a minimum, there is no system providing a form to recognise other pluralist systems and establish the legitimacy or validity of claims amongst them, there exists a vacuum without a satisfactory resolution. Similar critiques of legal pluralism focus on an apparent vagueness that hinders the differentiation between law and other non-legal normative orders as well as amongst them.[12] This is not insurmountable, and certainly the substance of the various orders goes some way to alleviating this issue; yet the question of substance appears to be left to the internal orders' remedy.

Although, nominally, each legal order may work independently, their interactions do not always necessarily fit simply within the hybrid model developed within global legal pluralism. The easiest example would be the use of force. It is difficult to reconcile the UN's monopoly on the legal use of force and its interaction with other autonomous regional and domestic orders that interconnect within the hybrid space, while not resulting in a hierarchal model. Indeed, in some areas multiple claims of jurisdiction, such as assertions for the control of decisions that impact on both trade and the environment, may not be answered easily in such

[12] B. Z. Tamanaha, 'Understanding Legal Pluralism: Past to Present, Local to Global' (2008) 30 *Sydney Law Review* 375.

a pluralist democratic system. While it is arguable that a hierarchal system provides a better solution this does not suggest that such a system actually exists, but rather that it would seem more practicable than an entirely non-hierarchal model. On the other hand, what pluralism does offer is an understanding not reliant upon a Security Council paradigm proffering an ability for the global legal order to see beyond a process that patently does not explain the entire operation of the use and location of force beyond the Charter. Further global legal pluralism makes some sense of the activities of the actors called upon to follow a variety of legal orders when contemplating the use of force.[13]

Global legal pluralism presents fewer questions with regard to legitimacy and democratic deficits than other approaches to global governance that tend to sidestep these issues. The central place of the democratic order in the global pluralist system, while settling some issues, also raises questions regarding the potential difficulties in establishing legitimacy, where overlapping jurisdictions operate without a preordained and enforceable supremacy within the system. Rationalising claims of multiple equal orders as they currently operate is difficult to reconcile with democracy. Currently, to ensure broad participation, there would almost certainly have to be a partaking of states, institutions and other actors that are partly or entirely undemocratic, or have a consistent democratic deficit. But non-democratic countries could not participate within the models presented. This is not to legitimate these states' existence but rather to acknowledge their current contribution to the operation of international law, raising issues for both global pluralism and constitutionalisation.

Legal pluralism is an important facet of several other theories, and it is very useful in explaining aspects of the interactions between certain systems. However, it does not appear to offer a perspective on which to build a system of legitimacy within international law or, as Klabbers describes it, a way in which to understand better the dialogue between the various claims of right or authority that are persistent in any legal order.[14] Global legal pluralism is supported by credible arguments, but in seeking to understand the global legal system it presents more questions at this juncture in its development than answers. It raises interesting queries regarding the levels at which norm creation occurs and evident blind spots in

[13] G. Teubner, "Global Bukowina: Legal Pluralism in the World Society" in G. Teubner (ed.), *Global Law Without a State* (Dartmouth: Aldershot, 1997), p. 3; Berman, *A Jurisprudence of Law Beyond Borders*, p. 4.

[14] Klabbers in Klabbers, Peters and Ulfstein, *Constitutionalisation*, p. 29.

international law's governance structures. It identifies and describes the potential deficits that some other approaches do not recognise as undercutting the global governance scheme.

Global legal pluralism is important in understanding elements of the global legal order. It does not offer, nor does it claim to offer, an absolute basis for understanding the entirety of the system. It must be recognised that the norms within which international law operates may result in a hierarchal order that settles claims within the system; nonetheless, global legal pluralism offers a reasoned basis for analysing some of these interactions. In particular, global pluralism offers a route to recognising that alternative normative legal orders can and do exist, that models beyond the classical are possible and that international governance compels an examination of the structures of which classical international law is unable to take account.

4.1.2 Fragmentation

Perceived as a process where sectors of international law become increasingly independent and ultimately stand alone, fragmentation has become a critical point of contemporary debate within international, regional and, at times, domestic law. While recognising that these fragmented systems possess degrees of overlap covered by 'general' international law, what differentiates fragmentation from other theories is that each maintains an internal order based upon the needs and the gradual developments occurring within it that is separate to both general and other sectors of that legal order. This amounts to a more appropriate description of the global legal order than claiming that it is one fully co-ordinated system based on an assumption that where conflict occurs it can be resolved through *lex specialis*. Accordingly, fragmentation as a discourse meets the needs of the future global legal order, as it recognises the complexities of an ever-divergent regime of law. The result is what is often referred to, as it is by Simma, as 'self-contained regimes within international law' that will become more and more apparent.[15]

Thus, fragmentation examines the relationship between general international law and the various specialised areas, as well as describing the internal orderings of these sectors. Although it shares some traits with global legal pluralism, such as the recognition of a multitude of legal

[15] B. Simma, 'Self Contained Regimes' (1985) 16 *Netherlands Yearbook of International Law* 112.

orders, it is possible to differentiate fragmentation, as it centres entirely on law and its orders, and does not offer itself within a particular theoretical framework. Following fears expressed by a former President of the International Court of Justice, the International Law Commission's decision to commission a report on the concept resulted in much space being attributed to its description.[16]

It has become more difficult to be a general public international lawyer. 'Public international law' courses are increasingly coming to resemble the introductory courses of domestic legal systems. In these introductory courses the tenets of how an order works, the basic constitutional order, the civil/common-law system, the officers of the law, the sources of law and so on are deliberated upon and outlined without providing a commanding knowledge of the varied areas of law that coexist within the legal arena; so too, international law. Fragmentation moves away from ideas of a coherent central order. This does not suggest anarchy but instead a more complex understanding of how law operates. Thus, depending on the form in which it is presented, fragmentation may stand in contrast to claims of constitutionalisation. This is particularly the case when constitutionalisation is based upon the notion of the UN Charter as the core constitutional document of a global legal order.

Alternatively greeted with fear or joy, the multiplicity of subsystems, be they trade, human rights or environmental law, suggests that international law is developing its own *sui generis* system, which may be fragmented or indeed both fragmented and constitutionalised.[17] While the links between sectoral constitutionalisation and fragmentation have not been abundantly critiqued, the potential for describing both processes as contemporaneous draws from their obsession in hiving off particular sectors or areas of law as different from the rest. Fragmentation may also have the opposite effect, making constitutionalisation improbable, as the legal order loses at least part of its coherence, but certainly there is room for both ideas to rest alongside each other.

[16] International Law Commission, 'Fragmentation of International Law: Difficulties Arising from the Diversification and Expansion of International Law', Vol. II, Part 2, *Yearbook of the International Law Commission* (International Law Commission, 2006).

[17] M. Koskenniemi and P. Leino, 'Fragmentation of International Law? Postmodern Anxieties' (2002) 15 *Leiden Journal of International Law* 553; G. Hafner, 'Pros and Cons Ensuing from Fragmentation of International Law' (2003–2004) 25 *Michigan Journal of International Law* 849; B. Simma, 'Fragmentation in a Positive Light' (2003–2004) 25 *Michigan Journal of International Law* 845; E. Benvenisti and G. W. Downs, 'The Empire's New Clothes: Political Economy and the Fragmentation of International Law' (2007–2008) 60 *Stanford Law Review* 595.

Human rights have a particularly important place in focusing attention on questions of governance in an ever-fragmenting system. In the global legal order, as it currently operates, human rights act as a system of rules and limitations restraining the activities of states and other international actors. Within fragmentation, it is these interactions, amongst human rights and other areas of law, that underpin many of the arguments made on its behalf.[18] Indeed, human rights may be described as the unifying element in the fragmentation debate. The norms established by human rights serve as a unifying base, which fragmented areas of international law are bound to, and deflect from areas of conflict that might otherwise arise. Thus, human rights often act as a core normative structure within an ever-fragmenting regime.

So while this process of specialisation within international law is hard to deny, this is not enough to justify a claim of detrimental disintegration. Rather it reflects the growing complexity of international law. Just as one course can no longer seek to give a full introduction to international law, neither can international law itself be described as one homogenous monolith where exactly the same rules and standards apply interchangeably to human rights or trade law. If the global legal order cannot function in a coherent manner it would be justification for maintaining claims of immaturity within international law, potentially standing to undermine any declaration of constitutionality.

Fragmentation moves away from any description of the global legal order as associated with an absolute statist hierarchal model that tended to see the International Court of Justice at its core. It accepts that the growth of these multiple systems moves international law into a post-statist arena, which recognises the complicated and nuanced nature of a more complex legal and accompanying court system. It quite legitimately argues that the older explanations of international and domestic law's interactions no longer suffice and are difficult to sustain.

Fragmentation reflects broader questions of legitimacy and accountability, as the Westphalia model recedes. During the nineteenth century, when states were considered the undisputed masters of international law, this lack of nuance meant that understanding the nature of the international legal system was a less complicated task. However, the emergence of a more complicated legal order, alongside a broader understanding of

[18] A. E. Cassimatis, 'International Humanitarian Law, International Human Rights Law, and Fragmentation of International Law' (2007) 56 *International & Comparative Law Quarterly* 623.

the actors involved in international law's creation, has led to a differentiated system.[19] This differentiated or fragmented system requires a more coherent consideration of how law works. Fragmentation does not dispute the legitimacy of discrete areas of law, but rather questions how they react when they come against each other, particularly when the actors involved have to choose which norms are the most prescient on a particular occasion. A current example of this would be the debate within trade law as to whether domestic and international environmental law should be considered as both part of the WTO system and its Dispute Settlement Understanding. Whether environmental law has protection within the WTO system or whether it and trade law should be regarded as entirely different and unconnected systems of law remains unsettled.[20] This exemplifies some of the difficulties associated within a differentiated system.

Klabbers correctly points out that international and domestic law are quite similar in their approach to fragmentation. Within domestic legal orders discrete areas function effectively, for example, intellectual property and family law, but rarely interact with each. Within international law this arguably is also the case.[21] The converse is also true. There are areas in domestic law, such as contract and company law, which frequently brush up against each other and so too, for example, trade and environmental law within international law.

There is no settled view as to whether areas such as international criminal or investment law are still attached to a more general systematic international law embodied in secondary rules or whether they have detached themselves. The ILC, in its Report, stated that

> [S]ome rules of international law are more important than other rules and for this reason enjoy a superior position or special status in the international legal system. This is sometimes expressed by the designation of some norms as "fundamental" or as expressive of "elementary considerations of humanity" or "intransgressible principles of international law". What effect such designations may have is usually determined by the relevant context or instrument in which that designation appears.[22]

[19] Benvenisti and Downs, 'The Empire's New Clothes', 595.

[20] The Dispute Settlement Body at the WTO is an inter-state settlement body, with a first instance (Panel) and appeal (Appellate Body) procedure. It is tasked with settling disputes between members of the WTO, where one state considers another state to have violated one of the treaties of the WTO, such as GATT, GATS or TRIPs.

[21] Klabbers in Klabbers, Peters and Ulfstein, *Constitutionalisation*, p. 11.

[22] International Law Commission, 'Fragmentation of International Law', para. 6 (31).

Fragmentation can successfully be combined with other approaches to the global legal order, even slants that regard the international law's development as an exercise in mutuality. As it complicates any linear explanation of international law's development, fragmentation requires a more sophisticated and nuanced consideration of the complexity emerging within the global legal order. If a broad understanding of global law is accepted that asks that the differential normative systems are recognised as such, and these are dealt with in a manner that gives due regard to their innate complexity, then recognition of the patterns of development should be more straightforward. Fragmentation is acknowledged as uneven, and this aspect of its nature should be considered central to a proper appreciation of international law's character.

Fragmentation may also form an important aspect of constitutionalisation. Fischer-Lescano and Teubner argue against extrapolating common usage of norms as an indicator of constitutionalisation across pluralist systems of international law, and the character of fragmentation in constitutionalisation is contentious.[23] Some argue that a pluralist legal system also recognises this differentiated law; but both theories move in different directions from their mutual starting point. The ambiguities that have emerged in the ever-expanding doctrines within international law are usefully discussed by those embroiled in the fragmentation debate, but it still leaves open questions regarding its position in the future of global governance. There are also issues as to the legitimacy of law's creation and of power within an entirely fragmented system. Acknowledgement of fragmentation's occurrence is somewhat different to basing an entire system on this approach or a full understanding of the nature of global governance.

4.1.3 *Global governance networks*

Global governance networks function on the assumption that since states have begun to co-operate at a sub-state level global legal practice is operational within domestic legal systems. The regulatory functions that these networks currently and increasingly operate establish what Slaughter describes as a New World Order. Thus, global governance networks have two underlying premises: first, government networks of regulators (including judges) interact and operate in a manner that establishes law

[23] A. Fischer-Lescano and G. Teubner, 'Reply to Andreas L Paulus, Consensus as Fiction of Global Law' (2004) 24 *Michigan Journal of International Law* 1059.

beyond the classical state paradigm; and, second, this has established a world order, 'a system of global governance that institutionalises cooperation and sufficiently contains conflict such that all nations and their peoples may achieve greater peace and prosperity'.[24]

The interactions that presently form and develop international law do not occur at the more commonly recognised inter-governmental points of governance within institutions such as the United Nations, the IMF, the WTO or the World Bank. Rather, the allocations of authority are as local as they are global, and the true nature of global law only becomes clear when both are considered. The less obvious links between domestic bodies that regulate and occupy regulatory spaces, for example, the various central banks that make up the Basel Committee, form the new global order.[25] Domestic to the extent that they are regulatory bodies created and legitimated through the state that establishes them but international in that there is a legal framework under which banking has become globally regulated, these bodies operate on the assumption that this global framework is the best option for tackling particular issues on an informal operation of subsidiarity.[26] This banking example is replicated across various sectors of governance and has created a web of global law that while not necessarily traditionally the concern of international lawyers increasingly must become so if the entirety of global law is to be recognised and examined. Consequently it is an existent order that it is advocated here, one that needs recognition to further its operation and to regulate some of its potential difficulties with legitimacy or hegemony but ultimately regarded by its proponents as a positive development in global governance.

Slaughter uses the example of the inter-governmental reactions and activities undertaken as a result of the attacks on 11 September and the more recent financial crisis as further examples of these governance networks. Following the attacks the already established governance networks tackled international terrorism as a stateless phenomenon and instigated co-operation at the regulatory level. The work of the G8 in tackling financial problems and creating new regulatory regimes is also an exemplar of how national officials and laws are used to pursue international aims.[27] These networks, it is argued, are regularly undertaken on a co-operative basis and are easily recognised when the focus is shifted from the state to the law itself. The argument follows that these networks are, in fact,

[24] A. Slaughter, *A New World Order* (Princeton University Press, 2004), p. 15

[25] Slaughter, *New World Order*, pp. 42–3. [26] *Ibid.*, p. 30. [27] *Ibid.*, pp. 1–2.

the predominant manner in which law is made and co-operation occurs, though arguably with some problematic opacity in their operation.

But it is within these bureaucracies that state practice within international law can, in fact, be found, and thus this horizontal activity is elemental to understanding the nature of global governance. This offers an understanding of law that recognises a legal system not necessarily as state practice and treaty, but rather focuses on the actual running of the global world order. The work of writers such as Slaughter and Chayes has brought close attention to the allocations of power in domestic institutions and law, not just on the national level but distributed throughout the entirety of the global legal system, creating what in Slaughter's words is a world order based upon a disaggregated state.[28] As well as dealing with the operation and generation of international law these various governance networks include a broad spectrum of distinct segments, such as environmental, trade and economic law, and the use of force, as well as networks of particular types of actors, such as judges or bankers.

The co-operation required amongst domestic agencies to achieve some of the aims of combating terrorism or regulating the financial world is often overlooked, as the bureaucracy of ministries involved are frequently obscure structures. In common and perhaps in tribute to the New Haven School, and certainly appearing to have roots in American Legal Realism, this approach includes elements of an interdisciplinary perspective.[29] Similar to the New Haven School, it also firmly relies on the various processes involved in governance and power to substantiate the claim that it has moved to this regulatory level of global networks.

This disaggregated focus recognises the involvement of a varied group of domestic institutions and actors in international activities while still centring the state as the prime point of governance from which these various networks gain their legitimacy to operate and, most importantly, to create international law. In contrast, the unitary state reflects traditional, sovereignty-based understandings of international law in which all interactions take place at the inter-state level within the classical legal framework. Yet, the state remains, not in the classical paradigm but rather functioning in the traditional setting in the frame of institutions, such as

[28] A. Chayes and A. Handler Chayes, *The New Sovereignty: Compliance with International Regulatory Agreements* (London: Harvard University Press, 1995); Slaughter, *New World Order*, p. 42.

[29] R. O. Keohane and J. S. Nye, Jr, 'Transgovernmental Relations and International Organizations' (1974) 27 *World Politics* 39; R. O. Keohane and J. S. Nye, Jr, *Power and Interdependence*, 3rd edn (New York: Longman, 2001).

the UN or IMF, while also establishing and regulating the varied bodies that carry out the majority of practice. The state thus remains essential, as it is here that democracy and accountability function, as a world government is regarded as being both unfeasible and unworkable even within a federal model.[30]

The descriptive force of this theory sets about recognising an existent practice as well as a future trend, and it is very much a Euro-American form of constitutional order that is being advocated. Certainly the type of state that has the capacity and wherewithal to enter into these varied networks and engage within them on an equal footing appears, in practice, to be largely Western-centric. In Slaughter's language, borrowing from company law, there is no right to pierce the veil of statehood but it is in looking inside the state that the reality of lawmaking becomes obvious, and it is this reality that this proposition seeks to bring forth for analysis.[31] Within these governance networks, power is exercised by what Slaughter describes as 'power with', mobilising others to achieve ends. Thus comity and co-operation form governance structures unless, of course, it is impossible to convince others to come along with the proposed ends or modes; then an alternative form of power, in a commanding form, must be utilised.[32]

Governmental networks are focal points of the modern world order. These less formalised structures are easily overlooked when examining the development of international law, particularly when that analysis is state focused. Such accounts are appealing, as they grant a basis upon which to understand a state's motivation in enabling and allowing for interactions at these often non-political, and thus perhaps less immediately controversial, points of administrative governance. A further attraction is the pinpointing of other actors in the international sphere, perhaps without political oversight. Critically all remain emergent from the state, eschewing any other points of materialisation.

Yet, there are difficulties in accepting such governance networks. In particular the very informality that forms the core of many of the propositions is problematic.[33] Although, certainly, sub-state actors are regulated

[30] Slaughter, *New World Order*, pp. 1–2. [31] *Ibid.*, p. 12.

[32] A. Slaughter 'Filling Power Vacuums in the New Global Order' (2013) 36 *Boston College International And Comparative Law Review* 919, 921–5.

[33] A. Slaughter and T. Hale, 'Transgovernmental Networks and Emerging Powers' in A. S. Alexandroff and A. Fenton Cooper (eds.), *Rising States, Rising Institutions: Challenges for Global Governance* (Baltimore, OH: Brookings Institution Press, 2010), p. 48.

within domestic administrative structures, these systems are established to consider the ramifications of activity within states and enable action to be taken when domestic actors go beyond their remit. The activities described by governance networks were not envisaged by domestic administrative law. The legitimacy of action beyond the state and the creation of international law are not within the purview of domestic law to either regulate or legitimate. This is not to suggest that the traditional inter-governmental structures provide for such legitimacy but rather to acknowledge that, if anything, there is even less available in these incidences. Thus accountability remains a problem. Further, the reliance on a particular form of state activity that engages in particular networks at this sub-governmental level and depiction of the development of international law here enable the omission or non-recognition of those states that do not wish, or perhaps are unable, to engage at this level. Within global governance networks it seems unrecognised that law created in the absence of a swathe of the world is as problematic now as it was 100 years ago. Even within traditional inter-state bodies, such as the WTO, there is an acknowledgement that continued asymmetry amongst delegations and their limited resources creates a problem with legitimacy within that organisation and so too arguably within global governance networks.

This is not to exclude the potential utility in recognising the phenomenon that Slaughter and others describe; indeed to do so would be dangerous to understanding the global legal order's operation. Rather, the question needs to be asked as to whether this occurrence is a positive development that enhances global governance. Potentially some answers lie within a constitutionalised system that develops an administrative accompaniment that would regulate these sub-state networks or alternatively within a vertical divisions-of-power model. But such a formulation has yet to be contemplated, though the Global Administrative Law movement does go some way in setting out the basis of such a possibility.

4.1.4 Global administrative law

Global administrative law also centres upon governance, but rather than seeing it as a conglomeration of networks or part of a constitutionalisation process, it regards recent developments within global law as based within an administrative framework. Accordingly the form that contemporary global law takes ought to be characterised as a type of administrative activity and, as such, needs to regulate the tools available within administrative law. Thus, global administrative law utilises principles such as transparency, participation, review and accountability as the basis for understanding and regulating much of the activity within the global legal order, all of which are also familiar notions within constitutionalism. While not aiming to rationalise fully the entirety of international law it does suggest that certain functions, often those considered problematic by international lawyers, such as accountability and legitimacy, may be secured through administrative processes. Thus it is not a totalising theory of the global legal order but rather one that regards the complications recognised by other current theories as partly soluble in administrative action.

Cassese, setting out how global administrative law emerged, focuses on structures created by treaty regimes over the past forty years. These regimes' schemes, such as those accompanying the UN Convention on the Law of Sea, establish bodies for their management and operation. These function within the specific treaty regime established but also within the broader area of international law in which the regime is situated.[34] In doing so, global administrative law sets itself within the expanding development of regulatory regimes abundant in certain areas of international law. Thus global administrative law does not supplant or replace existent international law nor does it propound a new global legal order, rather it suggests that this is a new form of law, developing alongside and out of aspects of the global legal order's more complex structure. In addition, symptoms of fragmentation, such as the emergence of *sui generis* and self-contained regimes of law, are an elemental aspect of administrative law, but one regarded as furthering the administrative process rather than necessarily problematic. As part of the fundamentals of its operation, global administrative law recognises the inclusion of non-state actors within these various regimes as well as the existent ambiguity between the private and public, though the latter's traditional place was probably not as firm as is perhaps suggested elsewhere in any case.[35]

The impetus for the materialisation of this field comes from the 'globalised interdependence' of various sectors of international law.[36] The momentum emerges from outside law, but globalisation is reflected within global administrative law's development and indeed perpetuates

[34] For more specific examples, see S. Cassese, B. Carotti, L. Casini, E. Cavalieri and E. Macdonald, *Global Administrative Law: The Casebook*, 3rd edn (New York: IIIJ, 2012).

[35] S. Cassese, 'Administrative Law without the State: The Challenge of Global Regulation' (2004) 37 *New York University Journal of International Law and Politics* 663, 668–70.

[36] B. Kingsbury, N. Kirsch and R. B. Stewart, 'The Emergence of Global Administrative Law' (2004–2005) 68 *Law & Contemporary Problems* 15, 16.

the process. Thus, global administrative law takes the complexities of the present operation of the global legal order and funnels elements of it into a form that, like constitutionalism, already exists, but adapts it for a globalised order.

As with several other recent theories on global governance, administrative law advocates recognise that the classical divisions between domestic and international law no longer suffice; thus a new form of legal analysis needs to be put forward that both recognises and systematises national, transnational and international law.[37] Indeed it argues that the reliance on domestic regulation, as global governance networks do, furthers the accountability deficit, which may only be remedied by its addition to its domestic counterpart. Thus much of global administrative law ought to be understood as what Kingsbury and Kirsch describe as administrative action, 'rulemaking, administrative adjudication between competing interests, and other forms of regulatory and administrative decision and management'.[38]

In setting the case for global administrative law, Cassese directly tackles the assumption that administrative law can only be domestic, while also clearly stating that the state itself remains a vital part of international law, though a law that is increasingly plural in its operation. For Kingsbury, Kirsch and Stewart, the fact that administrative tasks and functions are happening is enough to claim that administrative law exists.[39] Traditional administrative law aims to control government power, protect individual rights, ensure effective administration, assure governmental accountability and secure participation in decision-making processes.[40] While global administrative law recognises this heritage, it also suggests that the global version has developed its own features. Whether these distinct features are more akin to differences between states' operations of administrative law or are more substantive remains open to debate. Potentially, the biggest difference between the domestic administrative law and its global counterpart is the lack of a constitutional base from which to operate. Some, such as Cassese, are willing to anticipate a future relationship between global administrative and constitutional law, particularly with regard to the evolution of human rights and the rule of law, though this is not necessarily shared amongst all those that advocate for global administrative law's recognition.[41]

[37] *Ibid.*, 15. [38] *Ibid.*, 17. [39] *Ibid.*, 17.

[40] P. Craig, *Administrative Law*, 6th edn (London: Thomson Sweet & Maxwell, 2008), p. 3.

[41] Cassese, 'Administrative Law without the State', 687; Kingsbury, Kirsch and Stewart, 'The Emergence',15.

Critically, advocates of global administrative law see this as an emergent field, much as those that argue that constitutionalisation is an ongoing process, which has far from ended. Proponents of administrative law willingly admit that much research and legal development is required before a fully coherent body of global administrative law, immersed in a normative framework, can be said to be realised fully. Particular issues of accountability, democracy and legitimacy remain, as they do in many of the propositions for global law, but with the hope that global administrative law may, in fact, hold the resolution to at least some of these problems.[42]

Global administrative law's relationship to constitutionalism remains a difficulty that has yet to find a fully rationalised resolution. While, as with constitutionalisation, aping domestic law is unnecessary, the rationale for administrative law as an abstract legal order requires some consideration. The creation of global administrative law with a deficiency of constitutionalism or rather, in Kingsbury's words, in the absence of a 'rich constitution' remains problematic particularly if it stands in the place of normative constitutionalism.[43] In such circumstances it, rather than constitutionalism, ensures that the rule of law, democratic legitimacy and human rights amongst others are *in situ*, a task it regulates but does not provide the normative base for in domestic law. Unlike the other propositions discussed, such as global legal pluralism or governance networks, administrative law has always been intrinsically linked to another form of law, constitutionalism, thus making the latter's absence a rather difficult proposition to assert.

Global administrative law opens a space that recognises the complexities of relationships at the national, transnational and international levels. Like global governance networks, it partly describes present activity within international law, though not necessarily advocating that it is an ideal, and also recognises its reliance on interactions with other aspects of international law. In taking such a basis, contingent on broader international, transnational and national law, global administrative law sets a challenge to those that recognise a state-led more classical vision of international law that, as these various theories commonly recognise, does not appear to be entirely sustainable.

[42] D. C. Esty, 'Good Governance at the Supranational Scale: Globalizing Administrative Law' (2006) 115 *Yale Law Journal* 1490.

[43] Kingsbury, 'Concept of "Law"', 36.

4.2 What to do about global governance?

Global legal pluralism, fragmentation, global governance networks and global administrative law stand alongside constitutionalisation as attempts to grapple with a global legal order that no longer seems to fit into classical tropes of state-centrism.[44] While state-centred analysis was never universally accepted and certainly has always been heavily critiqued, what is interesting about these group of theories is that they also jostle the state out of its core role. None have gone so far as to suggest its death. Indeed most are quite adamant that the opposite is the case; the state remains, but in a new position in a global rather than international legal order; a change in moniker, which is perhaps best rationalised in the tension in grasping the state's role in global law, while also gaining an understanding of the fluidity between international, transnational and domestic law that naturally fits a more global model.

It is important to note that this consideration of approaches to the global legal order is in broad brush strokes and certainly not intended to explicate fully the intricacies or internal debates within each proposal. Nonetheless, in succinctly and often accurately pointing to the issues associated with the global legal system, these various approaches draw to the fore the complicated nature of contemporary global law. Individually, each points to a particular facet of the current global legal system and together illustrate its character, or at the very least, its potential nature.

The plethora of approaches helpfully set out an array of questions, though none fully answer them. The three categorisations outlined earlier – the purely theoretical frame aiming to establish a philosophical foundation to international law, theories combining the philosophical approach with descriptive proposals on the contemporary and future operation of global law, together with the purely descriptive discussions – provide a context for constitutionalisation but also suggest problems with some of its underlying premises. Global legal pluralism and fragmentation advocate a form of coherence, which the world order constitutionalists pursue, though perhaps not as obviously as is suggested by the latter. Both global governance networks and administrative law provide

[44] S. Marks, 'State-centrism, International Law, and the Anxieties of Influence' (2006) 19 *Leiden Journal of International Law* 339.

alternative models for understanding the governance activities occurring at the transnational level and are perhaps more suitable in their relative narrowness than making any grand claims of constitutionalisation. The honest portrayal of the gaps and failures described by these theories must be tackled by any theories claiming to settle governance questions. The difficulties in fully embracing any of these theories, including constitutionalisation, lie in the uncertainty as to what any of them in particular offer from a normative perspective.

What constitutionalisation puts forward is a method of co-option that attempts to clarify the governance order while incorporating aspects of each of these theories into its own system. Thus global constitutionalisation ought to be set apart in its willingness to co-opt their propositions within its own system. Although it may not be a desired choice, it is possible to argue for a fragmented constitutionalisation process, as trade law becomes constitutionalised but environmental law does not, or alternatively the emergence of a global administrative regime as evidence of the existence of an underlying constitutional order. In recognising the importance of these other proposals and what each provides by way of partial explanation of the present state of the global legal order, constitutionalisation could be described as a very welcoming doctrine. This is obviously not the case in all its iterations, but there is often more than a gleam of other theories within constitutionalisation that will increase since the complexities of the global legal order cannot be realised fully by one of these proposals alone. For example, the fragmented or administrative systems must function within an overall structure, and it is this acknowledgement that differentiates constitutionalisation from these other theories.

Constitutionalisation offers the ability to absorb aspects of each of these approaches and adopt them within its remit. Constitutionalisation does not start from a basis that requires it to be in competition with these other approaches, but rather one that seeks to explain and regulate the current global legal order. Yet, this may also be its underlying weakness. It is an all-encompassing approach that is really only matched by global legal pluralism in its ambition and, as such, opens itself to many more points of criticism. To appreciate fully the context in which constitutionalisation and these other theories emerged, it is also important to consider the historical circumstances in which they emerged. Two theories, Verdross and New Haven, are examined next and both have direct relevance to each of these theories though the focus will be on their role within global constitutionalisation.

4.3 Historical antecedents of global constitutionalisation

While Verdross' work on *jus cogens* makes his link to constitutionalism evident, the second, New Haven, is perhaps less obvious. The New Haven approach to both politics and process has become a facet of global governance. Not that it necessarily took a constitutional approach, perhaps an anathema to it, but rather its rationalising of certain legal tropes and transplanting of these to international law are important for the present debate. In both approaches the essential characteristics of their reasoning are discussed followed by a consideration of their influence on the present constitutionalisation debate as well as the broader contemporary context.

4.3.1 Verdross in the European tradition

As one of the leading international law scholars of the twentieth century, Verdross is widely acknowledged as having influenced the development of international jurisprudence, particularly in continental Europe.[45] Verdross' writing focuses on a range of international legal issues but his most important contributions to international law are those in the areas of universalism, monism,[46] *jus cogens*,[47] neutrality[48] and the United Nations Charter.[49] His work in these areas forms a clear foundation for assessing the impact of the United Nations Charter and the other elements of multilateralism that emerged after both World Wars. Most importantly, with a base in natural law, Verdross was able to establish a coherent theory of constitutionalism within international law.[50] As early as 1926 and the publication of *Die Verfassung der Völkerrechtsgemeinschaft* (*The Constitution*

45 In 1935, Janzen stated that Verdross' contribution to legal theory had not received as wide an audience as it deserved; he argued that this was owing to Verdross' non-adherence to the core principles of positivism, the personified state, sovereignty and the will of the state. H. Janzen, 'The Monism of Alfred Verdross' (1935) 29 *American Political Science Review* 387; also see B. Simma, 'The Contribution of Alfred Verdross to the Theory of International Law' (1995) 6 *European Journal of International Law* 33.

46 A. Truyol y Serra, 'Verdross et la théorie du droit' (1994) 5 *European Journal of International Law* 55; B. Conforti, 'The Theory of Competence in Verdross' (1994) 5 *European Journal of International Law* 70.

47 A. Verdross, '*Jus Dispositivum* and *Jus Cogens* in International Law' (1966) 60 *American Journal of International Law* 55.

48 A. Verdross, 'Austria's Permanent Neutrality and the United Nations Organization' (1956) 50 *American Journal of International Law* 61.

49 A. Verdross, 'General International Law and the United Nations Charter', 30 *International Affairs* 342.

50 A. Verdross and H. Franz Koeck, 'Natural Law: The Tradition of Natural Law and Reason' in MacDonald and Johnston (eds.), *The Structure and Process*, p. 17.

of the International Legal Community) he espoused the idea of an international constitution centred upon core principles of international law, particularly *jus cogens* norms. While his theory on how international law functioned and developed changed over the course of his writing, these core elements remained constant.[51]

Simma states that Verdross was the master of synthesis, bringing disparate elements and arguments together to create a coherent whole, and it is this that distinguishes Verdross from his contemporaries.[52] Fundamentally a natural lawyer, this clearly threads throughout his works and influences both his concept of the international community and its effect on law.[53] While several jurisprudential schools influenced his ideas (the Stoic and Kantian traditions are probably the most apparent), his approach comes within the Kelsian approach to law.[54] While he often tackled discrete areas of international law, he was very much concerned with the operation of the whole legal order.[55] It is these aspects of his work that are the focus here. The breadth of Verdross' writing, particularly his knowledge of legal philosophy, allowed him to make a coherent and strong argument for constitutionalism long before it became popular to embark upon a validation of an international constitution, though perhaps this in itself was problematic, and it suggests a slight utopianism in his writing.

4.3.2 Historical influences upon Verdross

Verdross' approach to the natural law instilled recognisable elements of Aristotle, the Stoics, Aquinas and Suárez.[56] In Verdross' idea of community, as in the Stoic tradition, the concept of allegiance moves beyond the state. Members have wider concerns, which as Cicero noted, must be considered when understanding the operation of a particular community; thus the state does not command the entire faithfulness of its citizenry.[57]

51 Truyol y Serra, 'Verdross et la théorie', 56.

52 Simma, 'The Contribution of Alfred Verdross', 35.

53 A. Verdross, 'Two Arguments for an Empirical Foundation of Natural-Law Norms: An Examination of Johannes Messner's and Victor Kraft's Approaches' (1975) 3 *Syracuse Journal of International Law and Commerce* 151.

54 J. L. Kunz, 'The "Vienna School" and International Law' (1933–1934) 11 *New York University Quarterly Law Review* 370.

55 *Ibid.*, fn. 28.

56 Verdross and Koeck, 'Natural Law' in MacDonald and Johnston (eds.), *The Structure and Process*, p. 18; and Simma, 'The Contribution of Alfred Verdross', 38.

57 A. Verdross, 'Fundamental Human Rights: The Journey of an Idea' (trans. J. D. Gorby) (1979–1980) 8 *Human Rights* 20; Verdross and Koeck, 'Natural Law', in MacDonald and Johnston (eds.), *The Structure and Process*, pp. 18–19.

This idea is linked to the writings of Aquinas and the notion of the false nature of the subordination of the individual to the state, a point of particular appeal to Verdross.[58] According to Aquinas, the individual is not inferior to the state's authority and could disobey the state if the natural law required the individual to do so, though this was only in the very rarest of occasions.[59] Verdross' firm disagreement with totalitarian regimes and the imposition of laws contrary to the natural law supplements his concept of its international counterpart.[60]

According to Douzinas, 'the Spanish scholastics school argued that natural law is a branch of morality and linked religious rules of conduct with moral reason'.[61] Within the Spanish School, the international community was considered akin to the already accepted community of individuals within the state, and Verdross was predisposed to this conception.[62] This community of individuals requires a legal order to govern their relations, and this is also the case within the international order.[63]

In contrast with his contemporaries Suárez considers *jus gentium* to be part of the natural law.[64] His colleagues considered the law of nations to have developed from the existence of human communities, and without these there would be no reason for the law of nations.[65] Communities required the development of this law. In contrast Suárez argued that these rules of the international order of reason predate the law of nations and are thus part of the natural law. International law did not develop by mere necessity. Community is thus linked to the natural law; it is not the reason for the law of nations but is an integral aspect of it. Suárez disagreed with the assertion that *jus gentium* is part of positive human law.[66] There

58 Verdross, 'Fundamental Human Rights', 20.

59 T. Aquinas, *A Treatise on Law* (trans. R. J. Egan) (Indianapolis: Hacket Publishing, 2000); T. Aquinas, *Selected Political Writings*, 2nd edn. (trans. J. G. Dawson) (Oxford: Blackwell, 1959).

60 Verdross, 'Fundamental Human Rights', 23.

61 Douzinas, *The End of Human Rights*, p. 63.

62 Verdross and Koeck, 'Natural Law' in MacDonald and Johnston (eds.), *The Structure and Process*, pp. 19–21.

63 Simma, 'The Contribution of Alfred Verdross', 33; R. S. Hartigan, 'Francesco de Vitoria and Civilian Immunity' (1973) 1 *Political Theory* 79.

64 G. L. Williams, A. Brown and J. Waldron, *Selections from Three Works of Francisco Suárez, S.J, De Legibus, ac deo Legislatore, 1612, Defensio Fidie Catholicae, et Apostolicae Adversus Anglicanae Sectae Errores, 1613, De Triplici Virtute Theologica Fide, Spe, et Charitate, 1621*. Vol. II: *The Translation* (Oxford: Clarendon Press, 1944); D. Kennedy, 'Primitive Legal Scholarship' (1986) 27 *Harvard International Law Journal* 1, 4.

65 Williams, Brown and Waldron, *Selections from Three Works of Francisco Suárez*, pp. 331–6.

66 *Ibid.*, p. 341.

are shared attributes in the natural law and *jus gentium*. They are, for instance, both common to all of mankind. However, their subject matter is exclusive, since the sources of natural law do not develop from necessity. They are therefore in Suárez's estimation, interchangeable. Suárez argues that one of the main differences between the natural law and *jus gentium* is that while the natural law can only serve the good, *jus gentium* may at times permit 'some evils'.[67] *Jus gentium* may be changed by the consent of men and is therefore not a constant.[68] It is thus possible to change *jus gentium* to the detriment of humanity.

Simma identifies Suárez's position on international law as a 'universal community-orientated' philosophy.[69] *Jus gentium* is not part of the natural law, but at the same time it is more than positive law. The same universal community identified by Suárez was evident to Verdross, though a more intricate and developed version owing to increasing constitutionalisation.[70] Verdross takes this idea of community based upon international law, which may be adapted or changed but remains an essential aspect of the functioning of that legal order, and adapts it for twentieth-century international law. Working from a strong history of state-based international law Verdross divided the international community into two distinct groups: the disorganised community and the organised community, with the community as identified by Suárez being part of the former.[71]

This philosophy of a universal community has not gone unopposed. The positivist approach of writers such as Hegel or Hobbes suggests that the notion of international community is not uncontroversial. Hobbes asserted that the lack of superior authority robs international law of its status of law.[72] The claim that the law of nations has not developed sufficiently to be truly law promotes the key distinction between positivism and the natural-law theories of the time. According to the positivists, international law is dependent on sovereign wills, with Hegel arguing that the nation-state is thus the highest order of power.[73] The state is the highest moral power, and law is thus always the law of the state; international law is but an unachieved norm. Hegel affirms that it is within the state that the individual's rights can be realised, and this is the only community of consequence.

[67] *Ibid.*, pp. 352–3. [68] *Ibid.*, p. 354.
[69] Simma, 'The Contribution of Alfred Verdross', 39.
[70] Verdross, 'Fundamental Human Rights', 23.
[71] A. Verdross, 'On the Concept of International Law' (1949) 43 *American Journal of International Law* 435, 438.
[72] T. Hobbes, *Leviathan* (Cambridge Classics, 1991), p. 244.
[73] Anon., 'Hegel's Political Philosophy', 78.

> The simple observation of the law has no virtue in it or an abstract view of the good *per se*, the law can be obeyed without a belief in the good, and a belief in the good is not a sure sign of respect for the law. The belief should be shown in a manner not entirely subjective, accidental, and temporal, but stably and substantially – that is, in ethical habit, ordinary action and custom.[74]

Universal justice is based on the state; international law is a derivative of state interactions based on the sovereignty and autonomy of states; thus Hegel would not recognise as legitimate transference of sovereignty to a higher authority.[75]

Hegel believed that the state, as the realisation of a moral idea, is legitimate simply as a result of its existence. He separates this from historical development, as this is the science of the state and as such deals more with distinct legal questions.[76] Thus, in order for Verdross' idea of community to be reconciled with Hegel's view of community, Verdross would have to identify a community similar to the one proposed by Hegel, that is a dynamic similar to the family, civil society and state.

If a civil society of states could be recognised as a layer above Hegel's idea of the state, what could follow is an international community. This would be necessary to create the moral idea of an international community in equity with Hegel's community and in accordance with his doctrine. This form of international community would need to deal with the historical science of community that leads to the state and then the international community. Verdross' answer to this is that the international community does not require this paradigm.[77] For Hegel, the state has no imposed limitations; sovereignty of the state does not allow any other interpretation. Verdross does not interpret sovereignty in this manner; his monist interpretation of municipal law and international law requires them to be one system, and thus the truncation of the development of community at the state does not arise.[78]

Simma, to illustrate the core differences between Hegelian philosophy and that of Verdross, uses the drafting of the Weimar Republic's

[74] Hegel, quoted in L. Miraglia, 'Comparative Legal Philosophy Applied to Legal Institutions' in *Modern Legal Philosophy Series*, Vol. III (trans. J. Lisle) (Boston, MA: Boston Book Company, 1968 [1912]), pp. 68–9.

[75] *Ibid.*, p. 69.

[76] Anon., 'Hegel's Political Philosophy', 78, 81.

[77] Simma, 'The Contribution of Alfred Verdross', 33, 42.

[78] Janzen, 'Monism of Verdross', 387.

Constitution as an example of these distinctions.[79] The debate centred on how to include international law in the new German legal system. One version proposed was Hegelian in its international individualism. It put the state at the core of its operation. This was ultimately rejected by the drafters following an article written by Verdross, which questioned its commitment to international law.[80] The Hegelian draft would have enabled Germany to choose when and in what manner to be bound by international law. Verdross argued that the validity of international law was not a question for domestic constitutions; the only matter left to domestic law was how international law was integrated into domestic law not the validity of international law itself.

This is a critical early example of how, from Verdross' perspective, the natural law is intertwined within international law. From a Hegelian position, the state is the ultimate arbiter of the law; the state is an individual actor in international law and is the master of its own commitment to international law. From Verdross' standpoint, this is incorrect: the community of states develops international law either through custom, treaty or via the other sources of international law, and adherence cannot be made or unmade by any individual state.[81] Verdross addresses the core differences between universalism and individualism, and argues that universalism derives from the notion of the moral unity of mankind as a norm, whereas individualism centred on factual occurrences is too caught up in their significance.[82] He argues that both must be accounted for in examining the law; that they are insubstantial without the other, but ultimately the state does not command international law.

4.3.3 *Verdross and* jus cogens

Verdross was a firm advocate of *jus cogens*.[83] Verdross regarded *jus cogens* as a non-negotiable and unalterable aspect of international law. According

[79] Simma, 'The Contribution of Alfred Verdross', 41. Simma writes that Verdross was influenced by Blackstone in his interpretation of the incorporation of international law into domestic law that is universalistic in tone.

[80] A. Verdross, 'Reichsrecht und internationales Recht. Eine Lanze für Art. 3 des Regierungsentwurfes der deutschen Verfassung' (1919) 24 *Deutsche Juristenzeitung* 291.

[81] Verdross did not accept the idea of instant custom; H. Mosler, 'Book Review: Die Quellen des universellen Völkerrechts; eine Einführung;' (1974) 68 *American Journal of International Law* 350, 351.

[82] Simma, 'The Contribution of Alfred Verdross', 40.

[83] Verdross, 'On the Concept', 435; Verdross, '*Jus Dispositivum*', 55; Verdross, 'Forbidden Treaties', 571.

to Verdross, *jus cogens*' decisive factors are that 'they do not exist to satisfy the needs of the individual states but the higher interest of the whole community'.[84] In his early work on the law of treaties, he accepts that there could be a debate as to the validity of *jus cogens*, but in questioning whether treaties may be in violation of international law, he argues that first *jus cogens* must be established.[85] Verdross suggests that only those wishing to rely entirely on the will of states, and thus only on treaty law can exclude the existence of *jus cogens*. Yet, the law of treaties itself presupposes the existence of public international law, and thus treaties alone are an insufficient basis on which to disregard *jus cogens*. He argues that if these norms exist they establish positive and negative modes of behaviour that are without prerequisites.[86] As such, Verdross discounts a positivist position as, if no international law may be created without relying on a pre-existing legal order, there can be no purely positivist international law that is not entirely reliant on the state.

In the pre-Charter era Verdross divides *jus cogens* into two groups, and the international law of this period is observable in his partition.[87] The first group consists of single compulsory norms, one-off examples of laws from which there are no derogations. An example of this would be the use of the high seas.[88] The second group are those norms that establish laws *contra bonos mores*. This group emerges from the commonality of all juridical orders that 'regulate the rational and moral coexistence of the members of a community'.[89] The exact nuance of this original division remains somewhat unclear. The 1937 standard is inward looking and not necessarily what is now understood as *jus cogens*. He maintains that there is no juridical order, including an international variant that accepts norms contrary to the principles of that community, here specifically the international community.[90]

Verdross argues that 'we must ask what are the moral tasks states have to accomplish in the international community' limiting these to universal ethics of the international community that establish an 'ethical minimum'.[91] This is not unproblematic as it reduces *jus cogens* to the lowest common denominator, and indeed it is this minimum that Verdross recognised in 1937, far lower than what he would distinguish when considering

[84] A. Verdross, '*Jus Dispositivum* and *Jus Cogens* in International Law' in L. Gross (ed.), *International Law in the Twentieth Century* (New York: Ardent Media, 1969), p. 220.

[85] Verdross, 'Forbidden Treaties', 571.

[86] *Ibid.*, 571. [87] *Ibid.*, 571. [88] *Ibid.*, 572.

[89] *Ibid.*, 572–3. [90] *Ibid.*, 574. [91] *Ibid.*, 574.

the proposed Convention on the Law of Treaties.[92] Verdross' central argument is that all communities create a positive legal system but that this system is based on a common ethical understanding of core standards of international law reflected in *jus cogens* or peremptory norms. These norms require a community.

Writing in 1949, Verdross addressed the relationship between norms and the community:

> As these norms are always created by an organized community of states, this writer calls them the 'internal law of the community of States' (*internes Staatengemeinschaftrecht*). Under this name this writer means such rules of private, criminal, administrative and disciplinary law as may be issued by a community of *states* for the regulation of the conduct of *individuals* immediately subject to this community of *states*. This group of norms must not be confused with the norms governing the conduct of the *states* united in this community. As the latter have as their object the organization of the particular community of states and form, therefore, its constitutional law, it is of a community of states.[93]

Verdross understood the Charter as disrupting the hitherto development of international law.[94] Acknowledging the altered international legal situation, he reconceptualised *jus cogens* into three distinct groups.[95] The first group protected third states from treaties encroaching upon their sovereignty. While this could be considered part of the single compulsory norm already identified, it is not as specific. It encompasses treaties that would, for example, include third states' right to make use of the high seas, as per the original group. However, it is also a narrower understanding, as aspects of the original first category are subsumed into two new sections.

In the second category, Verdross positions the norms that substantiate humanitarian ideals. These are specifically not for the protection of any state or states and are present to protect the individual. These come within the conception of *contra bonos mores*, but are more specific than in the 1937 group. The third group are firmly established in the post-Charter era, being introduced in the articles on the use of force.[96] This is the chief transformation in Verdross' explication of *jus cogens*. It introduces the

[92] Verdross' list of minimum standards include: maintenance of law and order within the states, defence against external attacks, care for the bodily and spiritual welfare of citizens at home, protection of citizens abroad. *Ibid.*, 574.

[93] Verdross, 'On the Concept', 438.

[94] *Ibid.*, 435. [95] *Ibid.*, 437.

[96] Verdross, '*Jus Dispositivum*', 58–60.

Charter into the core of international law and the newly organised community that Verdross is addressing.[97]

He believed these three groups to be incontrovertible aspects of international law, stating,

> a norm having the character of *jus cogens* can practically be created only by a norm of general customary law or by a general or multilateral convention. Indeed, the customary law of the former unorganized international society had already accepted certain limits on the liberty of states to conclude treaties by its recognition of the 'general principles of law recognised by civilised nations' as a subsidiary source of international law. Article 38, paragraph 3, of the Statute of the Permanent Court only codifies an old practice of international arbitration in this field.[98]

Thus, Verdross separates international law into the pre- and post-Charter era, which, of course, is not uncommon, particularly regarding the use of force. Nonetheless, it is rare to do so when discussing the development of *jus cogens*. For Verdross the Charter's adoption constitutes a significant moment of change within the international legal order.

An important feature of Verdross' position on *jus cogens* and one central to constitutionalisation is their pre-Charter status, though in what he describes as the 'disorganised community'.[99] Since the Charter 'organised' the community, this focuses the community and *jus cogens* into the operation and function of the UN, though Verdross broadens this slightly with references to the Permanent Court; yet the UN is not the originator of their form. Verdross also excludes other organisations such as the IMF or World Bank from such a central place within international law; albeit, the first category of *jus cogens* could encompass economic law.

4.3.4 Verdross, international organisations and constitutionalisation

Verdross' work on the international community also focused upon neutrality and the impact of the ambiguity in the law upon membership of the League of Nations.[100] Closely related to Verdross' differentiation of the pre- and post-Charter era into the disorganised and organised community, some conclusions may be drawn from neutrality as a common point

[97] Verdross also discusses these distinctions in '*Jus Dispositivum* and *Jus Cogens*' in Gross (ed.), *International Law in the Twentieth Century*, p. 220.

[98] Verdross, '*Jus Dispositivum*', 61. [99] *Ibid.*, 62.

[100] Verdross, 'Austria's Permanent Neutrality', 61.

in both organisations and thus membership of the international community. During this period neutrality went through a transformation from an accepted functionary of international law, to a period of desuetude and back to primacy once again, illustrated in Swiss relations with the League of Nations.[101] The Swiss joined the League of Nations as a neutral but afterwards changed the basis of its membership and eventually left when the incompatibility of neutrality and the League became clear.[102] It suggests something of the Charter's nature that Switzerland eventually felt compelled to become a member. The United Nations (UN) now represents the organised community, and through membership Switzerland contributes to the international community.[103]

Verdross argues that the aims of the Covenant and the Charter are the same neutrality should also be similarly regarded.[104] Although these organisations' ultimate aims were and are to maintain international peace and security, the UN contains far more. In making a point based upon the use of force, Verdross seems to be at odds with his own statements on *jus cogens*.[105] The laws of neutrality are *jus ad bellum* and thus within Verdross' third category of *jus cogens* norms. If the laws on the use of force under the Charter are indeed *jus cogens* norms as Verdross contended then surely there can be no 'opt-out' for individual states. While the Security Council may ask individual states to act, it also requires states to take collective action under Chapter VII, which may not result in active participation in the use of force, but may result in what in other circumstances would be a violation of the laws of neutrality.[106] It is true that states have maintained their neutrality alongside their membership

101 See, generally, J. L. Kunz, 'Neutrality and the European War 1939–1940' (1941) 39 *Michigan Law Review* 719; M. O. Hudson, 'Membership in the League of Nations' (1924) 18 *American Journal of International Law* 436. Upon joining the League of Nations, the League accepted Swiss neutrality; however, by 1938 it was clear that permanent neutrality and membership of the League were incompatible. Council of the League of Nations Resolution, 17 February 1920 (1920) 1 *League of Nations Official Journal* 57.

102 A. O'Donoghue, 'Neutrality and Multilateralism after the First World War'(2010) 15(1) *Journal of Conflict and Security Law* 169.

103 Jellinek asserted that there is no way to compel a state to join the international community but Janzen correctly points out that 'States join this community and abide by its rules because they have to do so. Life in international society can no longer be non-civic. Complete separateness of states is impossible because human interests can no longer be hedged in by state-frontiers.' Janzen, ' Monism of Verdross', 392.

104 Verdross, 'Austria's Permanent Neutrality', 68.

105 Verdross, '*Jus Dispositivum*', 55.

106 Verdross, 'Austria's Permanent Neutrality', 66–7.

of the UN; however, this dual position has never been given a satisfactory legal solution.

This theory of neutrality is more akin to what Verdross espouses regarding the pre-Charter disorganised community. In adding the Charter's regulation of the use of force to the pantheon of *jus cogens,* there is an assertion that the Charter is superior to other international legal obligations.[107] This characterisation of the Charter, or at least part of it, as superior law is an example of positivism or indeed individualism, and thus does not sit comfortably in Verdross' explication of international law and community.

Verdross maintains that law is hierarchal, the various levels in this pyramid being constitutional law, statutory law, executive decrees, administrative ordinances and decisions.[108] He prefers this grouping because it is 'immanent in law, not extraneous'.[109] This is core to Verdross' idea of monism but is also linked to his discourse of positivism versus the natural law. Verdross asserts that the positive law develops through a hierarchal system of norms, which are instituted by organs. The unwritten constitution is discovered by an examination of the legal acts at the bottom of the hierarchy and then tracing from whence these acts receive their authority.[110] This, as described by Kunz, incorporates two conceptions of sovereignty: '[s]overeignty as a presupposed conception and sovereignty as a conception deriving from the contents of inter-national law'.[111] As this places sovereignty within the realms of international law it implies that it is not an absolute but rather a creature of international law. This for Verdross makes the inter-relationship between domestic and international law unquestioned and unified.[112]

How international law is formed and created is central to understanding Verdross' perspective. Verdross argues that neither treaty nor customary law is based upon the will of the states, and therefore authority in international law is not based on the domestic constitutions of states.[113] If there is a higher branch of norms, such as *jus cogens,* then these supersede domestic constitutions. These higher norms form Verdross' international constitution. From Verdross' monist perspective these domestic constitutions form part of this international constitution. This does not

[107] Simma, 'The Contribution of Alfred Verdross', 41. Here Simma argues that this is the natural progression of Verdross' natural-law arguments.

[108] Kunz, '"Vienna School"', 398.

[109] Janzen, 'Monism of Verdross', 395. [110] *Ibid.*, 397.

[111] Kunz, '"Vienna School"', 398. [112] *Ibid.*, 400.

[113] 'Anglo-Norwegian Fisheries Case' (1951) *ICJ Reports* 116.

dismiss states or state constitutions; these are still vital to the development of international law as their bodies are subordinate in their own development. Jenzen argues that 'Verdross' theory … looked at from the pragmatic point of view; it appears to be more expedient, because it is not predicated on the dogma of sovereignty'.[114]

By the time of the publication of the third edition, after the death of Verdross, of *Universelles Völkerrecht: Theorie und Praxis*, the UN had almost universal membership.[115] Verdross argued that the UN Charter constituted the constitution of the international community, though not a world constitution. This claim is no longer as radical as it once might have seemed.[116] An evolution of the core understanding of international law, while not everyone has agreed on the extent of this development, has clearly occurred. The consent of states is not the lynchpin of all international law, and the norms established in *jus cogens* are an example of this change.

Kelsen, who shares some of Verdross' core tenets, argues that higher norms cover the creation of other norms, which are of lesser import.[117] The basic norm is what produces the constitution, and one should act as the constitution prescribes. However, Kelsen also acknowledges that first constitutions or revolutionary constitutions are not created as part of pre-existing or positive norms but are part of a 'basic norm' and that this comes from a presupposition that one ought to act as the constitution prescribes.[118] The basic norm is the foundation of an efficacious constitution, which remains binding as long as it remains effectual, a somewhat circular proposition.[119] Kelsen also states that the content of the norms created is not relevant, even where they conflict with the natural law. The constitution is a norm that is created through human action, which establishes other norms. Here Kelsen and Verdross depart. According to Kelsen's theory, any legal act maybe legitimated once it follows the norms

[114] Janzen, 'Monism of Verdross', 402.

[115] A. Verdross and B. Simma, *Universelles Völkerrecht: Theorie und Praxis*, 3rd edn (Berlin: Duncker & Humblot, 1984).

[116] Fassbender, *Security Council Reform*.

[117] Simma notes that Verdross in his early career was more Kantian and Kelsian in his writings than any affiliation to the natural law, though as also noted by Simma, Verdross' Catholicism as well as his education in the Austro Hungarian Empire makes his conviction in the natural law more understandable. In Simma, 'The Contribution of Alfred Verdross', 37. See also Truyol y Serra 'Verdross et la théorie', 59; Kunz, '"Vienna School"', 398; H. Kelsen, 'What Is a Legal Act' (1984) 29 *American Journal of Jurisprudence* 199, 201.

[118] Kelsen, 'What Is a Legal Act', 201. [119] *Ibid.*, 202.

established by the efficacious constitution. Kelsen's position rests on the idea that where states recognise each other as equal and are bound by norms that are intrinsically linked to the UN Charter as a treaty document, it cannot be the world constitution.[120] Verdross would debate this proposition.[121]

Carty argues that the most difficult part of the Verdross and Simma arguments on constitutionalism is the transition from 'pre-civil to civil society'.[122] Verdross and Simma had accepted Kant's argument of the *Völkerbund*, where the state is dependent upon the international community, and that this is embodied in the UN Charter. The norms established in international law, while not taking away from the parity of sovereign states, are not all encompassing. Norms must legitimate the international community for it to exist. This is not to suggest that Verdross or Simma believe the Charter to be a perfect constitutional document. Recognising the Charter as an ideal, as Carty points out, rejects any notion of politics as relevant to its evolution and functioning. It also belies the more general evolution of international law, which was an essential aspect of Verdross' work.[123]

Carty identifies in *Universelles Völkerrecht* a commitment to multilateralism and the UN as a constitution of the world community.[124] This Carty describes as idealistic, guided by Kantian normative political theory, and as a particularly German attitude to international law. This sums up Verdross neatly, though not amply enough in its understanding of Verdrossian constitutional law. Examining Verdross' thesis, based in the natural law, on *jus cogens*, and the development of the organised international community with the UN Charter as its basis, delivers an overall outlook of international law that is comprehensive. Thus the UN Charter developed into the constitution of the world community as a natural progression of Verdross' work but this is not to suggest it is complete. The omission of entire sectors of international law, such as economic law, is just one absence that requires Verdross' ideas to be developed further.

[120] A. Carty, 'Convergences and Divergences in European International Law Traditions' (2000) 11 *European Journal of International Law* 713, 716.

[121] Kelsen gives two examples of where the two would depart on this point. The first is acts that could be considered *ultra vires*, and the second is a revolutionary change. Kelsen's aversion to social theory and examining what actually happens to justify new constitutions would bring him into great conflict with the New Haven School; Kelsen, 'What is a Legal Act', 201.

[122] Carty, 'Convergences and Divergences', 716.

[123] A. Carty, 'Alfred Verdross and Othmar Spann: German Romantic Nationalism, National Socialism and International Law' (1995) 6 *European Journal of International Law* 78, 84.

[124] Carty, 'Convergences and Divergences', 715–16.

Simma argues that Verdross was the first to make use of constitutionalism with regard to international law; Verdross certainly was one of the first to use it in a systematic fashion with accompanying intentional meaning.[125] Simma suggests that by constitution Verdross means 'the norms that regulate the basic order of a community, that is, its structure, organisation, and allocation of competences'.[126] Mosler argues that the hierarchy of norms, *jus cogens* and the sources of international law is indicative of the 'constitutional principles established by Verdross and reflect his natural law inclinations'.[127] Verdross' central tenet is that the will of the state is not paramount. Fundamentally, the natural-law foundations of international law exclude a state-centred approach as improbable. The UN Charter is the epitome of the evolution of *jus cogens* at the core of international law. The categorical approach, as opposed to the comprehensive list methodology, is rooted in the natural law and allows for the growth of the international law through the Charter.

For Verdross, constitutionalisation was possible without a written document. It was only after the adoption of the Charter that the UN became so central to Verdross' constitutionalism. This suggests that Verdross originally saw international constitutionalisation as separate from any institutional/domestic familiar remit. Simma argues that when they came to write their textbook together this had been replaced by the UN Charter as the written constitution of the international community. Arguably, taken as a whole, Verdross' approach to constitutionalism does not inevitably lead to the UN Charter, but could alternatively result in a wider approach to global constitutionalisation.[128] Verdross enabled others that followed such as Simma or Fassbender to establish constitutionalisation without as much scepticism as may have otherwise been the case. While Verdross was elemental to the European tradition, across the Atlantic a quite different form of analysis was emerging.

4.3.5 *New Haven in the American tradition*

The New Haven School advocates a preference for understanding international governance on a continuum where questions of choice and judgement are part of an on-going process. Process is central, and the New Haven School's core tenet is to combine the study of law with policy.

[125] B. Simma, 'From Bilateralism to Community Interest' (1994–VI) 250 *Rec. Des Cours* 259.

[126] Simma, 'From Bilateralism', 259.

[127] Mosler, 'Book Review', 350.

[128] Simma also suggests that this is the structure on which their entire text depends.

There is a clear link here with legal realism and acting to understand how law operates in practice while appreciating the various non-law influences upon it.[129] The New Haven School's stance stresses that the law and the varied social processes that run in tandem are neither automatically identical nor harmonious, and indeed working within this framework makes most legal analysis somewhat lacking. Law and policy are each significant, and it is their interaction with each other that is an essential element of understanding law as composed of many different mechanisms.[130]

The founders of the School, McDougal and Lasswell, seeking to create a new approach to legal education, began their philosophical journey in the midst of the Second World War. Their aim was to present a new form of legal education, which no longer stressed formalism but taught law students to appreciate the entirety of the law. It would teach law students to see law as a process and not merely to approach legal education as the transference of a set of rules.[131] Fundamentally, it was an offer to see law not as rational set of laws, but as a product of an authoritative decision-making process.[132] This required a move away from case and statute legal education.[133] The case-centred approach is of particular significance to common-law legal education, which probably had reached its zenith in US law schools. In teaching law students to see law as a process and not merely approaching legal education as the transference of a set of rules, this would result in a better and more realistic understanding of law, including its international form.

McDougal and Lasswell's ancestry is amongst the American Legal Realists of the late nineteenth and early twentieth centuries, who argued that law is more than a set of rules. The American Legal Realists' position on law is based, to paraphrase Wendell Holmes, upon the life of the law being far from logic.[134] Holmes believed that the influence that those involved in the practice of law, particularly the judiciary, had on

[129] M. S. McDougal, W. M. Reisman and A. R. Willard, 'The World Community: A Planetary Social Process' (1987–1988) 21 *U.C. Davis Law Review* 807, 811.

[130] H. D. Lasswell and M. S. McDougal, 'Legal Education and Public Policy: Professional Training in the Public Interest' (1943) 52 *Yale Law Journal* 43.

[131] Koh more recently has made a similar argument about legal education, arguing that in American law schools the emergent transnational public law should be incorporated into legal education. H. H. Koh, 'The Globalization of Freedom' (2001) 26 *Yale Journal of International Law* 305, 307.

[132] R. A. Falk, 'Casting the Spell: The New Haven School of International Law' (1991) 104 *Yale Law Journal* 1991, 1992.

[133] Lasswell and McDougal, 'Legal Education', 43.

[134] O. W. Holmes, *The Common Law* (New York: Dover Publications, 1991), p. 3.

the interpretation of the law was immense. Holmes sought to abandon the formalist basis of law, as positivism ignores the actuality of law in action.[135] The personalities of and the influences on the protagonists involved in the creation and interpretation of law had a far greater impact upon legal interpretation and creation than positivists gave credit. The New Haven School, centred as it is at Yale, has taken the torch from the American Legal Realists and has run with it, to the extent that one would not imagine Holmes recognising his own progeny.

Borgen argues that the various strengths and weaknesses inherent in the New Haven School are, in part at least, derived from its place as an heir to the rationalism of the European Enlightenment.[136] Law is discovered through reason and discourse and not through the lens of strict formalism or positivism. Both claims can be correct and not necessarily contradictory. The direct line from the New Haven School through to legal realism is perhaps most obvious, but the nuance of a rationalist understanding of process as an aspect of law is also evident. Its original contribution was as one of the older and very much twentieth-century emanations of debate, but its reinvention and its current position will also be examined.[137]

While New Haven began within legal education, one of the central aims became to reconceptualise the 'World Public Order', and arguably it is within international law that the New Haven School has been most consequential. As has been mentioned process is paramount to New Haven, and this is echoed by many others including Higgins, who are not necessarily entrenched within the School.[138] The emphasis on seeing international law as process, rather than focusing on, for instance, sovereignty or *jus cogens*, requires reorientating analysis on law as part of a broader practice of influences, which cannot always easily be reduced to black-and-white rules. Process operates on a range of levels and should be understood as on-going, and therefore the law too must be regarded as such.

The New Haven School can be quite opaque in its use of language, though its more recent advocates have moved away from some of the language of Lasswell and McDougal. This mini-renaissance has been spearheaded by those such as Koh who argue that '[t]he New Haven School

[135] H. H. Koh, 'Is There a "New" New Haven School of International Law?' (2007) 32 *Yale Journal of International Law* 559, 561, fn. 14; Falk, 'Casting the Spell', 1991.

[136] C. J. Borgen, 'Whose Public, Whose Order? Imperium, Region, and Normative Friction' (2007) 32 *Yale Journal of International Law* 332, 333.

[137] Koh, 'Is There a "New" New Haven', 559.

[138] Higgins, *Problems and Process.*

consistently argued international law is not a body of rules, but a process of authoritative decision-making'.[139] While it is far from obvious if there is truly a 'new' school or simply a reinvigoration and reimagining of the New Haven School, as the political and legal climate in which it was born has changed, it has added another layer of analysis.[140] Although the Cold War may have ended, a neo-conservative analysis of international law, which is quite similar in its nihilistic approach to international law as positivist analysis, finds space here.[141] While these newer proponents of New Haven are more centred on international law itself, their approach, which advocates interdisciplinarity and awareness outside law's well-constructed façade, was and is an important element in answering the questions concerning global governance.

The New Haven School often offers more questions than it necessarily answers, but it presents a riposte to approaches to law that are entirely formalist or focus on the establishment of core rules without cognisance of the broader spectrum of influences and manipulation. It could be argued in seeing nothing but the manoeuvring, the actuality of law itself is obscured in favour of the multiplicity of other factors identified in interdisciplinary approaches. The New Haven School stresses that to understand law without policy is naive and leads to an incomplete understanding of the legal process. The New Haven School argues that '[l]egal process and social process are not comprehensively identical or rationally congruent' and therefore both are necessary to understand law in operation.[142] One without the other is insufficient; they are not the same and therefore both are vital to fully understanding law.

In undertaking analysis, the New Haven School purports to use five basic tools: goal formulation, trend description, factor analysis, projection of future decisions and the invention of alternatives.[143] Reisman argues that 'conventional legal analyses and jurisprudences that conceive of law as a body of rules look only at a limited number of texts characterized as legal, and those social events, "facts", to which the rules direct attentions ... the *what* of inquiry is necessarily broader than the *what* of conventional

139 Koh, 'Is There a "New" New Haven?', 559; Koh, 'Why Do Nations', 2620.

140 L. A. Dickenson, 'Toward a "New" New Haven School of International Law?' (2007) 32 *Yale Journal of International Law* 547.

141 J. K. Levit, 'Bottom-Up International Lawmaking: Reflections on the New Haven School of International Law' (2007) 32 *Yale Journal of International Law* 393.

142 McDougal, Reisman and Willard, 'The World Community', 811.

143 W. M. Reisman, S. Wiessner and A. R. Willard, 'Commentary, "The New Haven School: A Brief Introduction"' (2007) 32 *Yale Journal of International Law* 575, 576.

analysis'.[144] Goal formulation could be seen in several areas from treaty negotiations to the creation of international organisations and the legal structures that have been created to ensure institutions' productivity.

The New Haven School through what is described as cultural anthropology centres on law as a solution-orientated inquiry.[145] Examining pure law in isolation and regarding any change as merely a reflection of those who have the power to act does not explain all the interactions within the legal order. Traditional analysis of reform, from the positivist perspective, does not allow for an appreciation of the 'how' and 'why' of these decisions. According to Reisman, '[p]ositivism views law from the perspective of commands, the "political inferior"',[146] whereas the New Haven School looks beyond commands to all the interactions involved in the process of legal change. This concentration on commands is the core problem that the New Haven School seeks to rectify. As McDougal, Reisman and Willard wrote 'a treatment which takes "law" as a closed system, intermittently disturbed by "independent" naked power variables is hardly conducive to appraising the value effects of decision or recommending structural improvements'.[147]

This cultural anthropology involves examining social processes based upon those who participate in them, the perspectives that influence them, their resources, which according to the School are the basis of power, and finally how they use these resources, described as strategy, in their interactions.[148] A form of governance that is reflected in constitutionalisation theories based upon gradual growth and development around power.[149] This leads to the decisions that determine the law; however, all these processes must be understood before one can understand the law. Reisman states that 'the jurisprudential tools necessary for performing these tasks must address a wide range of issues, including: (1) the way one looks at oneself; (2) the way one looks at the social process and trying to understand and influence; and (3) the way one tries to influence it'.[150]

144 W. M. Reisman, 'The View from the New Haven School of International Law' (1992) 86 *American Society of International Law Proceedings* 118, 121.
145 Reisman, Wiessner and Willard, 'A Brief Introduction', 577, 580.
146 Reisman, 'The View', 119.
147 McDougal, Reisman and Willard, 'The World Community', 811–12.
148 Reisman, Wiessner and Willard, 'A Brief Introduction', 577.
149 C. E. Schwobel, *Global Constitutionalism in International Legal Perspective* (Leiden: Martinus Nijhoff, 2011).
150 Reisman, 'The View', 120.

This, according to the New Haven School, leads to a better understanding of attempts to achieve what all people wish to cherish. The achievement of human dignity is of central import, and the New Haven School goes a long way to define what this is: 'a public order of human dignity is defined as one that approximates the optimum access by all human beings to all things they cherish: power, wealth, enlightenment, skill, well-being, affection, respect and rectitude'.[151] Each category of what people cherish is defined separately by the School and not always in line with either common or legal parlance.[152] Human dignity is said to be the ideal to which the inter-relation between law and policy is aimed at achieving. In analysing whether this human dignity is achieved through current or future reform, the New Haven School insists on separating the myth system or pure legal analysis and instead makes use of functional analysis, accepting that what may be apparent in pure legal analysis may be absent in reality.[153] The interplay between formal structures, actual control and decision-making requires policy to be an integral part of analysis. Reisman states that '[w]hen the international arena is examined, the presumed congruence of formal and actual authority may or may not be sustained by the concurrence of exceptions necessary to justify a claim of actual constitutive authority'.[154] Or as McDougal argues '[l]egal process and social process are not comprehensively identical or rationally congruent'.[155]

It is not as straightforward as simply examining law with process. This interaction is not static. International law is where it is most generally utilised, but it 'provides an orientation toward law in any context'.[156] 'Summarizing these trends will orient the scholar and decision maker in the events affecting all particular problems, and perhaps suggest the potentialities of such a flow of orientation to observers who may remain dubious of the existence and operation of the world process.'[157]

Koh argues that the New Haven School is the school of international law for legal realists.[158] The focus upon community and its broad definition

[151] Reisman, Wiessner and Willard, 'A Brief Introduction', 576.

[152] W. L. Twining was particularly critical, stating that 'LSP [law and social process] is currently the jurisprudential counterpart of LSD: its effects on individuals vary from exhilaration, to deep depression, to indifference and nobody is quite sure to what extent it is habit forming. There are some who would make it the basis of a religion.' W. L. Twining, 'Pericles and the Plumber' (1967) 83 *Law Quarterly Review* 396.

[153] Reisman, Wiessner and Willard, 'A Brief Introduction', 577.

[154] *Ibid.*, 577.

[155] McDougal, Reisman and Willard, 'The World Community', 811.

[156] Falk, 'Casting the Spell', 1999.

[157] McDougal, Reisman and Willard, 'The World Community', 815.

[158] Koh, 'Is There a "New" New Haven', 561, fn. 14; Falk, 'Casting the Spell'.

is particularly relevant to international law.[159] McDougal wrote that the New Haven School could be used as a tool to focus upon 'a fundamental critique of international law in terms of social ends … that shall conceive of the legal order as a process not as a condition'.[160] Understanding international law not as a preconstructed end in itself, but as a progression that reflects and aids the social ends that the international community wishes to achieve, is reflective of an application-orientated as opposed to a rule-orientated vision of law. The main questions are whether it is possible to identify these social ends and how the community itself is constructed by the New Haven School.

4.3.6 *Community and the New Haven School*

Community is central to the New Haven School, as it claims to grant a place to non-state actors in international law.[161] The participants in constitutive decision-making processes make up communities that share values to the extent that in pursuing their own may account for others' objectives.[162] The New Haven School identifies the development of communities as one of the most important aspects of world history. It has been a great influence on the development of the state and international law. It is argued that the complete isolation of humanity's first communal life, before the creation of an integrated order, stands in contrast to the global communities that have developed.[163] This is not to suggest that there is but one community but rather there is a collection of communities existing simultaneously, most commonly in the form of states.[164] This may seem obvious but what is not so clear to the observer is whether these new global communities are on the same course as their predecessors. The earlier examples of community developed into states. In *Jurisprudence for a Free*

159 According to McDougal, Reisman and Willard '"Community" designates interactions in which interdetermination or interdependence in the shaping and sharing of all values attain an intensity at which participants in pursuit of their own objectives must regularly take account of the activities and demands of others.' McDougal, Reisman and Willard, 'The World Community', 809.

160 M. S. McDougal, 'International Law, Power and Policy: A Contemporary Conception' (1953) 82 *Rec. Des Cours*, 137, 157.

161 Reisman, Wiessner and Willard, 'A Brief Introduction', 576. When the New Haven School first emerged, this may have been a revolutionary concept; today it is much more broadly accepted.

162 McDougal, Reisman and Willard, 'The World Community', 809.

163 H. D. Lasswell and M. S. McDougal, *Jurisprudence for a Free Society: Studies in Law, Science and Policy*, Vols. I and II (New Haven, CT: New Haven Press, 1992), p. 151.

164 Borgen, 'Whose Public, Whose Order', 335.

Society Lasswell and McDougal assert that global communities are now 'entirely comparable to, though not yet as stable as, that today maintained in the more mature national communities'.[165] This is quite an assertion. To understand how the New Haven School has reached this point, the idea of community within the theory must be understood.

The New Haven School does not describe the world's different community decision-making processes through a dichotomy of national and international law, or in terms of the relative supremacy of one system of rules or their inter-relations. Instead, it describes the global order in terms of the inter-penetration of multiple processes in an authoritative decision of varying territorial compasses. A shared wish to achieve human dignity is essential to understanding this, and the New Haven School describes a 'homogenisation' of prospects amongst those who participate in the modern world, which sustains communal ideas.[166] The growing interdependence of global society and what has been described as the globalisation of freedom contributes to this notion of community.[167] Koh goes on to describe two more forms of globalisation: governance and terror.[168] For the purposes of constitutionalism, the former is the most important. If the global community has a parallel global governance process, it may be asserted that there is also a formal process of constitutionalisation. The interpretation of the different community processes of the world, from local through regional to global is the New Haven School's 'perspective of inquiry'.[169] Thus, community is an essential component of international law's legitimacy and development.

It is this community that, according to the New Haven School, has the ultimate power: '[a]uthority is sought not in some trans-empirical source of "obligation" or "validity" but empirically in the genuine expectation of the people who constitute a given community about the requirements for lawful decision in that community'.[170] It has been asserted that the School provides a form of empowerment 'for individuals not associated with the state, a class that classical international law all but disenfranchised'.[171]

165 Lasswell and McDougal, *Free Society*, p. 151.

166 McDougal, Reisman and Willard, 'The World Community', 840.

167 *Ibid.*, 972; Koh, 'Is There a "New" New Haven', 565.

168 Koh, 'Is There a "New" New Haven', 572. Koh argues that the challenge will be to balance the globalisation of freedom and governance against terrorism.

169 E. Suzuki, 'The New Haven School of International Law: An Invitation to a Policy-Orientated Jurisprudence' (1974) 1 *Yale Journal of World Public Order* 1, 30.

170 *Ibid.*, 31.

171 Reisman, Wiessner and Willard, 'A Brief Introduction', 576.

As the international community arguably now consists of international organisations, multinationals, non-governmental organisations and individuals as well as states, certainly, with reference to traditional international law, this is correct. Yet, this empowerment seems mooted as it does not necessarily grant to non-state actors any constituent power.[172] As late as 2007 the New Haven School seemed insistent in maintaining what appears to be the monopoly of state sovereignty. This may be owing to limitations in the School's theories. The New Haven School certainly does not have a monopoly in recognising non-state actors, nor is it credible for its proponents to suggest that otherwise such participants would be entirely disenfranchised. The inter-determination and interdependence, the shared values at an intensity that requires the account of others to be taken, may mirror the moment a community moves to a constitutional process as opposed to a loose alliance, though this is dependent upon how much account is taken of others in the decision-making process, and this extra step does not appear to have been taken within the New Haven School.

Community according to the New Haven School requires sustained reliance between members. 'It is the perception of interdependence in community process that leads participants to appreciate the relevance of pursuing common interests and motivates them to clarify it.'[173] This interdependence leads to co-operation amongst the members of the community to the extent that there is a common goal to which all members wish to attain. In determining what community means and is, the New Haven School is quite dismissive of other attempts to define it.[174] The School does acknowledge the contributions of the natural law, Marxism and the sociological theory, amongst others, but finds them all analytically wanting.[175] Each of these theories does not examine 'the global community' sufficiently and is thus unable to encompass all the developments or understandings within international law.[176] Critically, the Cold War impacted on the New Haven School's discussion of these other schools of thought as power-based realism, in contrast to legal realism.[177]

172 McDougal, Reisman and Willard, 'The World Community', 816.
173 *Ibid.*, 810.
174 Lasswell and McDougal, *Free Society*, p. 178.
175 McDougal, Reisman and Willard, 'The World Community', 812–13.
176 *Ibid.*, 813.
177 Berman, 'A Pluralist Approach', 305.

This begs the question of what, according to the New Haven School, constitutes the global community? It appears that 'The more comprehensive model of the world community which we propose, and will develop, is an expansion of the generalised image of social process as a continuing flow of interaction in which *people* strive to maximise *values* employing *institutions* affecting *resources*.'[178]

This does not fully answer the question. The School also refers to participation, and it is here where the members of the community may be identified. This community is quite beyond the nation-state.[179] It is imperative that all participants be identified in order that a true examination is undertaken. 'It is individual human beings, interacting both separately and as the ultimate actors in all groups, who comprise the global community, as well as its lesser component communities and various functional associations.'[180] This is far removed from state sovereignty and what was described in classical international law. For the followers of the New Haven School 'in many contexts the nation-state is virtually a superficial organisation sometimes used deliberately to conceal the loci and channels of effective loyalties which control the flow of indulgences and deprivations'.[181]

The New Haven School acknowledges that there is little agreement on what constitutes community in international relations.[182] It identifies the state as the vehicle by which power is exercised. The state is of utmost importance in order that all those within the community are identified in order that both the scholar and the decision-maker be aware of all those who impact upon the decisions that are made. This is closely related to the identification of holders of constituent power. While the identification is for a different purpose within constitutionalism it serves similar ends, recognising that in order to institute fully a legal order its entirety must be understood. To be relevant to understanding its operation, the New Haven School must regard all action within global governance connecting all actors to governance, though with a power-based rather than normative outcome.

4.3.7 Inter-governmental organisations

The New Haven School recognises inter-governmental organisations as the means by which states, through interdependence, achieve a number of

[178] McDougal, Reisman and Willard, 'The World Community', 814.
[179] Berman, 'A Pluralist Approach', 306; Lasswell and McDougal, *Free Society*, p. 149.
[180] McDougal, Reisman and Willard, 'The World Community', 818.
[181] *Ibid.*, 821. [182] *Ibid.*, 816.

aims or objectives.[183] They are also a facet of the global community; they deal with global issues that are transnational. Both the UN and the WTO are excellent examples of such bodies. International organisations can be to the disadvantage of the state as the state community is replaced by globalised communities. 'An intriguing and unsettled question is whether individuals are rearranging their larger-group loyalties to the disadvantage of the nation state.'[184] Human dignity, which is the aim of any community, has become more 'homogenised'.[185] The human dignity is the same for the varied global communities, and the aims of some of these communities are achieved in, amongst others, the United Nations and the World Trade Organization.

However, the New Haven School does not suggest that this process of globalised community has subsumed the state: '[a]n institution is a recurring and coordinated pattern of thought and behaviour which human beings establish to maximise what they perceive to be their own interests. Institutions are identified with those features of social process that are specialized to the shaping and sharing of particular values.'[186] This institutional framework reaches beyond international organisations to incorporate other systems of governance, enabling the co-ordination of thought and behaviour. As human dignity has become a global common aim, so too have the processes to achieve it. The 'base values' available to the several categories of participants and the 'strategies' that participants employ to manage the base values to maximise (or optimise) value outcomes are central. The 'outcomes' are the culminating events of 'increasing' or 'decreasing' power, wealth or other values.[187] These global common aims can be achieved through such organisations.

While the WTO and the UN are arguably the most obvious examples of such organisations, a constitutionalisation process could also be within this form of analysis. This process of constitutionalisation must be both beyond the state and institutions to come fully within the scope of the New Haven School. 'The culminating outcome of the process whereby power is shaped and shared is a decision, which includes the giving and receiving of support for particular choices.'[188] Within state communities this process resulted in constitutional orders, and therefore it would seem to not be entirely outrageous to suggest the same for the international community as understood by the New Haven School.

[183] *Ibid.*, 822. [184] *Ibid.*, 845. [185] *Ibid.*, 840.
[186] *Ibid.*, 853. [187] *Ibid.*, 814. [188] *Ibid.*, 815.

While the language of the New Haven School is no longer as prevalent in international law as it once was, the core of what is proposed by the theory is still relevant. The idea of an international community linked within a process of international law is apparent in any number of theories on constitutionalism and is considered in the next chapter. Human dignity as the aim of international law can be pursued through the process of constitutionalisation, but only one that eschews formalism for a legal order based in the relevant community. This must be beyond the legal rules of constitutionalism and embody the entirety of the transactions, including the political, into its remit. Global governance networks of authoritative decision-making may ultimately be constitutional but the New Haven School in its purest form would not have necessarily directly identified them as such. However, the forms of analysis that the New Haven School introduced have impacted upon how global constitutionalism is now perceived, particularly in regard to process.

4.4 Verdross and New Haven within constitutionalisation

Both Verdross and the New Haven School are influential in the development of contemporary theories of global law. In the global constitutionalisation debate, elements of both approaches are evident. Both theories' focus on understanding the overarching governance order within the global legal system law. Be it from the Verdrossian or New Haven perspective the need to see the global legal system as a coherent body of law, with central norms, based within a community, beyond any positivist understanding of a legal system, is apparent.

Verdross approached international law from firmly within the natural law. This natural-law perspective, combined with his understanding of *jus cogens*, established his constitutional approach to international law. As one of the first proponents of a coherent and fully realised constitutional insight into international law, Verdross' slant offers a rational understanding of the place of constitutionalisation within international law. While Simma has located this constitutionalisation within the UN Charter, arguably it is Verdross' reliance on identifiable central norms of a higher order than general international law that is most significant for the current constitutionalisation debate. The New Haven's influence is of a different order to Verdross but no less significant. It understands international law as a series of transactions that shuns formalism; it appreciates the role of politics within international law, without lessening the substantive nature of the legal order. This is particularly relevant in the discussion of the relationship between constituent and constituted power holders. While the New Haven School does not directly deal with the constitutionalisation debate, its focus on the nature of the actors involved in international law, as well as its core in interdisciplinary research, has pushed the understanding of international law beyond a purely statist consent-based legal order.

Both Verdross and New Haven are significant in understanding the development of international law in the twentieth century and, as such, both are important facets in understanding how it will develop into the future. Both are evident in the constitutionalisation debate, in considering process, *jus cogens*, community, politics and the norms of constitutionalism. While Verdross' influence is more readily identifiable, the recognition of the role of politics in a global legal order, which the New Haven School advocated, should not be underestimated.

4.5 Conclusion

Global constitutionalisation has firm roots both in the evolution of international law in the twentieth century, as well as a place amongst the present theories that attempt to explain what the outcome of that development is within contemporary global governance. While all six approaches, global legal pluralism, fragmentations, global governance networks, global administrative law, Verdross and the New Haven School, are different in their idealised notions of international or global law, what they all share is an understanding of the inadequacies of the classical vision of international law, which global constitutionalisation also seeks to remedy. While Verdross is clearly linked to global constitutionalisation, the others share both apparent and present threads of debate, evident in both their starting points as well as their content.

While the next chapter discusses the nuance of global constitutionalisation in some depth before moving on to the debate regarding its normative constitutional content, what is important is whether the form of purchase that constitutionalism brings is also evident in these other theories; whether the context of constitutionalism's purchase is paramount and thus the method taken is less important, or whether the very form is of such import that the advantages gained in constitutionalisation, if it is normative, cannot be sidestepped. Each theory roots itself in both governance and a shared space of operation, suggesting a broader need to take further account of these questions within contemporary global governance. The context from which constitutionalisation emerges is one concerned with legitimacy, power, democracy, politics and the rule of law, and each theory establishes a different account of how they can be balanced against one another. The next chapter outlines how the constitutionalisation debate has gone about this task.

5

The structure of global constitutionalisation

Habermas describes the basis of constitutionalism as 'the *terminus ad quem* of the process of juridification of political power ... the very idea of a constitution that a community of free and equal citizens gives itself'.[1] Linked to the preceding chapters on normative constitutionalism in relation to constituent power and present debates on the global legal order, this chapter uses these perspectives to consider the content and form of the global constitutionalisation debate. Reflecting on whether a normative proposal is being put forward, and if not, what alternative constitutionalism is suggested, this chapter seeks to consider whether constitutionalisation theories further entrench Westphalian values within the global legal order or if they pertain towards a break from international law's historical operation.

In considering the features of the global constitutionalisation debate, it first must be conceded that there is little agreement as to its content.[2] Depending upon the divisional method there may be as many as seven or eight schools of global constitutionalisation, making the identification of the theories that come closest to a coherent normative global constitutionalism difficult. Yet, such differentiation is also global constitutionalisation's strength, as it grants an opportunity to consider this form of governance order before it becomes entrenched. This chapter seeks to identify commonalities amongst global constitutionalists but in doing so will necessarily isolate aspects that may seem to undermine positions that otherwise appear coherent. Attempts to avoid such characterisations are made, yet in seeking to locate commonality within the debate they may be unavoidable.

1 Habermas, *Divided*, p. 131.

2 See, for example, the discussion of different forms of domestic constitutionalism and why certain models cannot be transposed. J. Rubenfeld, 'The Two World Orders' (2003) *The Wilson Quarterly* 28.

Dunoff rather witheringly refers to the increased use of constitutional imagery as lacking the practice to follow it; this chapter attempts to identify such constitutional practice amongst the variety of debates put forward.[3] The oft-casual use of constitutionalism, constitutionalisation and constitution creates confusion. These terms are not always connected to constitutional law but rather imply a further legalisation of international law or some form of constitutive force.[4] Instances where constitutionalisation is used simply as a synonym for legalisation will not be considered, as there is little commonality to be found beyond mere word use.

Qualms regarding the practicality and plausibility of constitutionalisation have not dampened enthusiasm for the theory. The aspiration towards global constitutionalisation could be characterised as a yearning for rigour or part of an evolution from a simplex to a complex legal system beyond the recognition of a fully constituted order.[5] Constitutionalisation enables global law to form a recognised structure of legitimacy.[6] If global law is constitutional, then it is as 'good' a legal system as any domestic or regional, for example, EU, equivalent; however, before this may be asserted, basic questions of suitability of constitutionalism and its components need consideration. Legitimacy ought not to underpin the debate, as the result will undermine any basis for adopting constitutionalism.[7] Further, those that dispute claims that global governance is politics should not use constitutionalisation simply as a buffer against such arguments.[8]

This chapter investigates whether global constitutionalisation makes room for constitutional norms. Thus, finding definitions of global constitutionalisation within various theories is not as essential as understanding the impetus driving both the normative and descriptive constitutionalisation debates. The form that global constitutionalisation theory takes

[3] J. Dunoff, 'Constitutional Conceits: The WTO's "Constitution" and the Discipline of International Law' (2006) 17 *European Journal of International Law* 647, 650.

[4] De Wet, 'The International Constitutional Order', 53.

[5] This is not to exclude a Hartian analysis that precludes the recognition of international law as a legal order, or other critical approaches. D. M. Johnston, 'World Constitutionalism in the Theory of International Law' in R. St. John MacDonald and D. M. Johnston (eds.), *Towards World Constitutionalism, Issues in the Legal Ordering of the World Community* (Leiden: Martinus Nijhoff, 2005), p. 3. Within institution-based constitutionalisation, for example, while the UN issues various reports on reform exemplifying the consensus that reform is necessary, there is a doubt as to how it could be achieved politically.

[6] Legitimacy can form part of the elements of constitutionalisation itself. De Wet, 'The International Constitutional Order', 63–4.

[7] Dunoff, 'The Politics' in Dunoff and Trachtman (eds.), *Ruling the World*, p. 179.

[8] A. Buchanan, 'The Legitimacy of International Law' in S. Besson and J. Tasioulas (eds.), *The Philosophy of International Law* (Oxford University Press, 2010), p. 79.

depends upon the theoretical perspectives underpinning its approach. For example, if constitutionalisation starts from a state-based community theory as opposed to a governance order, the test of its presence or effectiveness differs, but whether either is bound to constitutionalism must be adjudged from a normative perspective.

Numerous viewpoints on the role of constitutionalism within international law clamour for attention. For example, Allott regards global constitutional law as fulfilling the same function as any other law; thereby traditional international law is best understood as 'the minimal law necessary to enable state-societies to act as close systems internally and to act as territory-owners in relation to each other,'[9] which is founded on a 'delict-property-contract ethos'.[10] Thus, international constitutional law regulates international public law as opposed to merely being a subgenre.[11] Disliking the term 'constitution' as it implies a finished product Allott prefers to regard constitutionalisation as a process of development.[12] This is indicative of a form of constitutionalisation that is less concerned with recognisable structures of constitutionalism but rather focuses on the evolution of law within a particular order. Walker describes constitutionalism as 'a deeply contested but indispensable symbolic and normative framework for thinking about the problems of viable and legitimate regulation of the complexly overlapping political communities of a post-Westphalia world', a normative constitutionalism closer to what is proposed here;[13] while Fassbender's constitutionalism is a sub-discipline of public international law, 'the constitutional law of the international community',[14] but is also linked to the growth of multilateralism and the debate on the fragmentation.[15]

9 Allott, *Eunomia*, p. 324. 10 *Ibid.*, p. 335.

11 P. Allott, 'The Concept of International Law' (1999) 10 *European Journal of International Law* 31, 38.

12 P. Allott, 'Review Essay Symposium: Philip Allott's Eunomia and The Health of Nations Thinking Another World: "This Cannot Be How the World Was Meant to Be"' (2005) 16 *European Journal of International Law* 255, 269.

13 N. Walker, 'Post National Constitutionalism and the Problem of Translation' in J. H. Weiler and M. Wind (eds.), *European Constitutionalism beyond the State* (Cambridge University Press, 2003), p. 53.

14 Fassbender, 'We the Peoples' in Loughlin and Walker (eds.), *The Paradox*, p. 268. Peters also argues that the Charter is not a world constitution but rather that international constitutional law is a subset of international law containing its most important principles. Peters and Armingeon, 'Interdisciplinary Perspective', 387.

15 Fassbender, *Security Council Reform*; MacDonald, 'The Charter of the United Nations', 205; Trachtman, 'The Constitutions of the WTO', 623; Fassbender, 'The United Nations Charter'; Dunoff, 'Constitutional Conceits', 647.

Beyond an understanding of progression, these three constitutionalisation models are difficult to reconcile, and parts are based on normative values; thus constitutionalisation provides a coherent legal framework for transition from traditional international law to a modern counterpoint but others entirely rely on traditional frames of reference. Fassbender's approach, as it incorporates constitutionalism into international law on the same basis as human rights or international criminal law, implying an existent constitutional order resting upon the UN, is particularly problematic. If constitutionalism is not a higher form of international law, it cannot fulfil its purpose as a normative regulator of the governance order. Generally, and as can be seen in Allott and Walker, constitutionalisation perceives the entirety of global law as relevant, though not necessarily all global law as constitutional.

Critically, constitutionalisation embraces the political in a coherent fashion. Rather than conjecturing on the true nature of law when politics is clearly identified and understood, constitutionalisation should, theoretically, embrace the political forms of governance as substantiating a constitutional system. It balances the levers of power and provides a legitimisation forum for the workings of states, international institutions, global actors, individuals and civil society amongst others. This must work alongside a functioning political system.

Although this form of politics may not resemble what is found in domestic legal systems, and certain schools of constitutionalisation may be slower to embrace the political elements, it is a central aspect of constitutionalism. This could be seen as admitting to the charge that there is no international law but rather, to gain legitimacy, international politics masquerading as law. However, recognising that constitutional systems work in parallel with political systems presents an argument against those who claim that since international law does not resemble its domestic counterpart there is no legal order. Global politics is distinguishable from domestic politics and, as such, its constitutional structure. This is not an impediment to its existence. The law is separate from the politics of international relations but is still indelibly intertwined with it, as arguably should be the case in any functioning constitutional system. Thus, in contrast to other theories, one of the aims of constitutionalisation should be to regulate the relationship between law and politics. If this dualistic interplay is not in reality the case, then the constitutionalisation process is arguably still embryonic. The discussion of community, constituency, and constituent and constitutive power bears much relation to this.

Constitutionalisation as a system for understanding governance is an important factor in differentiating between the various theories of constitutionalisation, and between it and other schools of global law. While the diverse theories on constitutionalisation are discussed in detail, there is a difference between suggestions for autonomous constitutional orders, such as in trade, and alternative understandings that recognise an overall scheme of world constitutionalisation. This latter group tends to be less concerned with the content of the varied systems, meaning that the minutiae of trade law is less essential to its understanding than the overall system it helps to create. The internal legitimacy of trade law would have its source within constitutional law, but it is the governance structure that is paramount.

As discussed in Chapter 2, the use of constitutionalism beyond the state leads to varied reactions. The first is usually abhorrence at the very idea that an entirely domestic construct can be put to a use to which it was not intended. Another is to accept that constitutional regimes may have some keystone ideas that global law may utilise to enhance its structure. Broader visions of constitutionalisation propose that an understanding of the entirety of the governance of global law is essential. Those common elements, such as questions of sovereignty, sources of law, identification of the actors and the legitimate exercise of power must therefore be fully understood. Constitutionalisation offers a manner to do this in that it provides to the global framework a substantive basis on which the future of global law may develop along an already signposted route. Thus, it is governance that must be understood as forming an elemental part of constitutionalisation, a point often omitted or sidelined in others schools, particularly fragmentation and the global legal pluralist model.

Loughlines propos that constitutionalism is based upon a shift from a hierarchy to an understanding that constituted power is based upon the consent of the holders of constituent power or 'the people'.[16] He states that 'the process of constitutionalisation is born of the reconfiguration of values of constitutionalism, an extension of their reach and a loosening of the connection between constitutionalism and the nation state'.[17] Thus, constitutionalisation is characterised as a process by which a legal system (and must therefore be accepted to be a legal system and not merely a political one) moves from a position of consent or contract base to one where

16 M. Loughlin, 'What Is Constitutionalisation?' in Dobner and Loughlin (eds.), *Twilight*, pp. 47–8.

17 *Ibid.*, p. 68.

the remit of power and freedom of action has been curtailed and dampened by a multifaceted regime of law based upon key normative values.

Some schools of constitutionalisation aim to cover sectoral areas of international law; however, its true potential may lie in advancing a coherent overarching structure. The world order approach provides a vertical arrangement of governance delineating the constitutional elements of international law in conjunction with domestic law but would also provide a horizontal framework for understanding how areas of global law interact with each other. This horizontal structure is significant in many contemporary dilemmas as it provides methods for dealing with the ever more complex interactions between segmented areas of law, such as how international environmental law interacts with 'general international law' and domestic law as well as how it interacts with the other distinct branches of international law. While other schools such as fragmentation and global legal pluralism seek to identify the varied characteristics of each branch, constitutionalisation offers a more complete framework, which works for both the horizontal and vertical eruditions of global law.

5.1 Theories of global constitutionalisation

Global constitutionalisation does not offer a utopian vision of international law, nor does it aim to resolve all the structural or normative issues within the global legal order. Constitutionalism does not accomplish this in the domestic realm; indeed most constitutionalisation theories recognise a lack of current normative coherence in the actual structures it supports.[18] Yet, even if the constitutionalisation debate does not succeed in creating a coherent constitutional system it may offer an analytical tool for better understanding international law's nature thus justifying the ongoing debate.[19]

Johnston suggests several reasons why global constitutionalism appears threatening: jurisprudential misgivings on the need for legal formalism; cultural issues in attempting to find one legal order that is actually global; as well as political questions of whether a global constitutional framework is required.[20] Some of these concerns are well-founded. As was discussed

[18] For instance, Paulus and Habermas both agree that the current system has not evolved into a fully constituted order.

[19] Though there are theories, such as those of De Wet or Petersmann, that are more definitive in their assertions; Walter, 'Process of Constitutionalization' in Nijman and Nollkaemper (eds.), *New Perspectives.*

[20] Johnston, 'World Constitutionalism' in MacDonald and Johnston (eds.), *Towards World Constitutionalism*, pp. 18–20.

with regard to Walker's four factors – inappropriateness, inconceivability, improbability and illegitimacy – such anxieties need carefully consideration. Yet, this is a healthy position to be in, as it allows for a substantive debate before conceptions become entrenched.[21] A resolution to these objections depends on a notion of constitutionalism that is neither narrow nor constrained by domestic interpretations.

Often constitutionalisation theories recognise constitutional norms without constitutional structures.[22] Indeed, it could be argued that it is necessary for the debate to detach itself from certain international structures.[23] This does not deny the importance of institutions, particularly the UN, but rather recognises that a comprehensive global legal order must be broadly construed. Generally, constitutionalisation theories come in two guises: sectoral and world order constitutionalisation. However, it is not easy to divide one from the other. Indeed, any distinction between the two should be considered artificial. The aim of maintaining this division is to highlight the distinctions that have emerged in presenting international organisations, such as the UN or the WTO, or alternatively areas of law, such as human rights or environmental law, as constitutional within a broader global system.

Sectoral constitutionalisation combines procedural elements of constitutionalism in the guise of the organisational structures with substantive law emergent in particular fields. For example, within the WTO the substantive law is trade, within the UN the maintenance of international peace and security.[24] Thus, sectoral constitutionalisation requires alternate communities or constituencies, each directly linked to its substantive law. As such, the interests and the holders of constituent power within human rights or trade law would inevitably be different.

In the alternative, Paulus describes the creation of a world constitutional order as the move away from the formal notion of constitution unified around a central hierarchal system towards a 'substantive conception that deals with the emergence of formal and substantive hierarchies between

21 Peters also deals with some of the core objections from an international perspective such as the bestowing of legitimacy, the symbolic quality, lack of empirical evidence and that it oversimplifies a global order that is more complicated than is often presented. Peters, 'Merits', 402.

22 Peters and Armingeon, 'Interdisciplinary Perspective', 387.

23 Paulus, 'The International Legal System as a Constitution' in Dunoff and Trachtman (eds.), *Ruling the World*, p. 71.

24 Agreement Establishing the World Trade Organization, Article III, Functions; and Preamble, Charter of the United Nations, Article 1.

different rules and principles'.[25] Here, constitutionalism forms part of the emerging complexity within global law. This does not necessarily imply a grander project, but rather a description of international law's evolution, described by Fassbender as a *leitmotif* (reoccurring theme) common in many theories.[26] World constitutionalisation requires a constituency or community that encompasses the entire global order, and the attendant difficulties in establishing such on the global scale necessarily must be considered.

There are several alternatives to the sectoral or world constitutionalisation categorisations. For example, Slaughter and Burke-White focus upon constitutional moments, using the war on terror and particularly Afghanistan, as a moment that redefined the relationship between law and politics.[27] Fischer-Lescano decries their form of analysis as having nothing constitutional in its elements or purpose.[28] While Slaughter and Burke-White discuss the invocation of human rights, Fischer-Lescano describes the very dearth of law in their analysis as problematic. But what is missing from both arguments is a basis within constitutionalism itself where the actions of all actors may be adjudged. A constitutionalisation process cannot be identified in one moment. It should be acknowledged with regard to Slaughter that while it remains important, the aim of understanding the relationship of law with politics and the nature of networks of governance is outside the constitutionalisation debate.

Klabbers argues that the constitutionalist debate comes in two guises: first, global justice and, second, attempts to prove empirically that constitutionalisation is actually taking place.[29] In eliminating some of the more nuanced debates, this categorisation confines its scope and underestimates its multiplicity. Nonetheless, it raises important issues: if the global constitutionalisation debate is about showing its presence how is this adjudged or if it is about achieving justice, is constitutionalism the best method of achieving such an outcome?

[25] Paulus, 'The International Legal System as a Constitution' in Dunoff and Trachtman (eds.), *Ruling the World*, p. 71.

[26] Fassbender, 'We the Peoples' in Loughlin and Walker (eds.), *The Paradox*, p. 273.

[27] A. Slaughter and W. Burke-White, 'An International Constitutional Moment' (2003) 43 *Harvard International Law Journal* 1; A. Slaughter, 'International Law and International Relations Theory: A Dual Agenda' (1993) *American Journal of International Law* 205; and Slaughter, *New World Order*, p. 42.

[28] A. Fischer-Lescano, 'Redefining Sovereignty via International Constitutional Moments?', available at www.fb6.uni-bremen.de/uploads/ZERP/AFL/Publikationen/Lescano_RedefiningSovereignity_Chapter7.pdf, accessed 30 August 2013, p. 12.

[29] Klabbers in Klabbers, Peters and Ulfstein, *Constitutionalisation*, p. 4. Perhaps more important are the arguments that it is not, in fact, taking place.

Here, constitutionalisation theories are discussed in two forms: sectoral and world order constitutionalisation. Aiming to establish a coherent picture of the current state of global constitutionalisation debate, various theorists in both categories will be considered in relation to the development of a constitutional frame. Adding to the context established in the previous chapter, the following sections outline the basic characteristics of constitutionalisation before, in the next chapter, considering their relationship with constitutionalism, particularly the rule of law, divisions of power and democratic legitimacy.

5.1.1 Sectoral constitutionalisation

The momentum accompanying the sectoral constitutionalisation debate underpins the variety within constitutionalisation.[30] Two forms of sectoral constitutionalisation dominate. The first centres on potential constitutional institutional structures, such as the UN, while the second considers the normative values evolving within a particular area of law, such as human rights. At times, these two mix, as in the case of trade law, but usually they are stand-alone arguments. These two forms of sectoral constitutionalisation throw up numerous questions regarding their relative coherence as well as the justifications for entirely different processes of constitutionalisation occurring across a number of discrete areas of global law. Considering its relationship with world order constitutionalisation is also critical. The potential of multiple tracks of constitutionalisation, proceeding at different speeds across different parts of global law as well as within discrete areas, should not be discounted, particularly if global legal pluralism is taken account of within constitutionalisation.

Pluralism is an important facet in understanding the interconnected debates within sectoral constitutionalism.[31] Global legal pluralism focuses on non-hierarchal structures and democratic legal orders that are recognisable in claims regarding governance and the coexistence of different constitutional orders. Global constitutional pluralism identifies the emergence of different constitutional sites and processes on a horizontal and sometimes vertical basis realised in elements of sectoral constitutionalisation. Fragmentation, particularly its descriptive elements, could also be considered part of the sectoral constitutionalisation debate. Reliance by sectoral constitutionalists on the claims made for fragmentation and

[30] Dunoff, 'The Politics' in Dunoff and Trachtman (eds.), *Ruling the World*, pp. 178, 179.
[31] N. Walker, 'The Idea of Constitutional Pluralism' (2002) 65 *Modern Law Review* 317.

the adoption of their rationales offers a method of rationalisation between the various proposed constitutional orders. If constitutionalisation is coupled with global legal pluralism or fragmentation it may support the proposition that constitutionalisation can occur at different paces within different sectors of international law.

If pluralism is inoperative, then sectoral constitutionalisation will require a formal understanding of hierarchy; yet there is little agreement on such a structure. Most often, the UN is put forward as the most viable option for such a hierarchy. For example, the necessity of some form of representative body places the UN General Assembly as the easiest body to fulfil such a role. Yet, the connection between representative functions and democratic legitimacy remains unclear. The state interest as represented in the General Assembly does not necessarily map onto the wider global interests with which the General Assembly is concerned. While this issue will be returned to later, the lack of structures to support normative constitutional development should not be sidestepped within the sectoral debate.

While sectoral constitutionalisation is often associated with institutional law, in fact, it is much broader in scope. Sectoral constitutionalism attempts to describe the shift from a treaty-based institutional order to a more complex structure that, depending on the perspective taken on the role of a specific sector, in turn, impacts upon other constitutional and non-constitutional areas of global law. Whereas the entire shift is not always characterised as constitutional, it is, however, indicative of the main pillars of the global constitutionalisation debate. Except for those sectoral theories that claim a place at the apogee of the legal order, often the intended interaction of these various sectors remains unclear. This relational issue becomes a significant point of global governance, which may be resolved in a number of ways: a global pluralist vision based in democratic governance; an acceptance that this sectoral constitutionalisation is a form of fragmentation that needs to be treated as such; or by accepting Fassbender's assertion of the UN as a form of global constitutionalisation that establishes a hierarchy amongst other areas also internally constitutionalisationising.

Governance structures as epitomised in the UN and the WTO are at the forefront of debates on institutional constitutionalisation but rarely as intentional constitutional documents.[32] Discussions within sectoral

[32] The EU has also been at the vanguard of the recent sectoral debate, and while this development has both been influential and remarkable, and has greatly influenced the

constitutionalisation often regard the intent of the founders of the organisation as unimportant. For example, there is no evidence that there was a distinct intent by those negotiating in the Uruguay Round under the GATT to produce a constitutional organisation.[33] The fast-paced development at the WTO is remarkable considering that trade is not often considered central to general international law.[34] While there may be questions regarding the intent behind the creation of the UN Charter, whether constitutionalism as such was in mind is not at all clear.[35] For the UN Charter to be accepted as a constitution for the global community arguably depends upon a political move equivalent to the developments of 1945. Thus, the founder's intent provides little enlightenment on the nature of sectoral or institutional constitutionalisation.

Jackson's work, in concert with constitutionalists such as Fassbender, is emblematic of the theories that focus upon institutional structures. In Jackson's case, this is a constitutionalist understanding of the WTO. The WTO, and trade law broadly, has been the site of much constitutional deliberation. In fact, Jackson suggested a constitutionalist bent for trade law long before the creation of the WTO, which partly explains the rapid growth of the constitutionalisation debate within this sector since 1995.[36]

Jackson places himself firmly in the constitutionalisation camp, though he argues that the WTO still has some way to go before becoming a fully constitutionalised order. The basis for his discussion is firmly rooted within broad public international law but his claims remain attached to trade law. Jackson considers the move in trade law from a power to a rule based system central to its constitutionalisation. This process, he believes, emerged prior to that organisation's creation but

direction of the current discussions, it will not be considered here in any great detail; as a regional development, though not unrelated, considerations must be borne in mind that are beyond the purview of this debate. For a discussion of the relationship between the EU and the WTO, see L. R. Helfer, 'Constitutional Analogies in the International Legal System' (2003) 37 *Loyola Law Review* 193.

33 Dunoff, 'The Politics' in Dunoff and Trachtman (eds.), '*Ruling the World*, p. 178.

34 D. McRae, 'The Legal Ordering of International Trade: From GATT to the WTO' in MacDonald and Johnston (eds.), *Towards World Constitutionalism*, p. 543.

35 For a discussion of the text of the Charter and its drafting, see B. Simma, *The Charter of the United Nations: A Commentary*, 2nd edn (Oxford University Press, 2002); or regarding judicial review by the ICJ, B. Sloan, 'The United Nations Charter as a Constitution' (1989) 1 *Pace International Law Review* 61, 72–6.

36 See, for example, J. H. Jackson, *The World Trade Organization: Constitution and Jurisprudence* (London: Chatham House Papers Series, 1998); J. H. Jackson, *Restructuring the GATT System* (New York: Council on Foreign Relations Press 1990); J. H. Jackson, *World Trade and the Law of GATT* (New York: Lexis, 1969).

came to fruition with the WTO's formation culminating in the formation of the Dispute Settlement Body alongside its wider economic structure. Aspects that for Jackson remain unachieved include both increased transparency and participation in decision-making (including civil society).[37] He is a key figure in instituting the contemporary constitutionalisation debate but from a position that recognises the shortcomings in this sector of law.

Petersmann, also firmly based in trade law, takes an international human rights discourse and couples this with a focus on the rule of law and separation of powers. His analysis centres on the WTO but seeks to extend the standard UN human rights purview to international economic law. In doing so he broadens both the general debates within trade and economic law but also opens up the possibility of various sectors of international law feeding off each other's constitutional momentum. Petersmann identifies eight core principles as constitutional: the rule of law, separation of powers, democratic self-government, national constitutionalism, (inalienable) human rights, international constitutionalism (international legal restraints), social justice and finally cosmopolitan constitutional law.[38] This list, as Petersmann regards it, requires a multilayered constitutional system of governance that ensures the place of human rights. He also insists that international organisations, such as the WTO, need to develop and acknowledge that human rights are core constitutional principles before constitutionalisation can be present.[39] Thus, international human rights are inalienable and exist with or without constitutionalisation, but for Petersmann at least, constitutionalism cannot exist without human rights.

Drawing support from both the workings of the EU and domestic courts, Petersmann takes a distinctly liberal economic view of rights. Alston resoundingly and convincingly disapproves of Petersmann's use of human rights in this liberal economic context. Alston does not necessarily critique the broader constitutionalist agenda but argues against certain economic values trumping other normative claims such as the right to development or environmental sustainability.[40] For Petersmann,

[37] J. H. Jackson, 'The WTO "Constitution" and Proposed Reforms: Seven "Mantras" Revisited' (2001) 4 *Journal of International Economic Law* 67, 76, though, for example, Krajewski disagrees that NGO participation would have such an impact upon the WTO. M. Krajewski, 'Democratic Legitimacy and Constitutional Perspectives of WTO Law' (2001) 35 *Journal of World Trade* 167, 171.

[38] Petersmann, '21st Century', 11–16. [39] *Ibid.*, 18.

[40] P. Alston, 'Resisting the Merger and Acquisition of Human Rights by Trade Law: A Reply to Petersmann' (2002) 13 *European Journal of International Law* 815. For further

governance structures must have a human rights basis, and using these principles it is easy to be critical of other constitutionalisation theories. For example, he places the right to democracy at the core of his argument, which could be contrasted with Fassbender's identification of the General Assembly as a representative body. The General Assembly fails to incorporate democratic self-government, and thus Fassbender's constitutional order would fail Petersmann's test of constitutionalism.[41] This rights-based approach is even more prevalent in Petersmann's most recent writing, and while he does not entirely abandon the institutional arguments of Jackson and Fassbender, the context of the argument is certainly skewed away from structural or institutional aspects towards a more normative constitutional approach within trade law.

Besides its invocation by those such as Petersmann, human rights constitutionalisation, as a process in itself, also claims a place in sectoral constitutionalisation. The argument is that bills of rights or human rights treaties with global application are of such significance that they could rightly be called constitutional.[42] Indeed, this is also where the interactions between domestic constitutional and international human rights can be most clearly seen within sectoral constitutionalisation, though in their domestic form, which is firmly rooted in existent constitutional structures, they may also point to a working frame of subsidiarity in a wider constitutional process.[43]

Claims that *jus cogens* norms or obligations *erga omnes* supply the common hierarchal basis within sectoral constitutionalisation have some traction and are echoed in Verdross. Yet, even in combination both only possess limited coverage and certainly would not meet the requirements of normative constitutionalism.[44] Further, when compared with substantive areas within the UN and the WTO *jus cogens* norms or obligations *erga omnes* may be of little use in settling competing claims of superior-

criticism, see R. Howse 'Human Rights in the WTO: Whose Rights, What Humanity' (2002) 13 *European Journal of International Law* 274.

41 Petersmann, '21st Century', 21–3.

42 Gardbaum, 'Human Rights', 749.

43 C. O'Cinneide, 'Human Rights and within Multi-Layered Systems of Constitutional Governance: Rights Cosmopolitanism and Domestic Particularism in Tension' (30 March 2009). University College Dublin Law Research Paper No. 12/2009. Available at SSRN: http://ssrn.com/abstract=1370264, accessed on 9 December 2013; also the UK Human Rights Act 1998 forms part of British constitutional law, while also being intrinsically linked to the European Convention on Human Rights.

44 Fassbender, 'We the Peoples' in Loughlin and Walker (eds.), *The Paradox*, pp. 285–6.

ity within sectoral constitutionalisation, beyond the most fundamental of questions.

One rather simplistic question is whether these sectors can successfully have such a different basis for constitutionalisation. The ordering of these systems must be considered. The questions of whether the legal order described by Fassbender or Jackson needs to be constitutional, which arguably it must, or whether it could remain part of traditional international law, which is doubtful, are left unanswered in both their approaches. Within states there is a broad array of forms and structures of constitutionalism; yet, as has been established, there is a core that is required and must be present across all normative constitutional orders. The identification of a constituency to rectify the disconnection between domestic and global interests is also necessary. Perhaps as a result of competitive rhetoric, a system in which these elements operate within each area appears absent from the workings of sectoral constitutionalisation theories.

5.1.2 World order constitutionalisation

Under world order constitutionalisation there is a single legal order based around a sole constitutionalisation process. Commonly it focuses on a reordering of global law as part of the movement towards a more sophisticated and usually hierarchal order. Most theories do not require the entirety of international law to become constitutional, but rather aspects, by necessity, must adopt constitutionalism in order to support a sophisticated legal system. For example, De Wet bases her constitutionalism on the assumption of an ever 'increasingly integrated international legal order',[45] and the end result of Paulus' theory is not a centralised constitutional order but rather a decentralised or 'constitutional lite' regime.[46] Both require a sophisticated understanding of constitutionalisation. While some suggest that existing structures within international law may sustain constitutionalisation, particularly as it is often recognised as a non-linear trajectory, substantive progression is most often advocated.[47] There does not appear to be any consensus between the advocates of world order constitutionalisation as to the degree of

[45] De Wet, 'The International Constitutional Order' 53; E. De Wet, *Chapter VII Powers of the United Nations' Security Council* (Oxford: Hart, 2004), pp. 92–115; alongside the emergence of regional value systems, De Wet, 'The Emergence of International', 611.

[46] Klabbers in Klabbers, Peters and Ulfstein, *Constitutionalisation*, p. 30.

[47] Peters, 'Merits', 398.

formalised structure required. Yet, the end result for the constitutionalisation process must be the submission of power to law.[48] The question then is whether the world order theories have either proven that this has occurred or at least that global law is on this trajectory. As world order theories are not one homogeneous group this is difficult to answer; however, certain themes have emerged.

World order constitutionalisation sees two potential roads for global constitutionalisation. One is to base changes within international law as part of the global legal order and adapt constitutionalism into this fold. The second is to base the developments in international law with constitutionalism as a concept (and not as an ideal) that assesses global law and identifies whether it has some or all of the necessary attributes to be constitutional. The latter is closer to establishing a normative constitutional order. The impact of the political in the guise of constituent and constituted power should be recognised as problematic. Within world order constitutionalism the holders of constituent power will be more difficult to ascertain on a world basis that covers all global interests rather than within a sector with more limited interests. Yet, this issue is largely only dealt with in passing by world order theories.[49]

Paulus bases global constitutionalisation within established constitutional norms. If, he argues, the arguments in favour of domestic constitutionalism are similar to those at the international level it would seem reasonable that it is correct to use similar principles when discussing constitutionalisation as a movement within law as a whole.[50] This is linked to Paulus' view that constitutionalisation within international law should not be regarded simply as indicative of 'bindingness'.[51] Paulus suggests that any international constitution needs to be based on both form and substance, as without the latter (or normative constitutionalism) there are

[48] Habermas, *Divided*, p. 132.

[49] This will be apparent in the sections that follow, which deal with questions of governance, democracy and the basic themes of constitutionalism.

[50] Paulus, 'The International Legal System as a Constitution' in Dunoff and Trachtman (eds.), *Ruling the World*, p. 91. This would be in agreement with the earlier chapter where constitutionalism was considered more broadly as symptomatic of a form of legal system, alongside Walker's arguments against displacing the domestic principles in the international sphere, which at first glance may appear to be easily done but is nonetheless incorrect. Bingham, *Rule of Law*, chapter 10.

[51] Paulus, 'The International Legal System as a Constitution' in Dunoff and Trachtman (eds.), *Ruling the World*, p. 75; or as Peters argues to be used in an inflationary manner, Peters, 'Merits', 403.

few constitutional elements to be fulfilled, but that form is also required to ensure the constitutionality of conduct.[52]

As with the sectoral account, the debate on world order constitutionalisation is closely linked to fragmentation. World order constitutionalisation suggests that fragmentation is a symptom of a more multifarious legal order, which is becoming constitutionalised at the centre but also compels the process of fragmentation. This may be contrasted with those who argue that fragmentation may be considered as unconstitutional and even an antagonistic trend within international law.[53] As previously discussed, this combination of both theories goes some way to describe present trends but without the substantive theory that underpins other approaches such as pluralism.

Walter advocates somewhat of a halfway house between sectoral and world order constitutionalisation. Regarding the constituent treaties of international organisations and their core rules as a partial constitution of the world community he places the constitutional processes of each sector as a part of a broader constitutional order. The global order manages relations between these partial constitutional orders.[54] Walter's compromise brings to the fore the difficulties in settling the relationships between the constitutional structures associated with sectoral constitutionalism. Walter's solution, to understand sectoral constitutionalism as a part of broader global constitutional order, includes some elements of global legal pluralism. Arguably, Fassbender's approach is nearer to Walter's as it also proposes a mixed sectoral/world order constitutionalism; however, in placing the UN at the centre, it is elevating its law to a status that Walter does not advocate.

If Walter's solution is adopted, constitutionalisation must be harmonised to enable a coherent system, within the confines of the rule of law, divisions of power and democratic legitimacy, to emerge. This raises issues of certainty, coherence and parallel development. To answer questions relating to the purpose and content of sectoral constitutionalisation the shape of a global system into which these sectors may fit must first be ascertained. It may be possible to have each constitutionalisation process

52 Paulus, 'The International Legal System as a Constitution' in Dunoff and Trachtman (eds.), *Ruling the World*, pp. 87–8.

53 Peters and Armingeon, 'Interdisciplinary Perspective', 390.

54 C. Walter, 'Constitutionalizing (Inter)national Governance – Possibilities for and Limits to the Development of an International Constitutional Law' (2001) *German Yearbook of International Law* 170, 191.

happen at different speeds, but this may inculcate discrepancies into the system.

Within world order constitutionalism, global governance theories tend to hold sway, and arguing for such a constitutional infrastructure most readily connects with domestic constitutionalism. A constitutional world order would establish one umbrella structure under which the various sectors of international law could operate. In establishing a hierarchal structure with clear substantive norms, world order constitutionalism appears more appealing than the sectoral model. Yet, it is also the more difficult to demonstrate succinctly. In seeking to prove a global process is underway, disparate areas of international law need to be brought together in a rational fashion. This is easier to do within one sector such as trade law; however, it is more difficult to find all the necessary elements of constitutionalism in one sector. World order constitutionalism makes more room for the debates on normative constitutionalism. The rule of law, divisions of power and democratic legitimacy are more readily identifiable in the entirety of global law than in individual sectors.

Although the differentiations between the two forms of constitutionalisation are not completely satisfactory, they should be borne in mind when considering global constitutionalisation. Throughout the proposals the identification of the rule of law, divisions of power and democratic legitimacy lack uniformity and this is partially owing to the sectoral and world order divide, a point returned to in later chapters. World order constitutionalisation theories are often based upon an ever-increasing understanding of the need for substantive co-operation and global law's response to this need. This can be achieved through the recognition of an existing constitution that is evolving or alternatively by maintaining that there is a move towards a future constitutionalised legal order, but both must be rooted in constitutionalism if their arguments are to be substantiated.

5.2 Coherence, competence, consistency and hierarchy?

If the UN provides the global constitution, as advocated by Fassbender, then it is at the apex of a hierarchy and other orders such as the WTO must submit to its law, or, at the very least, areas of dual competence, when conflict arises.[55] As mentioned, such conflict already occurs and various

[55] Such as with the UNDP or ECOSOC.

judicial bodies respond, with varying degrees of success, to settle competing claims. Nonetheless, constitutionalisation adds an extra tension to rival orders that current theories, world order or sectoral, neglect.[56] Such tensions feed towards questions of coherence that certainly constitutionalisation, as a normative project, ought to address.

Ulfstein suggests two possible alternatives for establishing constitutionalisation between organisations (though not between sectors of law): one is to integrate the organisations in the areas where they overlap, and the second is to establish a hierarchy amongst them.[57] Ulfstein argues that it is unlikely that states will change the founding treaties of these organisations, and therefore it will be left to the organisations to make arrangements between themselves. Why this is a more politically palatable solution is unclear, as surely those who opposed changing the founding treaties would equally oppose a treaty between organisations that would achieve the same end.

This imbalance of power between organisations working in trade offers a good example of this issue. As Ulfstein suggests, the WTO with its strong dispute settlement arm (even with the existence of the Trade and the Environment Committee within the WTO) versus UN-backed environmental law in the form, for instance, of the United Nations Framework Convention on Climate Change and the Kyoto Protocol, would seem to require the establishment of a hierarchal structure to consider which one takes precedence.[58] Alternatively, it supports the arguments made regarding the fragmentation of international law. If both systems are separately constitutionalised, this becomes ever more complicated. In practice, thus far the Dispute Settlement Body has attempted to avoid such clashes, but it is unlikely that such platitudes can continue indefinitely.[59] If the choice

[56] See, for example, the multiple cases regarding the Mox Plant: R. Churchill and J. Scott 'The Mox Plant Litigation: The First Half-Life' (2004) 53 *International and Comparative Law Quarterly* 643; J. G. Merrils, 'The Mosaic of International Dispute Settlement Procedures: Complementary or Contradictory?' (2007) 54 *Netherlands International Law Review* 361.

[57] Ulfstein in Klabbers, Peters and Ulfstein, *Constitutionalisation*, pp. 68–73.

[58] United Nations Framework Convention on Climate Change (1992) *UNTS* 1771; Kyoto Protocol (1997) *UNTS* 30822.

[59] *United States – Import Prohibitions of Certain Shrimp and Shrimp Products*, WT/DS58/R (15 May 1998); *United States – Standards for Reformulated and Standard Gasoline* WTO WT/DS2/R (29 January 1996). These cases have led to the DSB of the WTO finding environmental measures undertaken by States as ultimately for trade protectionist purposes, and while states may make exceptions within their trade regimes for environmental measures, these exceptions must be in full compliance with the law of the WTO trade system. The membership of both organisations overlap, and this in itself may lead to a solution.

is made to follow Fassbender's approach, then the UN is already establishing itself as at the apex of this order; however, without other organisations' co-operation, it is hard to see how, in practice, it can develop any form of coherence.

Trachtman suggests that the solution to incoherence is relying upon the allocation of power amongst the agents of states.[60] He proposes that the WTO should be considered an avatar of trade. This relies on the WTO yielding monetary or other compensation to developing and lesser developed states for accepting inappropriate or unsuitable WTO law, and this would in turn establish a level playing field. This seems to be at odds with the general values of both the WTO as an organisation as well as the aims of the Doha Development Round, which focuses on making the substantive law of the organisation fairer for developing members who were considered to have ceded more than what was received under the Uruguay Round, which established the WTO.[61] Nor does the proposal deal with the conflicts that arise within Trachtman's constitutional WTO, as it only seeks to improve upon the existing rules and not bring about any radical shifts towards a more normative understanding of trade law. It is unclear whether Trachtman considers this model as suitable for other global constitutional systems or indeed whether this compensation could be paid where WTO constitutional law would permit it, but UN constitutional law would not.

Sectoral constitutionalisation requires some global order to address competing interests. While some succour may be gained from pluralism or fragmentation, the nature of constitutionalism would seem to require a more substantive system to allocate preference or superiority. Yet, with the exception of the UN's virtual monopoly on the use of force, how to settle clashes between constitutional human rights, trade or environmental orders, amongst those not championing a pluralist approach, remains unclear. It remains difficult to imagine members of the WTO, in cases of conflict, agreeing to have another constitutional order decide whether its own constitutional regime will be substituted or take precedence.[62] It is hard to see how, in practice, sectoral constitutionalisation can develop any form of coherence within the global order.

[60] Trachtman, 'The Constitutions of the WTO', 634.

[61] S. P. Subedi, 'The Notion of Free Trade and the First Ten Years of the World Trade Organization: How Level Is the "Level Playing Field"?' (2006) 53(2) *Netherlands International Law Review* 273; and Doha Ministerial Declaration, WT/MIN(01)/DEC/1, 20 November 2001.

[62] J. G. Collier, *Conflict of Laws*, 3rd edn (Cambridge University Press, 2001).

Thus, a quandary remains. As the arguments in favour of sectoral constitutionalisation currently stand, consideration does not appear to have been given to the problems of coherence, competence and hierarchy that inevitably are thrown up should this form of constitutionalisation come to fruition. Certainly for those that argue it already subsists, the answer is that it is already functioning successfully; however, constitutionalism should offer a level of certainty approximate with the rule of law, which should not allow for simply muddling along. World order constitutionalisation does appear to offer an answer to this question but also requires an acceptance that global law as it currently stands needs to be tested against normative constitutionalism, such as the rule of law, divisions of power and democratic legitimacy, a task attempted in the next chapter.

In a constitutionalisation process the norms of a fully constitutionalised system must, by definition, be partially absent. Crucially, if global constitutionalisation is an aspirational process that either has yet to begin or to take firm root, then it is a process where some particular norms are present, others nascent and others non-existent, while still others merely have the potential to emerge as the system matures. If global constitutionalisation exists, it must lie on this spectrum. Indeed, similar constitutional evolutions over several hundred years can be found in domestic constitutional orders.[63] Nonetheless, this still leaves open the question of the place of constitutional norms within the global constitutionalisation debate. To understand how constitutionalism, community and constituency interact with normative constitutionalisation, a broad appreciation of global constitutionalisation is necessary. The next chapter considers the guises in which constitutional norms are part of the global constitutionalisation debate and the extent to which these norms are considered elemental by global constitutionalisation's proposers.

[63] See, for example, Van Caenegm, *An Historical Introduction*; Tomkins, *Republican*; Vile, *Constitutionalism*; Alexander, *Philosophical Foundations*.

6

The development of a constitutional approach

For Allott constitutions are three in one – the legal, the real and the ideal.[1] The legal constitution relates to power, both its allocation and implementation, whereas the real constitution is its present operation. The ideal constitution is what a society could be, which, while inherent in both legal and real constitutions, remains but a possibility. Allott argues for a present constitution constantly aiming for an ideal. Therefore, as there are gaps in the operation of the rule of law, divisions of power and democratic legitimacy, its full realisation as a constitutional ideal is uncertain. Depictions such as Allott's leave room for a normative analysis of the vagaries of the global constitutionalisation debate. The hortatory language of global constitutionalisation does nothing to bring together the strands of propositional theories, nor does it question the overtly progressive characterisation of law's evolution.

Allott's language hints at the broader consequence of the global constitutionalisation that forms part of a wider trend of an ever-positive Whiggish attitude to global governance. Such proclamations see an optimistic inclination that sidesteps contemplation of the underlying normative rationales underpinning such apparent trends. Global constitutionalisation is a crucial example of tendencies towards constant sanguinity on the future of global law. A step back towards normative constitutionalism, as discussed in Chapter 2, may temper such zealousness towards progress, though with the realisation that such inclination is also apparent in constitutional scholarship. The rule of law, divisions of power and democratic legitimacy form the basis of analysis not as a test that global constitutionalisation is bound to fail, but rather taking from Allott the recognition that constitutionalism's 'nous' is its multifarious occupation of the legal and political that must be part of any proposition seeking to insinuate itself into a global legal order, that to

[1] Allott, *Eunomia*, pp. 134–6.

adopt constitutional purchase as worthwhile has implications beyond the natural progression of the global legal order.

6.1 The rule of law and constitutionalisation theories

As described in Chapter 2, while the symbolic value of the rule of law remains important there needs to be something binding governance beyond avoiding arbitrariness or Raz's political rhetoric. It is easy to invoke Henkin's famous statement that 'almost all nations observe almost all principles of international law and almost all of their obligations almost all the time' and argue that this provides evidence for the existence of the rule of law.[2] But this statement does not demonstrate how the rule of law is manifested within a normative constitutional system, nor does it necessarily distinguish between it and rule by law. As discussed with regard to domestic constitutionalism, the rule of law requires law to be applied equally, created openly and administered fairly. Within the global legal order, that should be no different. Thus, international constitutional law should be obeyed, consistently applied and actions taken in light of it if the global legal order is to adopt it on to itself. An entrenched rule of law suggests a bounded legal system of good governance. Besides any considerations regarding a global constitutional order, international law should possess a rule of law ethic distinguishable from constitutionalisation.[3]

First, the rule of law will be addressed in general terms; it will then be discussed with relation to judicial activism, and finally with regard to human rights and constitutionalisation. The latter two are exemplars of the wide use of the rule of law within constitutionalisation and offer contrasting approaches to the constitutional imperative behind its presence. This analysis offers an answer to whether the rule of law is as elemental to global constitutionalisation as it is to domestic constitutionalism.

Brownlie argues that the 'moral purpose of the United Nations was the promotion of the rule of law'.[4] While he is not arguing that the Charter established an international rule of law, Brownlie suggested that an aim in formulating the Charter was its institutionalisation and, as such, it is not alien to global law. Indeed, to suggest otherwise would be to accept that international law is subordinate to international politics, although

[2] L. Henkin, *How Nations Behave: Law and Foreign Policy*, 2nd edn (New York: Colombia University Press, 1979), p. 47.

[3] Though see Bianchi on ad hocism. Bianchi, 'Ad-hocism', 263.

[4] I. Brownlie, *The Rule of Law in International Affairs: International Law at the Fiftieth Anniversary of the United Nations* (The Hague: Martinus Nijhoff, 1998), p. 1.

this claim, in itself, is not necessarily undisputed.[5] For instance, the use of Security Council terror lists certainly raise important questions for the employment of the rule of law to legitimise action.[6] While the role of the rule of law in the constitutionalisation theories is central, its wider significance for the global legal order ought to be borne in mind.

The framing principles of global constitutionalisation are instrumental in understanding how the theory developed. For instance, from Allott's perspective, constitutionalism is based on the notion that public power is subject to law. His constitutionalisation focuses on the curtailment of power by the rule of law.[7] He links the subjugation of governmental structures to a constitution to the subjection of subjects to those same governmental operations. The constitution is the fulcrum around which power and duty emerge for both the governed and the government, or as it could also be described mutually for the holders of constituent and constituted power.[8] The case in favour of substantive rule of law may in fact be easier than in domestic law. While acknowledging the arguments made by writers such as Posner, that international law does not provide much curtailment of power, it is proposed that the rule of law ought to be recognised as a central element of global constitutionalism. If the rule of law exists within a global constitutionalisation process, then there must be consistency, coherence and predictability within the law; otherwise accusations of arbitrariness will abide.

This is fundamentally what the rule of law within a constituted system provides. For example, Bianchi queries the ad hoc nature of international law.[9] Broaching important questions regarding exceptionalism and the rule of law, he points to Iraq in the period running up to the 2003 invasion as an instance treated as exceptional to enable it to be dealt with outside of normal international law. He argues that the continuation of this ad hocism undermines any constitutionalisation.[10] International law must have some consistency where the debate is not characterised by hard cases such as Iraq but is rather based upon normative discussion of the law. A concern with ad hocism should be visible in both the substantive and

[5] For a discussion on this point, see Georgiev, 'Politics or Rule of Law', 1.

[6] See, for example, E. Cannizzaro, 'A Machiavellian Moment? The UN Security Council and the Rule of Law' (2006) 3 *International Organisations Law Review* 189; O. Schachter, 'Self-Defence and the Rule of Law' (1989) 83 *American Journal of International Law* 259.

[7] See, generally, Allott, *Eunomia*; P. Allott, *The Health of Nations: Society and Law Beyond the State* (Cambridge University Press, 2002).

[8] P. Allott, 'The Courts and Parliament by Whom?' (1979) 38 *Cambridge Law Journal* 79

[9] Bianchi, 'Ad-hocism', 263.

[10] *Ibid.*, 270.

structural arguments in favour of the rule of law as it constrains the arbitrariness fundamental to ad hoc actions.

Fischer-Lescano and Teubner suggest that the most important task that global constitutionalism can fulfil is to ensure the independence of law against any oncomers such as politics, economics or religious pressures.[11] Arguably, this is already the task of law, whether constitutional or otherwise, but also underpins the necessity of a legal order maintaining the rule of law. Linking the rule of law to divisions of powers and democratic legitimacy, within international law, Bingham proposes substantive equality as a necessary element of the rule of law, but such calls are yet to be considered critically within global constitutionalisation.[12] For instance, while organisations such as the WTO or treaty-based legal regimes regard sovereign equality as paramount, this does not fully translate into the ability of constituent power holders to exercise their rights or institute a substantive rule of law.[13]

Allan argues that both citizens' and judiciaries' abidance by the rule of law do not require absolute obedience to the legislature, creating a point of debate between various constituent and constituted power holders inculcated within the process.[14] Similarly, Tomuschat proposes that a constitution and community are intrinsically linked: 'a legal community presupposes as a minimum that the relationships between its members be defined by law so that it does not confine itself to a purely factual juxtaposition of the individual actors'.[15] De Wet posits that the international constitutional order consists of an international community, an international value system and a basic structure for its enforcement.[16] This pins

[11] Fischer-Lescano and Teubner, 'Reply to Andreas L Paulus', 1067–1968.

[12] Bingham, 'The Rule of Law', 73. The role of equality in international law is complicated by the notion of sovereign equality as epitomised by the decision-making processes of international organisations, the formation of international law, and the debate in sub-altern movement and equality as understood within international human rights law or feminism. See Anghie, *Imperialism*; Charlesworth and Chinkin, *A Feminist Analysis*.

[13] See, for example, Subedi, 'The Notion of Free Trade' 273. See also the Doha Declaration, para. 44, 'Special and Differential Treatment'. See, for instance, Posner's book on climate change, which argues against differentiated treatment. E. A. Posner and D. Weisbach, *Climate Change Justice* (Oxford: Princeton University Press, 2010). This form of differentiated equality is tied to the arguments of the subaltern movement, which will be discussed in more detail in Chapter 7.

[14] Allan, 'Fairness, Equality, Rationality' in Forsyth and Hare (eds.), *The Golden Metwand*, p. 17.

[15] Tomuschat 'Obligations' 219.

[16] De Wet, 'The International Constitutional Order', 51; though a more recent piece moves somewhat away from this argument, E. De Wet and J. Vidmar, 'Conflicts between

constitutionalisation to a value-orientated scheme, which relies upon *jus cogens* norms as underlying principles of constitutionalism and as the basis for the rule of law. Thus the rule of law is both structurally and substantively important to constitutionalism, a point reflected in some constitutionalisation proposals but by no means universal.

Raz argues that 'the law may … institute slavery without violating the rule of law'.[17] This would be remedied by a substantive rule of law capable of acting as a safety valve within global constitutionalisation, particularly where other elements of normative constitutionalism are, as yet, unincorporated. While it is important to be mindful of the warnings of Fuller's substantive rule of law, the apparent lack of judicial activism within international law favours this approach. Further, substantive rule of law would be more important within the global legal order than in a domestic order based in long-established democratic processes. Within global law, balancing the weakness of the divisions of power necessitates a substantive system to ensure the rule of law is central to a global constitutional order. The question is whether the rule of law is integrated and imperative to the extent necessary to endorse the presence of constitutionalism within constitutionalisation. The next two sections on judicial activism and human rights draw attention to some of the difficulties associated with its presence within the constitutionalisation debate.

6.1.1 *The rule of law, judicial activism and substantive content*

In domestic constitutional orders judicial activism, with the court standing as guardian of constitutional norms on an equal and non-deferential basis to other branches of government such as the legislature or executive, is central to both the rule of law and divisions of power. It is reasonable to suggest that courts could play a similar role in global constitutionalisation or, at least, that another structure should perform this role. The present particularity of the global judicial system, the differences between the form of judicial settlement available in each sector and the positions that these judicial institutions play within the institutions or areas of law with which they interact do not necessarily mean that they cannot form part of a normative constitutional order but rather suggest their operation will be specific to the global order. As well as being fundamental to any claims regarding the rule of law, judicial and quasi-judicial bodies play an

International Paradigms: Hierarchy Versus Systemic Integration' (2013) 2 *Global Constitutionalism* 196.

[17] Raz, *Authority*, p. 221.

important role in authoritative interpretation, settlement of disputes and the establishment of global law.[18] Employing judicialisation to substantiate claims that a constitutionalisation process is underway plays a significant role in the constitutionalisation debate.

Cass argues that the Dispute Settlement Body (DSB) of the WTO contributes to the latter's constitutionalisation in a number of ways: by amalgamating techniques from other constitutional systems, instituting a new system of law and incorporating issues traditionally considered to be of a domestic constitutional character.[19] Judicial norm generation in the form advocated by Cass lies squarely within a common-law constitutional court methodology linked to the rule of law.[20] As such, Cass relies upon a particular interpretation of the role of the DSB at the WTO.[21] Common to most if not all sectoral claims for constitutionalisation is the issue of choice of law. While the DSB accepts that general international law may be used, this has not resulted in the acceptance of other sources of law beyond the specific treaties within the WTO system.[22]

Thus far the DSB rebuffs any constitutional claims in its proceedings. In *India–QRs* the DSB rejected an Indian argument that a separation of powers existed within the WTO.[23] Reconciling Cass' claims with either the Panel or the Appellate Body's position in *India–QRs* is difficult without also accepting that this drift cannot be explained in the text of DSB decisions. Thus, claims to constitutionalisation must be justified either as part of a broader WTO institutional change or within economic law. The DSB's attitude in *India–QRs* suggests a lack of interest at the WTO in subjecting the governance structure to any form of restraint from its dispute settlement arm. It is difficult for the Appellate Body to be transformative or make constitutional changes without a major sea change

[18] Helfer, 'Constitutional Analogies', 197.

[19] Cass, *World Trade Organization*, p. 203.

[20] Intriguingly the common law would suggest a system of precedence that does not exist within the DSB.

[21] Cass, *World Trade Organization*, p. 177.

[22] See Article 3.2 of the Annex 2, 'Dispute Settlement Understanding, Agreement Establishing the World Trade Organization', which refers to the rules of interpretation of general international law. See also *United States – Standards for Reformulated and Standard Gasoline*, WTO WT/DS2/AB/R.

[23] *India – Quantitative Restrictions on Imports of Agricultural, Textile and Industrial Products (India–QRs)* WT/DS90/AB/R (23 August 1999); for a discussion of judicial review and constitutionalisation, see J. Klabbers 'Straddling Law and Politics: Judicial Review in International Law' in MacDonald and Johnston (eds.), *Towards World Constitutionalism*.

in its findings, or reform of the Dispute Settlement Understanding in renegotiation at the WTO.

Some consider the establishment of the DSB to be a 'constitutional moment'.[24] This view depends upon the WTO portending towards constitutionalism from the outset rather than relying, as in Cass' argument, on the jurisprudence of the DSB. The DSB rejects any constitutional form in its own Reports and thus for it to be leading the constitutionalisation surge, it must be doing so out of confluence with other WTO bodies. General compliance, despite Henkin's suggestion, cannot of itself be evidence of the inculcation of the rule of law into WTO procedures. The DSB must go beyond applications of the text of treaties and take wider substantive governance issues into account if the rule of law is to become part of its jurisprudence. It does not appear, at this point, willing to do so.

The European Courts have a significant impact on global constitutionalisation theories. For example, Petersmann relies on the transformative nature of judicial activism of both the European Court of Justice and the European Court of Human Rights. Yet, the nature of the transformative effect is dependent upon the regional and wider normative developments across Europe. Still, it remains an important source of analysis in judicial constitutionalisation. For instance, the manner in which judicial organs mediate between conflicting norms is central to constitutionalisation at the WTO, and this sub-categorisation could reasonably be placed at the feet of several other sectoral constitutionalisation ideals.[25]

Sloan maintains that the International Court of Justice (ICJ), in establishing the UN's legal personality in the 'Reparations' case, was acting constitutionally.[26] Further, he argues that the method of interpretation employed by the ICJ is similar, if not identical to that undertaken by the US Supreme Court.[27] Yet, the finding of legal personality, while it was

[24] Trachtman, 'The Constitutions of the WTO', 632–3. He quotes Buchanan and Tulloc's definition of a constitutional moment as the Harsanyian 'veil of uncertainty', which allows individuals, or in our case states, to agree on constitutional change even though they are uncertain of the possible future. J. M. Buchanan and G. Tullock, *The Calculus of Consent, Logical Foundations of Constitutional Democracy* (Ann Arbor: University of Michigan Press, 1962).

[25] Dunoff, 'Constitutional Conceits', 665; the other two are based upon institutional architecture or a set of normative commitments.

[26] 'Reparation for Injuries Suffered in the Service of the United Nations' (Advisory Opinion) (1949) *ICJ Reports* 174.

[27] Sloan, 'The United Nations Charter', 69–71. Sloan does go on to contend that while the ICJ may have constitutional elements it ultimately is not seriously considered to be more than a special treaty, 81.

monumental, could also be said to be in line with the development of institutional law. Evidence for this may be found, with the exception of the Commonwealth, in the legal personality attributed to other international organisations. For example, it is found in the Agreement establishing the WTO.[28] The 'Reparations' case confirms that the ICJ does not take a literal approach to interpretation but this does not make its actions necessarily constitutional without a broader normative change in the Court's operation.

The lack of judicial review at the ICJ must be considered.[29] The ICJ's lack of jurisdiction to enforce the rule of law is detrimental to a core role as a constitutional mechanism. As already mentioned, judicial activism forms part of the rule of law, and judicial review is central to such action. As one possible variant on judicial review, Ulfstein ascribes some weight to the process of advisory opinions, under which the General Assembly may have regard to actions taken by the Security Council, under Article 96 of the Charter. However, as Ulfstein admits, owing to their non-binding character, cases such as 'Certain Expenses'[30] and the 'Legality of the Use of Nuclear Weapons'[31] are of little use in substantiating constitutional norms.[32] The 'Lockerbie' case was probably the closest the Court has come to undertaking a judicial review; however, as this case never went to the Merits, the position of the ICJ remains inconclusive as an enforcer of the rule of law.[33] In common with the DSB, to find constitutional character similar to domestic constitutional or superior courts, a tremendous amount of extrapolation is required.

Thus, there is a gap between the normative claims made by some constitutionalisation theories and actual judicial action. Ulfstein describes this as historically linked to the lack of control exercised by international organisations over individuals that, of late, has come to be transformed.[34] He points to the UN Security Council's targeted sanctions regime and

[28] Agreement Establishing the World Trade Organization, Article VIII, Status of the WTO, 'The WTO shall have legal personality ...'

[29] Sloan argues this was an intentional approach by the drafters of the UN Charter. Sloan, 'The United Nations Charter', 74–5; Klabbers, 'Straddling Law and Politics' in MacDonald and Johnston (eds.), *Towards World Constitutionalism*; J. Alverez, 'Judging the Security Council' (1996) 90 *American Journal of International Law* 1.

[30] 'Certain Expenses of the United Nations' (1962) *ICJ Reports* 151.

[31] 'Legality of the Use of Nuclear Weapons in Armed Conflict' (1996) *ICJ Reports* 66.

[32] Ulfstein in Klabbers, Peters and Ulfstein, *Constitutionalisation*, p. 64.

[33] 'Questions of Interpretation and Application of the 1971 Montreal Convention Arising from the Aerial Incident at Lockerbie' (Preliminary Objections) (1998) *ICJ Reports* 9.

[34] Ulfstein in Klabbers, Peters and Ulfstein, *Constitutionalisation*, p. 77.

its Counter-Terrorism Committee as prime examples of a more individualised approach to international law.[35] Certainly, the UN's peacekeeping operations have long since given the UN direct contact with individuals and their rights.

Judicial activism plays a significant role in human rights constitutionalisation theories. The focus on human rights transcends many if not all institutions and presents a challenge in understanding the relationship between the various sectoral constitutional systems. For example, Petersmann, focusing on the WTO and liberal economic rights requires organisations to overcome their constitutional deficiencies and fulfil their human rights roles. He suggests that human rights come within the UN's purview but also within global economic law in the guise of the WTO.[36] Yet, as Dunoff correctly notes, although there is some scope to do so within trade agreements, the DSB has also not chosen to take a human rights approach to WTO law.[37] Petersmann argues that the UN's focus on sovereignty over human rights combined with the international judiciary's underdevelopment mean that it is inaccurate to describe the UN as either a constitution for itself or the global legal order.

Petersmann argues that institutions are often based upon 'sovereign prerogatives of the power-holders' and not upon human rights claims.[38] Utilising this analysis, it could be asked whether, regarding human rights, the UN would pass a test of constitutional rigour. On the basis of sovereign prerogatives versus human rights, it probably would not. In contrast, Fassbender and Dupuy both argue that constitutionalisation is founded within the UN. Since their focus is not upon a rule of law, which protects individuals from arbitrariness, but upon institutional arrangements their arguments appear unsound as constitutional stalwarts. Ulfstein argues,

[35] The Counter-Terrorism Committee and questions regarding the extension of human rights norms to the Security Council are discussed by Fassbender; B. Fassbender, 'Target Sanctions and Due Process' (20 March 2006), commissioned by UN Office of Legal Affairs, available at www.fb6.uni-bremen.de/uploads/ZERP/AFL/Publikationen/Lescano_RedefiningSovereignity_Chapter7.pdf, accessed 9 December 2013.

[36] Petersmann, 'Constitutional Justice', 769. See also Petersmann, '21st Century'; E. Petersmann, 'Time for a United Nations "Global Compact" for Integrating Human Rights into the Law of Worldwide Organizations: Lessons from European Integration' (2002) 13 *European Journal of International Law* 621; E. Petersmann, 'The WTO Constitution and Human Rights' (2000) 3 *Journal of International Economic Law* 19; E. Petersmann, How to Reform the UN System? Constitutionalism, International Law, and International Organizations' (1997) 10 *Leiden Journal of International Law* 421.

[37] Dunoff, 'Constitutional Conceits', 659.

[38] Petersmann, '21st Century', 23.

in a similar vein to Petersmann, that it would be far better if international organisations took on the protection of human rights in their own governance structures. This he argues is particularly the case within the UN where the relative parity of Article 103 of the Charter and human rights is unsettled.[39] The ICJ's paralysis with regard to the actions of the Security Council, in particular, further underpins this lack of rigour.

If one of the main functions of domestic governments is the protection and promotion of human rights as part of a structural rule of law, which includes a judicial action, then for global constitutionalisation such processes are vital. While Ulfstein recognises some constitutional elements, such as aspects of the rule of law in adjudication, within the WTO, he argues that it, alongside other international organisations, lacks judicial human rights vigour. The varied elements of potential reform, such as an advisory parliament or civil society institutions, are as applicable to the UN as they are to the WTO; however, judicial elements cannot be siphoned away from broader arguments regarding constitutionalism.[40]

The critical aspect of these debates is the degree of extrapolation required to find the rule of law within these judicial bodies. Rarely, if ever, is there a direct link between judicial activism and the establishment of a consistent rule of law analysis linked to constitutionalisation. Judicial activism forms at least part of the panoply of arguments in favour of constitutionalisation. But this does not suggest that the rule of law has been established as a form of constitutionalism. As is often the case, these bodies seem loath to take on such a role for themselves, or even to admit to its potentiality, so it is one of the easiest constitutionalisation claims to criticise. This leaves the rule of law as an element of constitutionalism reliant on other aspects of constitutionalisation theories to establish it existence.

6.1.2 *The rule of law,* jus cogens, *consent and curtailing constituted actors*

If the rule of law is incoherent with regard to judicial activism, it may be present in other aspects of global constitutionalisation, for example, within human rights. Gardbaum makes three claims on behalf of human

[39] Ulfstein in Klabbers, Peters and Ulfstein, *Constitutionalisation*, pp. 78–9. See also A. Orakhelashvili, 'R (on the application of Al-Jedda) (FC) V Secretary of State for Defence' (2008) 102 *American Journal of International Law* 337.

[40] Petersmann, '21st Century', 35.

rights. First, international human rights are constitutional in their own right and run in tandem with domestic constitutional law, with both possessing identical constitutional status. Second, in the same manner as the EU, human rights are a constitutional system of international law. Third, human rights substantiate the move of international law beyond a horizontal consent-based system.[41] This places human rights at the centre of both a substantive rule of law and a constitutionalisation process. Petersmann argues for the universal place of human rights as a normative claim privileging them over other entitlements.[42] This, he argues, should be based upon rights as well as the rule of law, separation of powers, social justice and democratic peace. However, in making this claim he intimates a hierarchy.

Paulus stresses basic constitutional principles shared with domestic constitutional orders. As such, his theory is rights based, though perhaps not in the same vein as Petersmann's or *jus cogens*-based proposals.[43] He mixes both structural and substantive constitutionalism, in a manner reminiscent of Bingham, to identify what is necessary for constitutionalism in the global sphere. Indeed, Paulus specifically references both structural and substantive elements as indicative of the rule of law and democracy. Interestingly, he also includes state's rights. In doing so Paulus both acknowledges that global constitutionalism will not always mirror domestic constitutionalism as well as acknowledging states as actors within global constitutional law, the kernel around which much international law continues to occur.[44]

If human rights are distinct constitutional norms, then consideration of their relationship with both *jus cogens* and *ergo omnes* norms must be critiqued. *Jus cogens* norms, while often the basis of controversy, have steadily eked out a role as a consistent aspect of international legal theory. The place of *jus cogens* within constitutionalisation varies between those that argue they are a central element, such as Verdross and his successors, and others that contend that they represent part though not all elements of the process. *Jus cogens* are suggested as a replacement for other more familiar constitutional norms such as the rule of law, since

41 Gardbaum, 'Human Rights', 752. 42 Petersmann, '21st Century', 3.

43 Paulus, 'The International Legal System as a Constitution' in Dunoff and Trachtman (eds.), *Ruling the World*, p. 92. The French Declaration of the Rights of Man is a clear example.

44 This echoes some of the arguments made by Allott in this regard and also of Peters, who sees these institutional developments, together with what she describes as world order treaties, as evidence of the erosion of the theory of state consent. Peters, 'Compensatory', 588.

it is argued they establish a normative basis for governance. It is possible that the rule of law may be replaced with norms that achieve the same ends, and the question then is whether *jus cogens* or *erga omnes* norms are a workable alternative or, on the other hand, do *jus cogens* fulfil some constitutional elements but not encompass the entirety of the rule of law?[45]

According to Klabbers, *jus cogens* were used in the 'Yusuf' and 'Kadi' cases by the Court of First Instance to suggest a fundamental unity on the basis of 'shared and common values'.[46] Whatever the final outcome of these cases they underpin the manner in which *jus cogens* norms and, at times, *erga omnes* norms are utilised to maintain the existence of a global constitutional order or at a minimum an international community. As such, *jus cogens* are often presented within constitutionalisation theories as a ready-made solution to the question of the presence of the rule of law. These theories posit that a hierarchal constitutional order exists with *jus cogens* in priority over *erga omnes* obligations, human rights and other elements of international law. While *erga omnes* obligations tend not to play as significant a role as *jus cogens*, they are an important factor in considering the constitutions established by the latter, in particular negotiating between the role of the state and the restraint of the classical governance order. Verdross originated constitutionalisation based upon core value systems, and this tradition is followed, though not necessarily in an identically fashion, by Simma, Tomuschat and De Wet.

Mosler's constitutionalisation centres on a common public order, with *jus cogens* and *erga omnes* obligations as intrinsic but not identical traits. *Erga omnes* obligations establish the minimum uniformity central to any society.[47] While *jus cogens* are 'a cogent law limiting freedom of contract', *erga omnes* norms' broader application means they establish the common public order.[48] Mosler, followed by De Wet, considers *erga omnes*

[45] Peters argues that the most fundamental norms may correspond to an international constitutional order; Peters, 'Compensatory', 579. Paulus contends that *jus cogens* may form part of a constitution but that not all peremptory norms are necessarily constitutional. He argues that as mostly negative principles they are too limited in scope to be characterised as the entirety of a constitutional entity. For Paulus the lack of completeness rules *jus cogens* out as a constitution of the 'international community' but does not rule some out as being part of the constitution. Paulus, 'The International Legal System as a Constitution' in Dunoff and Trachtman (eds.), *Ruling the World*, p. 89.

[46] Klabbers in Klabbers, Peters and Ulfstein, *Constitutionalisation*, p. 2.

[47] H. Mosler, *Rec. Des Cours* (1974–IV) (Leyde: A.W. Sijthoff, 1976), p. 33.

[48] *Ibid.*, p. 33.

obligations to underpin international constitutional principles.[49] Any action by a state or a group of states contrary to the public order is invalid as it is contrary to the very foundations of international law.[50]

The differentiation between consensual and non-consensual elements of international law is central to Tomuschat's description of its evolution and his constitutional model and where the Mosler ancestry is clearest. Tomuschat developed Mosler's common public order and focuses upon core generally human rights and principles contained within peremptory norms.[51] Conceding that consent-based notions of international law remain pivotal, he posits that this is not without dissenters.[52] Referencing the ICJ's contention in the 'Nicaragua' case,[53] that consent remains central to international law, Tomuschat argues that this did not reflect contemporary developments.[54] Further, he argues that the reliance on ICJ-recognised norms as everlasting pillars of international law is misplaced since the world has moved on since these cases were heard.[55] As such '[j]udicial precedents do not have an eternal life as *rochers de bronce*'.[56] In contrast to Mosler, consent is not a central feature of his constitutionalisation, though critical to understanding the operation of constituted power holders within the rule of law.

Tomuschat argues that states exist within a system of law that has a fixed set of underlying rules that 'determine[s] their basic rights and obligations with or without their will'.[57] Thus, states may be the sole constituted power holders but their actions are curtailed by the rule of law; '[o]ne may call this framework, from which every State receives

[49] Indeed as Fassbender has pointed out such constitutional arguments are values orientatated; Fassbender, 'The Meaning of International Constitutional Law' in MacDonald and Johnston (eds.), *Towards World Constitutionalism*, p. 845.

[50] Mosler, *Rec. Des Cours*, p. 34.

[51] Tomuschat, 'Obligations', and Tomuschat, 'Ensuring the Survival of Mankind', 10; A. von Bogdandy, 'Constitutionalism in International Law: Comment on a Proposal from Germany' (2006) 47 *Harvard International Law Journal* 223, 225.

[52] Tomuschat, 'Obligations', 209. He reiterated this in 2001; C. Tomuschat, 'Constitutive Elements of the Present Day International Legal Order' (1999) 241 *Rec. Des Cours* 25. He considered Henkin and Weil to be prime examples of consent–based international law.

[53] 'Military and Paramilitary Activities in and against Nicaragua' (*Nicaragua* v. *United States of America*) (1984) *ICJ Reports* 392.

[54] Tomuschat, 'Obligations', 212–16. While Tomuschat's outline of the regulatory needs of international law may be outmoded in twenty-first-century international law, the basic premise, that the world is at a point where territorial jurisdictions are no longer a valid basis for establishing interest in a particular issue, is correct.

[55] Tomuschat in particular mentions the 'Lotus' case, Tomuschat, 'Obligations', 210.

[56] *Ibid.*, 210. [57] *Ibid.*, 211.

its legal entitlement to be respected as a sovereign entity, the constitution of international society or, preferably, the constitution of the international community, community being a term suitable to indicate a closer union than between members of a society'.[58] Though Tomuschat is not as wedded to *jus cogens* and *erga omnes* obligations as Mosler, they certainly form a core of Tomuschat's meta-rules. This lends itself to criticism on several points, with the charge of legal neo-imperialism, as well as peremptory norms' very limited and contested nature making them unrealistic as a basis for developing a consistent constitutional law.[59]

Both Tomuschat and Mosler are statists in their models of constitutionalisation but not necessarily to the exclusion of other potential constituted power holders. While the state remains significant, for Tomuschat international law's constitutional role permeates the domestic realm.[60] This suggests that the place of the state may evolve as a normative constitutional order is established and other international actors become both objects and subjects of the global legal order. He describes a shift from a society to an interdependent community with shared responsibility and solidarity.[61]

Simma is reliant upon the ICJ in his analysis of constitutionalisation and argues that the existence of an international community is linked to its interests.[62] He uses familiar examples of exaltations to the community of states, such as the cases of 'Barcelona Traction'[63] and 'Tehran Hostages'[64], as well as peremptory norms under the Vienna Convention on the Law of Treaties, to establish that a community puts higher interests at its heart, thereby making it different from '[a] mere society'.[65] He considers that the international legal community puts law as the binding force

[58] *Ibid.*, 211. Tomuschat also identifies several other jurists whom he identifies as being of similar stance with regard to this form of constitutionalisation, including Charney, Dupuy, Mosler and Pellet. Tomuschat also points to developments in the pre-Second World War era, particularly in humanitarian law and international labour law, as earlier indications that states alone could not be considered to be the only interest of international law. Tomuschat, 'Constitutive Elements', 58–61.

[59] M. Koskenniemi, 'International Law in Europe: Between Tradition and Renewal', Florence, 14 June 2004 (keynote address at the inauguration of the European Society of Law).

[60] Tomuschat, 'Ensuring the Survival of Mankind', 305.

[61] Cottier and Hertig, '21st Constitutionalism', 270–1.

[62] Simma, 'From Bilateralism', 244–245; Bogdandy, 'Proposal from Germany', 226.

[63] 'Barcelona Traction, Light and Power Company Limited' (1970) *ICJ Reports* 32.

[64] 'United States, Diplomatic and Consular Staff in Tehran' (1980) *ICJ Reports* 43.

[65] Simma, 'From Bilateralism', 245.

holding it together.[66] Thus, the community of states cannot emerge simply because there is law to outline its parameters. Simma's limited interpretation of the Court's actions perpetuates its innate problems. Simma's constitutionalism is still firmly attached to the post-Second World War era, centring on the state and the UN as the fulcrum around which international law operates. This position leaves open the question of the rule of law versus rule by law at the core of the post-Charter era. Following events such as the intervention in Kosovo, Koskenniemi considers it astonishing that Simma and others still consider the Charter to be so critical to legitimate action in international law, and indeed it is difficult to reconcile Simma's theoretical approach with the examples he then utilises.[67]

De Wet treats the hierarchy established in *jus cogens* and *erga omnes* obligations as embedded in the Charter. The Charter, in turn, articulates the norms core to global constitutionalisation.[68] Human rights as characterised in the International Bill of Rights, the ICC and the ad hoc tribunals in Yugoslavia and Rwanda are central to this perspective. De Wet presents *jus cogens*, which by definition are *erga omnes* obligations, as sitting on top of this hierarchy. These are then followed by norms that are only *erga omnes* obligations and finally those norms of customary international law that are characterised as emerging *erga omnes* norms.[69] She states that '[i]t is of a layered nature as it includes the (sometimes overlapping) layers of universal *ius cogens* norms and *erga omnes* obligations'.[70]

So while at first the arguments presented by Simma, and in many ways by Tomuschat and Mosler, may appear all encompassing, in reality, their coverage of global law is limited. The governance structures that are dense within international economic law, as an example, are rarely, if ever, referenced. De Wet's focus on *erga omnes* obligations may be contrasted with Simma's and Tomuschat's concentration on *jus cogens* to the exclusion of the former. De Wet includes trade liberalisation and democracy as potentially joining the ranks of *erga omnes* norms; though democracy is regarded as a domestic human right and not as part of the governance of the constitutional order itself.[71] But while their focus is on the non-

66 He rejects the idea that an international community could ever be held together simply by law, as community remains central.

67 M. Koskenniemi, '"The Lady Doth Protest Too Much": Kosovo and the Turn to Ethics in International Law' (2002) 65 *Modern Law Review* 159, 160, fn 6.

68 De Wet, 'The International Constitutional Order', 57.

69 *Ibid.*, 62; though this third category is omitted from the list in another article on the same theme, De Wet, 'The Emergence of International', 617.

70 De Wet, 'The International Constitutional Order', 57.

71 *Ibid.*, 63–4.

consensual nature of these norms, this does not necessarily translate to a broader system that would recognise an elimination of any remnants of the rule-by-law process of pure state consent. The focus on human rights as an element of the rule of law is limited by the constitutionalisation theories of Mosler, Tomuschat, Simma and De Wet to the already established *jus cogens* and *erga omnes* norms. While certainly *jus cogens* norms are necessary as core rules from which there can be no shift, the rule of law should act to limit constituted power. As such *jus cogens* norms do not possess the necessary breadth to ensure governance in accordance with the rule of law.

6.1.3 The rule of law in constitutionalisation

What is most apparent from the preceding discussion is that the rule of law is rarely, if ever, explicitly referenced. Nonetheless, the underlying rationale and purpose of the rule of law are observable in the debates on judicial activism, *jus cogens* and consent.[72] Yet, this does not mean it is established to the extent necessary to argue that a normative constitutionalism is present in these theories. Paulus probably comes closest but this is very much centred on his argument that constitutionalisation is a slow progressive process.

When Dunoff criticises constitutional imagery as lacking the practice to substantiate the constitutional claims, this may be answered by the focus of these constitutionalisation theories on the ICJ.[73] But a court with state-only clients and limited in its jurisdiction does not have the basis to make claims that could be interpreted as constitutional or substantiate the rule of law. This is exemplified in the 'East Timor' case, where the Court limited its ability to enforce *erga omnes* applications to the consent to its jurisdiction.[74] The ICJ establishes a community that is undefined and state-centric, and thus its use of *jus cogens* to establish the rule of law is also limited.[75]

The lack of a coherent place for the rule of law in constitutionalisation theories is also evident in the absence of a discussion of equality. Equality is one of the surest buttresses against the arbitrary use of law in governance

[72] The rule of law is also observable in some of the elements of the separation of powers and democratic legitimacy discussed next.

[73] Dunoff, 'Constitutional Conceits', 650.

[74] 'East Timor' (*Portugal* v. *Australia*) (1995) *ICJ Reports* 90.

[75] Simma, 'From Bilateralism', 298. Simma limits *erga omnes* as obligations owed to states; this is particularly acute in their limitations to ICJ decisions and not the wider field of international legal sources.

by the holders of constituted power and should be a central tenet of the global rule of law. Admittedly, this is a somewhat vague invocation that does not consider equality as a personalised right within the international human rights context. As equality currently applies within the WTO or the UN system or regarding state consent, it is without a rule-of-law content and missing from the constitutionalisation debate where even sovereign equality is left unresolved.

Neither the practice of the dispute settlement mechanisms nor the discussions on *jus cogens* appear to encourage a constitutionalisation debate partially based on the rule of law. This is not to suggest that it is not present, but rather that the theories put forward are not grounded in an understanding, discussed in Chapter 2, that the law should be applied equally, created openly or administered fairly as a minimum for constitutionalism. Rather, this is a happy by-product of international law in operation, and as such can only be relied upon under very particular circumstances. For constitutionalisation theories to withstand a test for the presence of constitutionalism, the rule of law needs to be more prominent in the formulations of what the law should be in a global constitutional order.

6.2 Divisions of power

In global constitutionalisation, it is not always obvious whether governance is based upon institutional structures, normative values or indeed both. For instance, whether it is the WTO's structure, the development of economic rights or some combination of both that is essential within sectoral constitutionalisation, or whether the UN's structure combined with Article 103 provides a division of constituted power for world constitutionalisation remain unsettled.[76] Unlike the rule of law, a division of power, or more often the separation of powers, is frequently name-checked by proponents of global constitutionalisation. In such instances, it is frequently existing bodies of law that are relied upon to provide the necessary fettering of power. Constitutionalism requires a check upon unfettered governing, and this section considers whether such a process of restraint is present within global constitutionalisation theories.

As discussed in Chapter 2, the requisite divisions of power are not centred on finding a classical triumvirate of legislature, executive and

[76] J. P. Trachtman, 'Constitutional Economics of the World Trade Organization' in Dunoff and Trachtman (eds.), *Ruling the World*, p. 206; J. O. McGinis and M. L. Movsesian, 'The World Trade Constitution' (2000) 114 *Harvard Law Review* 511.

judiciary. Instead, they focus upon the division of constituted power to ensure that it is not centred in one point and thus open to abuse by particular constituted power holders. Approaches to divisions of power come in several guises, three of which will be discussed here: the move away from a statist regime; a potential relationship with domestic and regional law; and organisational structures, each of which provides a basis for understanding the role of constitutional division within these debates.

6.2.1 Divisions of power, the state and domestic orders in international law

Either the state's slow demise or its constant presence often forms a central part of debate within global constitutionalisation. Any shift away from a statist order raises issues of constituency or community associated with a shift in constituted power, though this discussion will be left largely to the next chapter. Nonetheless, if global constitutionalism is to compensate for the ebbing away of state constitutionalism, then the interests that an ever-stronger global constitution represents must be recognised. The three following examples, Fischer-Lescano, Allott and Peters, suggest three variations of the potential shift of the state as the fulcrum of constituted power within a constitutionalisation process.

Fischer-Lescano argues that sovereignty and statehood remain central to any understanding of global constitutionalisation.[77] He contends that international law and sovereignty are reliant upon each other, as one does not exist without the other, and as such global constitutional law is entwined with statehood. International law constitutes states, and vice versa, and thus they are mutually reliant. Yet the identification of a move away from a solely statist regime is also present in these theories; for example, Allott recognises the importance of states, but not in the absolutist fashion advocated by Fischer-Lescano. Thus, while not advocating an end to sovereignty, Allott does not consider the relationship to amount to a zero-sum game.[78] This may be owing to Allott's existing constitution that does not have to bargain to either move states out of the equation or entrench them permanently, as they are already the sole actors in his constitutionalisation process. Yet, both positions ask questions of the fulcrum of constituted power in international law.

[77] A. Fischer-Lescano, 'Redefining Sovereignty', 12.
[78] P. Allott, 'Review Essay', 264.

Peters claims there is a process of de-constitutionalisation within states, which underpins a move away from the Westphalian or the statist model of consent-based international law, and that the fundamental norms present in a global constitutional order will make up for this loss of state authority.[79] A form of a compensatory constitutionalism, this reconstruction of global law does not unavoidably result in the destruction of the state, though it certainly requires a realignment of governance powers into a differentiated division-of-powers model.[80] It is conceivable that state and global interests do not as easily transform one to the other as may be suggested by compensatory constitutionalism, but this is not to suggest that the possibility of such a form of subsidiarity does not have some merit.

These three examples represent the potential for understanding the state in a constitutionalisation process, while also presenting difficulties for traditional state tropes such as sovereignty. If, as Peters asserts, state constitutions no longer possess the totality of governance, this suggests that there was absolute state control at some previous point. This is an absolutist Westphalian model and assumes that states had 'total constitutions', which is hardly an unquestioned claim.[81] In addition, such propositions result in a form of domestic constitutional regime, which is pushed up and compensated for at the global level.[82] This system for the divestment of constituted power amongst different points of governance is firmly linked to state consent and, as such, does not represent a radical change from the current international legal order nor a fully formed divisions-of-power model, as the single constituted power at the centre holds all control.

Peters argues that the de-constitutionalisation of the domestic sphere is or will be filled by constitutionalisation at the global level, which she links to globalisation. This implies a balance of constitutionalism. In Peters' model the representation of interests can move between orders, from the state to the international level. As discussed earlier, this is somewhat close to a vertical separation-of-powers model. In this theory the same or at the very least quite similar forms of constitutionalism are easily transposable and contemporaneously present within domestic and international law. This requires the dispersal of governance beyond the horizontal into a

[79] Peters, 'Compensatory', 579.

[80] Peters, 'Compensatory', 579. This is related to Tomuschat's arguments that see international constitutional law as indelibly linked to domestic public law; see Tomuschat, 'Ensuring the Survival of Mankind', 10.

[81] Munro, *Studies*. [82] Peters, 'Compensatory', 580.

vertical stream that could theoretically shift as it develops in a different form of constitutional order. This perspective opens a number of possibilities for constitutionalisation and the realisation of a separation of powers.

In Peters' compensatory constitutionalism, although constituted power is dispersed, there does not appear to be any system for one holder of constituted power to hold another to account, an essential of power division. This may be owing to Peters' rejection of the notion of a formal constitution, as she regards the essential norms of the international legal system as the basis for constitutionalism. This she combines with judicial activism for realising these norms in practice. This requires a strong judicial arm to be present to divest the holders of constituted power within the bounds of the divisions-of-power model, though where Peters locates this role remains unresolved.

Habermas links sovereignty to the legitimatisation of the use of force within international law, placing him apart from other more structural claims on the division of power. If world constitutionalism is, as Habermas argues it should be, limited to securing peace and protecting human rights, it makes for a more reasonable object to attain. However, in limiting the global constitution to this, and jettisoning other elements of constitutionalism, Habermas limits the possibility of really achieving constitutionalisation.[83] The development of a normative constitutional order that regulates the exercise of constituted power beyond the state necessitates a broader interest than human rights and the use of force. A concentration on these two elements dismisses entire areas of international law, where constituted power is exercised, from gaining the legitimacy necessary to operate within a normative constitutional order.

Habermas argues that constitutionalism offers an ideal system for the global legal order, one legitimised as a constitutional order with multi-level governance and political structures. In keeping with Paulus, he considers that constitutionalisation is not, as yet, fully realised. This does not imply that Paulus or Habermas claim that global constitutionalisation will be akin to the emergence of constitutionalism within the state.[84] The needs and thus the process are dissimilar, and as such development is not and will not occur in the same manner. However, for both theorists, the state remains a core element of any realised constitutional future, but amongst other subjects or constituted power holders in a constitutionalised system.

[83] Habermas, *Divided*, p. 143. [84] J. Habermas, 'Constitutionalisation of International Law and the Legitimation Problems of a Constitution for World Society' (2008) 15 *Constellations*, 444, 448.

For Habermas a distinction between world organisations, observable in an imperfect form in the guise of the UN, is at odds with what must be present in an international constitutional order. Organisations, such as the UN, may carry out functions that historically were situated within the state but presently the political system operates at both the transnational and inter-state levels. Habermas contends that some networks and interactions within the global system are unrepresented by the statist model. Although governance occurs in multilateral forms, at present, international law does not contain the 'legislative competences and corresponding processes of political will formation' that would be necessary in a fully functioning constitutional order.[85] Governance beyond the state is not characterised as divestment of power, although this may be how it will eventually manifest itself. Governance or constituted power, as situated at different points in international and domestic governance, ensures a shared structure of power that may form part of a constitutionalised legal order.

Tomuschat is at pains to point out that while discussions on customary international law are usually centred on how it is formed and its legitimacy, 'the great bulk of customary rules are a normative fact'.[86] This is besides *jus cogens* norms, which, as they are part of a higher order, will only come into play in certain circumstances. States cannot exempt themselves from customary international law. Tomuschat argues that states cannot 'leave that cage of golden rules'[87] and asserts that customary international law remains relevant to ensure that the international community remains attached to its rules.[88] The very existence of *jus cogens* norms establishes that there is an international community that is based upon 'axiomatic premises other than State sovereignty'.[89] But the community is still entrenched with values that are embodied in *jus cogens*.[90] Tomuschat takes particular issue with the New Haven School

85 J. Habermas, *Between Naturalism and Religion* (trans. C. Cronin) (Cambridge: Polity Press, 2008), pp. 323–4.

86 Tomuschat, 'Obligations', 275.

87 *Ibid.*, 278; this is true even for those states that emerged in the decolonisation period. This has echoes in the subaltern debate on how community perpetuates the colonialist system.

88 *Ibid.*, 307; this is also clear in the analysis of Wyler and Papaux who consider *jus cogens* to be 'miserably short of applications ... [i]ts contents remain vague and undefined yet no one disputes its quality as positive law'; E. Wyler and A. Papaux, 'The Search for Universal Justice', in MacDonald and Johnston (eds.), *Towards World Constitutionalism*, p. 290.

89 Tomuschat 'Obligations', 307. Although Tomuschat makes various uses of community to serve a variety of purposes, the concept is not as embedded as it is within Simma's constitutionalism. Bogdandy, 'Proposal from Germany', 223.

90 Tomuschat, 'Ensuring the Survival of Mankind', 75–6.

and Higgins' view of international law as other than a set of pre-existing rules ripe for application.[91] He describes how meta-rules, the rules that lay out how other rules are to be made, enter into force and are implemented. These, he argues, together with executive and judicial functions, form the constitution of any system of governance.[92] Yet, Tomuschat does not require a major shift in the practice of existing international law; as such, the impact of his understanding of constitutionalism would, in reality, be unremarkable.[93]

Tomuschat runs through a number of sources in seeking to establish the existence of an international community beyond states.[94] The necessity in establishing the parameters of community is based on the assertion that while mankind is a factual phenomenon, 'the concept of international community has a juridical connotation'.[95] This community is based upon international legal developments, which while constructed as a community of states indirectly include mankind (and one would assume womankind).[96] This brings to the fore issues surrounding the attachment of community's interests to the holders of power and whether this would reflect a governance structure in line with the rule of law. He acknowledges that there are different interests within the global order, but he does not appear to recognise a disconnection between it and potential holders of both constituent and constituted power. The community, as recognised by Tomuschat, would resolve this issue. However, there is no clear guide as to how to identify subjects of community beyond states.

De Wet argues that there is an increasing move away from the state as the sole perpetrator of public decision-making, though she regards this as part of a much broader scheme where a core value system is supported by structures at national, regional, international and functional levels.[97] This

[91] Tomuschat, 'Constitutive Elements', 25; R. Higgins, 'International Law and the Avoidance, Containment and Resolution of Disputes' (1991) *Rec. Des Cours*, 230.

[92] Tomuschat, 'Obligations', 216, 195. Tomuschat identifies the language of Hart and argues that these meta-rules are the equivalent of rules of recognition. He goes on to state that all systems of governance consist of administration, adjudication and lawmaking.

[93] Fassbender, 'Rediscovering a Forgotten Constitution', in Dunoff and Trachtman (eds.), *Ruling the World*, p. 136.

[94] He finds evidence in the Draft Articles on State Responsibility. Tomuschat also describes the developments surrounding the work of the ILC with regard to Crimes against Peace and Security, though this has since been overtaken by the International Criminal Court; Tomuschat, 'Ensuring the Survival of Mankind', 305, Tomuschat, 'Obligations', 223–5.

[95] Tomuschat, 'Obligations', 226.

[96] *Ibid.*, 228–30. He also discusses community in the context of the functioning of UN bodies, where it indicates worldwide concern in an issue.

[97] De Wet, 'The International Constitutional Order', 53; De Wet, 'The Emergence of International', 612.

does not exclude states from the international constitutional order but rather realigns the governance structures to broaden and reassign decision-making. De Wet's approach to the realignment of public decision-making does not conform to an absolutist model, but recognises that it can move between systems of governance.[98]

In considering the move away from a statist regime and the concentration on the relationship with domestic law these constitutionalisation theories have encapsulated the notion that governance does occur at multiple levels, that the holders of constituted power do not have to be at the same level of governance and that divisions of power as an element of constitutionalism should be present in a debate on constitutionalisation. The actual models of division's regimes are often found within institutions, which is the subject of the following section, but what is evident is that within constitutionalisation theories, the points at which governance occurs is central, and that states remain core to these structures of constituted power.

6.2.2 Divisions of power and organisational constitutionalisation

Arguments in favour of constitutionalisation often present governance structures in organisations as ready-made points of governance. Yet, in terms of on-going discussions on the necessity of reforming some of these very organisations, caution should be exercised in inserting constitutional rigidity into these regimes. For this reason Trachtman cautions against finding organisations as imbued with constitutional norms.[99] He argues that such a finding risks setting their organisational regimes in stone thus leaving unresolved institutionalised problems. Nonetheless, governance structures are presented in constitutionalisation debates often as framed to presuppose constitutionality.

Bowett, in *The Law of International Institutions*, proffered that '[t]he development of international organisations has been, in the main, a response to the evident need arising from international intercourse rather than to the philosophical or ideological appeal of the notion of world government'.[100] If Bowett is correct, then constitutionalisation may offer a remedy for this lack of forethought. In reviewing the first edition of Bowett's book, Franck argued: 'the law of, or about, international organizations is

98 De Wet, 'The International Constitutional Order', 53.

99 Trachtman, 'The Constitutions of the WTO', 623–4.

100 D. W. Bowett, *The Law of International Institutions*, 2nd edn (London: Stevens & Sons, 1970), p. 1.

essentially constitutional law. This is true not only because it is descriptive of the internal rules, governing the operation of institutions and societies, but because it is treated by lawyers in a manner different from other law ... treated as capable of organic growth.'[101]

This view certainly places the discussion of constitutionalisation squarely within the bounds of organisations, and it is indicative of a division between sectoral and world order constitutionalisation. The first regards constitutionalisation to be transformative, as it will change the terms on which international institutional law is discussed, and the latter regards treaties, usually the UN Charter, as a higher-order regime.[102] Both Bowett and Franck recognise that these organisations require a discussion of their philosophical bases. The question is whether normative constitutionalism and particularly divisions of power are present in these constitutionalisation theories and form part of these bases.

Dunoff rejects the constitutionalisation of international institutions. He argues that these institutions often, if not always, lack core constitutional attributes, such as elements of a 'constitutional court', a 'constitutional convention', a 'constitutional drafting process' and a 'readily identifiable constitutional moment' that he deems necessary for a constitutional system to exist.[103] In contrast, Trachtman uses the language of 'transaction costs', 'strategic problems' and 'efficient exchanges of authority' to explain the rationale behind ordaining these organisations as constitutional and to suggest that the domestic language, which Dunoff takes up, is, at best, unhelpful.[104] While these are two extremes, they do present the matrix within which debates on divisions-of-power arrangements tend to take place.

Fassbender is one of most ardent advocates of the UN as a constitution for the global legal order.[105] He regards the UN Charter as central to any understanding of constitutionalisation, seeing its identification

[101] T. Franck, 'Book Review' (1964) 17 *Harvard Law Review* 1565.

[102] This latter category does not come within this discussion but is indicative of the broad array of proposals that are espoused in this field. For a discussion of the nature of treaties as constitutional documents, see S. Rosenne, *Developments in the Law of Treaties (1945–1986)* (Cambridge University Press, 1989). See, for example, M. Happold, 'Security Council Resolution 1373 and the Constitution of the United Nations' (2003) 16 *Leiden Journal of International Law* 593; or Sloan, 'The United Nations Charter', 61.

[103] Dunoff, 'Constitutional Conceits', 650.

[104] Trachtman, 'The Constitutions of the WTO', 631.

[105] Fassbender, 'The United Nations Charter'; Fassbender, *Security Council Reform*; Fassbender, 'Rediscovering a Forgotten Constitution' in Dunoff and Trachtman (eds.), *Ruling the World*; Fassbender, 'The Meaning of International Constitutional Order' in MacDonald and Johnston (eds.), *Towards World Constitutionalism*, p. 845; Fassbender,

as coming 'out of the fog' of indistinct constitutional rhetoric.[106] The significance of this approach, placing the UN beyond sectoral constitutionalisation, is that it assumes the UN is on a different plane to, for example, the WTO. Fassbender suggests a number of constitutional features within the Charter as proof of its place at the core of not only its own but also global constitutionalisation.[107] According to Fassbender, the benefit of placing the UN at the core of international law is that it establishes the relationship between general international and UN law.[108] Thus, he places a high burden upon the Charter as the centre of constitutional governance.

The recognition of UN governance structures as symptomatic of constitutionalism is critical to this form of constitutionalisation. One of the consequential features of Fassbender's approach is the functioning of UN governance. How law is made and adjudicated, and whether this makes the UN system constitutional and, further, whether the UN system establishes a hierarchy of norms are all open to debate. For example, Ulfstein regards the General Assembly as the closest comparison to a representative organ that exists in international law.[109] However, there are issues with this approach to community and constituency, and the question ought to be whether it is accurate to designate the General Assembly as representative of the world when it is dependent upon state officials in a state-centric model. Certainly, it is representative of state views, but it is unrepresentative of a global community or constituency and does not enable states, as holders of constituted power, to exercise authority in reality, as it carries little lawmaking power. Fassbender argues that the place of state sovereignty within international law is clarified by the UN Charter, placing it above any questions on the nature of representation. But his state-centric form of constitutionalism places a particularly flawed governance system at the core of both the UN and global constitutionalism.

Fassbender's view that the UN is core to world constitutionalisation is shared by others, and it is not a particularly new assertion.[110] In contrast, this is not the case with regard to the WTO. While arguments

'We the Peoples' in Loughlin and Walker (eds.), *The Paradox*, p. 268. See also M. J. Herdegen, 'The Constitutionalization of the UN Security System' (1994) 27 *Vanderbilt Journal of Transnational Law*, 135.

106 Fassbender, 'We the Peoples' in Loughlin and Walker (eds.), *The Paradox*, p. 282.

107 *Ibid.*, pp. 281–5. 108 *Ibid.*, p. 281.

109 Ulfstein in Klabbers, Peters and Ulfstein, *Constitutionalisation*, p. 56.

110 Sloan, 'The United Nations Charter', 61; H. Waldock, 'General Course on Public International Law' (II 1962) 106 *Recueil des Cours* 20.

in support of it having a constitution are many, rarely is the argument made that it is a constitution for the global order outside of economic law.[111] In contrast to Fassbender's UN and state-centric approach, Cass argues that the constitutionalisation debate in economic law, which generally focuses upon the WTO, can also be largely based upon governance structures and judicial action.[112] Yet, this does not resolve the necessity of a division of power beyond arguing that more than one international organisation may possess constituted power. The New Haven School identifies the Charter as a constitutive decision and part of the constitutive process, with the UN at the centre of the international legal order. This places the UN, its formation, its evolution and its current place within the global legal system as an element, albeit an important element, of the broader development of international law.[113] This disparity, between Fassbender and the New Haven School, is important in helping to identify whether the UN can fulfil a role within constitutionalism.

Walter argues against the UN Charter as a constitution for the global community.[114] While he acknowledges its place as the constitutive document for the organisation, as its membership limits constitutionalism to states it cannot fulfil any purpose beyond its own parameters. If all the subjects of the community must be bound by the Charter this means there is little connection to the holders of constituent power. Importantly, from the perspective of divisions of power, it also limits constitutional norms to the UN's partial membership.[115] De Wet dismisses the Charter as the constitution of the world community but does acknowledge it as central to the emergence of a constitutional order. The Charter fails as a world constitution because the global community, and as such the holders of constituted and constituent power, extends beyond states, and thus the membership of the UN, as entirely state-centric, cannot fulfil a role as a constitution.[116] De Wet regards the UN Charter as a connecting factor

[111] Petersmann, 'Constitutional Justice', 769.

[112] See Cass, *World Trade Organization*; D. Z. Cass, 'The "Constitutionalization" of International Trade Law: Judicial Norm-Generation as the Engine of Constitutional Development in International Trade' (2001) 12 *European Journal of International Law* 39.

[113] Fassbender, 'The United Nations Charter', 545.

[114] Walter, 'Process of Constitutionalization' in Nijman and Nollkaemper (eds.), *New Perspectives*, pp. 195–6.

[115] The EU is a member of the WTO and this breaks the most obvious statist element of institutional law.

[116] De Wet, 'The International Constitutional Order', 54.

of central importance to the global constitutional order.[117] For De Wet the Charter remains central for structural enforcement of the value system of the constitutional order, but its own organisational structure cannot stand for a separation of powers within international constitutionalisation.[118] For De Wet the international community is wider, and while this does not necessarily remedy the disconnection between governance structures within international law, it does acknowledge that such a gap is problematic within global constitutionalisation.

Simma puts 'community interests' at the forefront of his approach to constitutionalism and argues that the UN Charter is an 'embryonic constitution of the world community'. Linking global constitutionalism to domestic constitutionalism, Simma argues that the similarities between the two include the following: both the rules for the activities of the organisation and also its substantive principles; the traditional if extremely truncated separation of powers; priority over other institutions; and the monopoly on the use of force with the exception of self-defence.[119] This excludes a normative approach to constitutionalism and more specifically a more in-depth discussion of whether the UN possesses a method of fettering constituted power. Relying heavily on the domestic elements of constitutionalisation, Simma, in seeking to identify constitutional forms, limits the possibilities available to global constitutionalism. While it is possible to identify shared qualities, identifying minimum shared substantive characteristics leaves international law wanting in stature, particularly when this form of global constitutionalisation is applied to institutions.

Simma sees a constitution as combining two elements, first the constitution has precedence over other law, and second it sets out a basic governance structure.[120] Simma applies this test to the UN Charter and finds that the Charter fulfils the criteria.[121] Yet the test appears to be based entirely on the Charter rather than normative constitutionalism. It is not an assessment that could be applied to another treaty document, such as the WTO, nor to a broader conception of constitutionalism that could be identified across several doctrines, documents or institutions. As such, Simma's characterisation of constitutionalism is based upon the assumption that it will be the Charter that will fulfil the criteria.[122] In connecting global constitutionalism to domestic understandings and establishing

[117] *Ibid.*, 56. [118] *Ibid.*, 64–7.
[119] Simma, 'From Bilateralism', 258–9.
[120] *Ibid.*, 258. [121] *Ibid.*, 261. [122] *Ibid.*, 261.

criteria that are conditioned by the Charter, Simma is reducing constitutionalism to finding the General Assembly to be a world parliament and the Security Council an executive. Although Simma does later acknowledge that constitutionalism cannot simply be assessed in this fashion, nonetheless, this is the basis on which his analysis proceeds, and he does not suggest any satisfactory alternatives.[123]

Mosler does not assert that there is one unifying constituent document thus he did not recognise the Charter as part of general international constitutional law; yet he did agree that at some point in the future it may be recognised as such. In arguing that the Charter may in future fulfil a constitutional role, Mosler is not seeking to establish an idealised constitutional order, but rather, as with Paulus or Habermas, considers constitutionalisation to be an on-going process. Mosler observes that the difficulty with treaties such as the UN Charter (and arguably the WTO Agreement) is that their object was essentially restricted compared with the traditional understanding of the subject remit of a constitution.[124] While this marries global constitutionalisation to the domestic evocations of what a constitution must represent, it does raise issues earlier considered with regard to fragmentation or pluralism. From Mosler's standpoint if we take a common object of domestic constitutionalism, that of the sovereignty of the state, this concept is not an essential element of the global constitutional order. Following this, other objects may also, if they are of little or no relevance to international constitutionalism, be omitted. Nonetheless, there are aspects of constitutionalism that must, according to Mosler, always be present and are not as core as a lack of omnipotence.[125]

Within institutions regarded as representing constitutional structures or normative values within global constitutionalisation theories, what is disconcerting is the common disregard for the underlying rationale of normative constitutional structure. The need for a division of constituted power as an aspect of constitutionalism is evident; however, the manner in which this is or will be achieved within these organisations, and particularly the UN, is not as evident as may first appear since the majority of these theories skirt the lapses in substantive constitutionalism or fear, as Trachtman does, the entrenchment of lacklustre structures.

123 *Ibid.*, 283.

124 Fassbender, 'The United Nations Charter', 547; though Mosler did acknowledge that it was becoming common to refer to statutes of various international organisations as constitutions, and indeed they possess some of the essential features of a constitution. Mosler, *Rec. Des Cours*, p. 32.

125 *Ibid.*, 32.

6.2.3 *Divisions of power within global constitutionalisation theories*

Unlike the rule of law, divisions of power often are explicitly dealt with by proponents of global constitutionalisation. Yet, questions of governance are considered in the abstract, often in the context of international institutions, without mapping how these fulfil the underlying rationales of constitutionalism. Potentially, this is owing to the lack of a classical horizontal divisions-of-power model anywhere in international law, and thus it is more difficult for constitutionalisation theories to press home its presence within global law. But, this need not be critical to constitutionalisation; as was discussed previously, alternate models are possible.

Amongst some advocates of constitutionalisation, there is evidence of a vertical or geographical proposal for the emergence of a system of governance that would divide constituted power. Yet, neither in Peter's compensatory constitutionalism nor in placing institutions at the centre of governance orders is the core idea of division of powers satisfactorily dealt with. In the description of the relationship with domestic constitutionalism, some valid observations of vertical separation of powers are evident, but not to the extent that would suggest a fully substantiated system of governance beyond what presently functions. Nor is subsidiarity seriously dealt with as a model of fettering power beyond the traditional separation-of-powers model. The potential of combining a vertical and horizontal division of power offers some options to global constitutionalisation but one that is currently under-theorised.

The constitutionalisation arguments presented here do not disburse constituted power beyond the state, and in such instances where they do, the actual identification of these other operators in the division of power is left open. Divestment of governance power is often considered central, but not to the extent that its lack of actual operation dampens the ability of a regime to be nominated as constitutional. Constituted power forms a central focus of constitutional governance, and its potential within global law must be recognised in combination with the rule of law and democratic legitimacy. Constitutionalism itself may offer alternative models to global law, but this requires a serious commitment to divestment of constituted power as a core feature of a constitutionalisation process.

6.3 Democratic legitimacy

As is discussed in Chapter 2, democratic legitimacy is a core norm of constitutionalism. The rationale behind maintaining democratic legitimacy and the accompanying governance structures at the centre of constitutionalism is to ensure that the holders of constituent power are sanctioned to exercise their warrant. This section discusses democratic legitimacy within global constitutionalisation theories. It will discuss whether democratic legitimacy is embedded into constitutionalisation debates and, in instances where it is ingrained, the guise in which it functions. The question of democracy is, in itself, a single issue, but democratic legitimacy is also bound to the rule of law and divisions of power as well as broader political human rights. Within global constitutionalisation theories human rights, the rule of law, checks and balances, and 'possibly democracy' are on occasion identified as vital to the constitutionalisation debate.[126]

As with the previous sections on the rule of law and divisions of power it is important to consider how democratic legitimacy interacts with these other norms of constitutionalism. Democratic legitimacy is first discussed as a broad concept within the wider international constitutionalisation debates, including a discussion of the positions of Habermas, Paulus and Allott. This is followed by an examination of the place of democratic legitimacy within the international community and the works of Mosler, Tomuschat and Simma, as examples of how community and democratic legitimacy interact.

Habermas, stressing democracy's absence from the international legal order, questions whether those within the global constitutionalisation debate advocating an existent constitutionalism are writing off democracy from the global constitutional order.[127] He argues that such disregard for democracy stems from the perception that international law has never in fact been, nor potentially ever will become, democratic. For those advocating a present global constitutional order, democracy's absence must be accepted as the fundamental difference between domestic and global constitutionalism.[128] Democracy's inclusion in the global constitutionalisation debate, even if it is to dismiss ultimately its relevance, points towards its relevance to discussions of constitutionalism. Further, it is suggested that democratic legitimacy cannot be ignored, its normative place within constitutionalism has been accepted and, as such, its absence from a global governance order precludes a fully constitutional model from becoming entrenched at the global level. As discussed in Chapter 2, democratic

[126] Peters and Armingeon, 'Interdisciplinary Perspective', 385.

[127] Habermas, 'Legitimation Problems', 445.

[128] A good example of this position is that of De Wet; see De Wet, 'The International Constitutional Order', 51.

legitimacy is of vital import in making out those entitled to participate in the process that ensures constitutionalism is sustained, and therefore is fundamental to the operation of constituent and constituted power. Constitutionalism and democratic legitimacy are mutually critical to any course of change to a constitution, and it is only through democracy that the benefits accrued by constitutional purchase may be distributed correctly. Only with democracy in place can a legitimate governance order operate with the moniker of constitutionalism.

Democracy is at the core of Habermas' argument and he makes democratic legitimacy a point of departure for all theories of constitutionalisation. He points to the gap between the actuality of governance beyond the state and the procedures that serve nation-states as the sole subjects of international law.[129] Habermas requires models of institutional arrangements to be established that enable governance within transnational spaces. He argues that the identification of this transnational space is necessary to enable the continued legitimisation of the political constitution. This transnational space forms part of the discussion on community and constituency within international law, considered in the next chapter, but also represents the difficulties present in most theories of global governance: identifying the mass to which a constitutional order is attached and, as such, considering who is to exercise their democratic warrant.

Suggesting a move away from the monopolisation of international law by the state is an important historical factor central to understanding present constitutionalisation. Habermas identifies two subjects of a future world constitution; states and individuals.[130] This accepts that global constitutionalism functions differently in form to its domestic counterpart but stresses that both possess the same underlying rationale. Acknowledging states and individuals as subjects in combination with international organisations and structures for the maintenance of the legal order is perhaps a more realistic proposition than is at first apparent. It is also preferred to those arguing for a contemporary constitution that either accepts the states' status quo or alternatively presses their demise too far. Constitutionalisation does not require the displacement of the state but rather recognises that the more classical interpretations of its role no longer serve to describe the position of states as law presently functions or ought to in a constitutional order. The potential of a vertical and horizontal division of power or the operation of subsidiarity also

129 Habermas, 'Legitimation Problems', 444–5.

130 *Ibid.*, 444, 449.

forms part of this constitutional dislocation of states as sole constituted power holders.

Habermas openly relies upon Kantian international law, which he regards as approximate with his own conclusions.[131] Kant's description of international law relies on one global unified system ensuring peace.[132] While Kant appears, at times, idealistic, Habermas' approach, in working within the confines that do subsist and towards a form of constitutionalisation rooted in the present, may answer some of the Romanticism charges. For instance, Habermas argues that European citizens do not, as yet, recognise each other as citizens of a larger political body. Thus, even the EU is somewhat off a full constitutional pace, a significant point for the global constitutionalism project.[133] Identifying subjects of the global constitution and their recognition of each other mirror other solidarity arguments made, for example, by Paulus. They are also of great significance in establishing, or at least identifying, either a community or constituency that will be bound to a sectoral or world constitution, before concluding that they exist.

Critically, Habermas does not regard the UN as the only possible institution or institutional form central to constitutionalism. Yet, as they currently operate, international organisations such as the UN or indeed the WTO do not possess the necessary features for world constitutionalism to be entirely legitimate. Resting upon three normative approaches, Habermas considers the constitutional nature of the UN within the broader order: first, the combination of safeguarding peace and human rights; second, the dislocation on prohibition on the use of force combined with sanctions and potential prosecution; and third, the universality and inclusiveness of UN law.[134] For Habermas it is not the UN as it stands, but rather the UN as part of his future ideal regime in which the cosmopolitan and the national citizen legitimate the process of constitutionalisation, that matters. But presently, the lack of democratic rigour holds the organisation back from fulfilling Habermas' theory. Rather, the UN serves as the world organisation with competence for peace and human rights within the global legal project that Habermas favours. But it lacks the necessary constitutional attributes for such a project to be complete.

[131] This is besides a world republic; see Habermas, *Divided*, p. 115.

[132] I. Kant, *Perpetual Peace* (New York: Cosimo Press, 2005).

[133] Habermas, *Divided*, p. 55. [134] *Ibid.*, pp. 160–1.

Whether the other constitutionalisation theories fully adopt and realise democracy's role remains debatable.[135] The relationship between the democratic legitimacy of treaties and international organisations is indicative of the place of states within governance. Tomuschat argues that 'world order treaties' are of a different nature than others. Such world order treaties protect the basic interests of the international community and have binding force. The passage of certain Security Council resolutions have a similar effect and he argues that it 'is the ultimate reversal of what is meant by concluding a treaty under a system of sovereign equality, namely an act freely decided upon by the responsible government'.[136] The international legal order has developed to the extent that it is no longer appropriate to discuss the more traditional forms of lawmaking as subsuming all possible modes of law creation. If the Security Council requires states to change their law then the argument that states are only bound by law that they consent to as sovereign equals is not entirely accurate. Tomuschat concedes that treaties, as an instrument of state-based law creation, remain fundamental and as such their democratic legitimacy is as obscure as it is in other areas of international law. In its stead, Tomuschat focuses on ensuring the state's compliance with what the community considers to be the core standards of law and ostracising those states that fail to comply.

Several proponents, including Trachtman, Paulus and Peters, focus on solidarity and commonality as a model for the interactions of the subjects of global constitutionalism. These characterisations are not set in opposition to a democratic bent but rather as an explanation of how legitimacy may be achieved within the global legal order. Trachtman suggests that in allocating democracy to member states the nature or character of the WTO's democratic credentials in a constitutional order becomes less consequential.[137] However, this fails to settle the central issue of the WTO's or indeed the UN's scope of interest and whether this matches interests of the state or those it purports to represent. If states do not, then an alternative structure is required. The community or constituency that both organisations address is a different one to that which states represent, and the disconnection between the two is not

135 For example, for a discussion of this with regard to Tomuschat, see Bogdandy, 'Proposal from Germany', 223.

136 Tomuschat, 'Obligations', 272–3.

137 R. Howse and K. Nicolaïdis, 'Democracy without Sovereignty: The Global Vocation of Political Ethics', in T. Broude and Y. Shany (eds.), *The Shifting Allocation of Authority in International Law* (Oxford: Hart, 2008), pp. 168, 184.

addressed in constitutionalisation. Paulus argues that the democratic deficit within international law cannot be resolved through domestic democratic principles alone, as 'international decisions have different effects on different national or international constituencies'.[138] In contrast, De Wet acknowledges the importance of democracy but as a human right to be enforced domestically, and presupposes that domestic constitutionalism satisfies the need for democratic legitimacy in international law.[139]

Paulus links constitutional principles to the need to identify members of a community and in turn the relationship between the community and the constitution. He suggests that besides the debate on global constitutionalisation, solidarity is explicitly or implicitly also a basis of domestic constitutional orders and as such 'indispensable to international law'.[140] Whether Paulus is arguing that this also must be linked to a vision of community or constituency is unclear. Such an acute basis in solidarity could be undermined, for example, by claims of US hegemony. Paulus considers the ramifications of a community basis for world order constitutionalism only in the context of solidarity. Arguably, the constitutionalisation process should seek to identify the concentrations of power and understand how they are dispersed; whether the rule of law prevails or democratic legitimacy is present ought to be brought to the fore.[141] Such notions of solidarity sit alongside Peters' reliance upon community interests. Peters' community is not founded upon the solidarity that Paulus advocates but rather upon identifiable elements of international law, which she describes as global goods or common assumptions.[142] This is not linked to an identification of the content of such a community or constituency but firmly places states at the centre of Peters' arguments, which rest on a retrospective and present constitutionalism. Paulus, by contrast, is far more prospective in his approach and as such is more

[138] Paulus, 'The International Legal System as a Constitution' in Dunoff and Trachtman (eds.), *Ruling the World*, p. 94; this is similar to Macdonald and Macdonald's arguments regarding constituencies and the gap between state and international interests. Macdonald and Macdonald, 'Non-Electoral Accountability', 89.

[139] De Wet, 'The International Constitutional Order', 63.

[140] Paulus, 'The International Legal System as a Constitution' in Dunoff and Trachtman (eds.), *Ruling the World*, p. 93.

[141] See, for example, the discussion in Fischer-Lescano and Teubner (eds.), 'Reply to Andreas L Paulus', 1071.

[142] Peters, 'Compensatory', 589.

likely to resolve the current issues regarding democratic legitimacy in international law.[143]

Allott identifies the subjects of society as individuals who are self-constituting and, as such, international society contains these self-constituting human beings.[144] Accordingly, constitutions are indelibly linked to the societies behind their creation. While he does not identify exact parallels between international and domestic law, he does claim that they all form part of the same system. Specifically, he argues that international law contains three elements: international constitutional law, international public law and the laws of nations.[145] International constitutional law grants to states the ability to enter into legal relations, establishing the relationship between international public law and the law of nations as well as the horizontal relationship between the law of nations and international public law. Accordingly, international public law mainly deals with inter-state relationships, and this suggests that international constitutional law will determine when other legal entities such as individuals and international organisations may participate. The law of nations mainly consists of the internal law of states. Thus international constitutional law determines who the subjects of international law are in this very hierarchal and integrated understanding of present international law.[146]

Like Peters the relationship between the international and domestic legal orders is central, though unlike Peters, Allott does not recognise a need to de-constitutionalise the state sphere to create an international constitutional order. The international constitutional order already operates and stands above, but not in contest, with domestic constitutional orders. Allott's system reconciles these systems as the common interest of all humankind.[147] This perspective fits well with the idea of geographic divisions of power where governance may move from one level to another but not necessarily to the exclusion of another constitutional level. It also suggests that democratic legitimacy must give space to the holders of constituent power within this constitutionalism.

Democratic legitimacy is an aspect of many constitutionalisation debates; however, its nature and obligatory character as essential to

143 Though Peters also recognises what she describes as micro-constitutionalisation in the guise of the EU and further the WTO. This brings some of her discussion within the realms of sectoral constitutionalisation debates.

144 Allott, 'The Concept of International Law', 33.

145 *Ibid.*, 38. 146 *Ibid.*, 38.

147 Allott, *Eunomia*, p. 190, and Allott, 'The Concept of International Law', 38.

constitutionalism is not as evident as may be presupposed. Habermas and Paulus in recognising the future development of constitutionalism within a constitutionalisation process are clear that democracy is an essential aspect of such evolution. Yet, asserting that either democracy is unnecessary or may be identified within processes linked to states, means that democratic legitimacy has yet to find a home in many constitutionalisation theories. The next section will specifically deal with democratic legitimacy within constitutionalisation theories linked to community to decipher whether democratic legitimacy is better served therein.

6.3.1 Democratic legitimacy and the international community

The international community lies at the very core of several constitutionalisation theories, some of which have already been considered. Discussing them here again, within the rubric of democratic legitimacy, aims to highlight the reliance on community to establish the constituent power holders and further, how such instant dependence retards the development of a more nuanced identification of the actors who ought to hold constitutional purchase. Mosler regards constitutionalisation as having a transformative effect: it introduces the rule of law into society and grants a permanency, which he sees evoked in the community. He describes the international society as a legal community developing over time.[148] For him, this society includes states and institutions operating under law, thus widening the accounted subjects beyond the state, but still maintaining the order as it stands. Further, he argues that '[t]he constitution of a society, whether it regulated life within a state or the coexistence of a group of states, is the highest law in society. It transforms a society into a community governed by law'.[149]

For Tomuschat, sovereign equality remains the centre of the international community's constitution. While he acknowledges some of the shortcomings related to establishing international constitutional law on community, he argues that most of these difficulties are related to identification of the community beyond states. There is no discussion of the issues related to community and democratic legitimacy. Democratic legitimacy, in looking beyond the lawmaking processes to establish the members of the community, maintains community and constitution as firmly interdependent. Constitutionalisation introduces curbs on a state's

[148] Mosler, *Rec. Des Cours*, p. 17, There is much in common here with Allott's vision of an international society; see Allott, 'The Concept of International Law', 31.

[149] Mosler, *Rec. Des Cours*, p. 31.

freedom of action but these are driven by the need for more 'discipline'[150] in the international community, as law tries to balance the interests of states and the international community. Certain rules are resultant of this and accordingly are part of the constitutional foundations.[151] Alongside sovereign equality, Tomuschat argues that common values of mankind are part of the constitutional principles of the international community.[152] Tomuschat identifies three ICJ cases as particularly important to this community argument: the 'Barcelona Traction' case, 'Southwest Africa/ Namibia' case and the 'Tehran Hostages' case.[153] These cases, Tomuschat claims, reassert the notion that the community acts as a guarantor. He concludes that the jurisprudence of the ICJ identifies an international community governed by a constitution.[154]

For Tomuschat the emergence of non-state actors in international law forms part of the change in the subjects of international law and the evolution of the international community. Tomuschat argues that states have to act to the betterment of all human beings within their jurisdiction and accordingly rules have emerged, driven from the constitutional principle of the common values of mankind, to substantiate these needs.[155] Nonetheless, this retains the state as the focus of global law. States ensure compliance with these laws and states take action against those who do not. This is not to discount other actor's involvement but to acknowledge that states retain a key role. If the community is established as Tomuschat suggests, the next question is in what manner democratic participation by the members of that international community is established.

Since all states are required to be part of the international community for the constitution to exist, Tomuschat questions whether states can actually opt out of the community.[156] He argues that while states have a right to reduce their contact with the outside world, in accordance with sovereign equality, this does not mean that such a state is not bound by the core rules of the international constitution. In joining the community,

150 Tomuschat, 'Obligations', 292

151 *Ibid.*, 293–4. This includes the non-use of force, principles of environmental law and the use of nuclear weapons; no state can disregard the interests and rights of another state.

152 *Ibid.*, 300, 303. Tomuschat prescribes a sober discussion about whether rules actually derive from the unwritten international constitution, which also has 'deductive inferences'.

153 *Ibid.*, 230–2. 154 *Ibid.*, 236.

155 An example is international humanitarian law, *ibid.*, 301–2. This is somewhat similar to Fischer-Lescano's arguments that sovereignty and statehood are core to international constitutionalisation; A. Fischer-Lescano, 'Redefining Sovereignty', 10.

156 Tomuschat, 'Obligations', 306.

if they can persuade other states, states are free to attempt to change the constitution. This is not entirely convincing. While sovereign equality, as described by Tomuschat, is the basis on which a state can isolate itself and require other states to respect this isolation, his position does not satisfactorily explain the decolonisation process or advances made within environmental, human rights or trade law. A state must accept all the rules, however unjust, upon membership of the international community, and then they are free to attempt to change the content, however unlikely the reality of such an outcome. States do not equally participate in the creation of international law, nor do many of the other international actors. A new constitutional regime, in a democratic process, would need to ensure that, in the future, all participants can exercise their constituent power within a regime that recognises the necessary continued re-identification of constituent actors.

This places international organisations in a strange position within Tomuschat's constitutional remit. He references the law formed by international organisations as 'secondary law'.[157] Focusing on sovereign equality and the different voting procedures of these organisations, be they consensus, majority or otherwise, he argues that whenever a state joins an organisation that passes binding resolutions, then the state gives up some of its own rights. Tomuschat relies on an analogy with domestic systems – a group of persons coming together to guarantee the rule of law and submitting to a higher body give up some of their personal rights and freedoms.[158] However, within the state this goes hand in hand with democratic legitimacy and the exercise of constituent power. Thus, in reality, it is the democratic legitimacy formed at the domestic level that for Tomuschat also suffices at the global level. One process bleeds into the other and forms the legitimacy for an order possessing different interests and subjects. Like Habermas, Tomuschat recognises the shortcomings of international institutions as democratic entities but does not appear to recognise the disconnection between the two orders.[159]

In contrast to Tomuschat's more statist approach, Simma regards international law as having moved beyond the traditional state-centric

[157] *Ibid.*, 325–48.

[158] *Ibid.*, 328; this relies on state-based contract theory. Tomuschat is restricting himself to a state-based description of international organisations, which means they will always fall short of a standard that was not intended for them to be measured by in the first place.

[159] Habermas, *Divided*, p. 140 and Tomuschat, 'Ensuring the Survival of Mankind', 10.

and bilateral legal structure.[160] Simma describes this classical vision of bilateralism, which was understood by Verdross to be relative, as international law not requiring states to makes obligations to the world at large or, as he describes it, '*urbi et orbi*', but rather to other states.[161] This traditionalist view of international law maintains through consent the prohibition on intervention supported by state sovereignty and reciprocity. Simma points to the development of community interest as the antithesis of bilateralism in international law.[162] This community interest he defines 'as a consensus according to which respect for certain fundamental values is not to be left to the free disposition of States individually, or *inter se*, but is recognized and sanctioned by international law as a matter of concern to all States'.[163] This form of community interest expands its force and significance throughout international law. Simma asserts that community interest is fundamentally a new development; while its nascence may be observed in earlier periods of international law's growth, it is couched in the common interests of the international community, where traditional bilateralism has no place.[164] He deals with the constitutional elements at the macro-level, though he considers all the various modes of international law to be inter-related and not self-contained or within fragmented regimes.[165]

Simma argues that the most significant manifestation of the move away from bilateralism is the emergence of international organisations.[166] This he argues is based upon states reconciling their own interests with those of the community. Accordingly, Simma argues that the articulation of interests undertaken continually at the UN and other international bodies, including non-governmental organisations (NGOs), becomes critical to international law.[167] Yet, such a perspective does not consider the negative impact of these political institutions or the capacity of states for full engagement with setting their agendas. These agendas are not set by any objective standard emphasising the interests of the global community. As was discussed in Chapter 3, community interest very often means nothing more than what the stronger members or indeed the more conservative members of a group claim. Though his theory remains reliant upon community interests, as Simma admits, the tools for identifying such interests are not at all clear, particularly if states' and the international

[160] Simma, 'From Bilateralism', 229–30.

[161] *Ibid.*, 230. [162] *Ibid.*, 233–4. [163] *Ibid.*, 233.

[164] Though whether on Simma's definitions the substance of the law has moved is questionable; *ibid.*, 234–5.

[165] *Ibid.*, 252–3. [166] *Ibid.*, 236. [167] *Ibid.*, 235.

orders' interests are not identical.[168] In contrast, Tomuschat argues that community should be '[a] synthetic abstraction derived from a number of elements suggesting that, notwithstanding the principle of sovereign equality, humankind constitutes a unity which is held together by many ties, both of a factual and legal character'.[169] This detaches community from interests; though in preserving the state, Tomuschat cedes the remit of state interest as legitimate and above the interests of the rest of the global community. The differing attitudes may be based upon what Bogdandy alludes to as Tomuschat's acceptance of some of the imperfections within both international law and the institutions that support it, albeit that Simma is less willing to accept the deficiencies. [170]

Simma's approach to establishing interests is based within community, without necessarily fully identifying who the members of the community are or how their interests are to be ascertained. This precludes any form of democratic participation by the holders of constituent power, even if these holders were limited to Simma's community. In relying on the global legal order as it stands to establish the community and its interests, Simma sidesteps any attempt to remedy its present failings in establishing the holders of constituent power and the exercise of their warrant.

De Wet's vision of the international community moves beyond the state though in some ways remains faithful to the more traditional sources of community recognisable in Simma. De Wet argues that the ICJ in the 'Barcelona Traction' case or the Advisory Opinion on 'Legal Consequences of the Construction of a Wall in the Occupied Palestinian Territory' established a community-orientated jurisprudence in the guise of obligations *erga omnes*.[171] She suggests that the Articles on State Responsibility and elements of criminal and human rights law further exemplify this progression.[172] While extending the community beyond the state, De Wet limits its remit to inter-governmental regional and

[168] Simma decries occasions, such as the NATO intervention in Kosovo, when the constitutional order embodied in the Charter is ignored. B. Simma, 'Comments on Global Governance, the United Nations and the Place of Law' (1998) 9 *Finnish Yearbook of International Law* 61, 65, discussing the NATO intervention in Kosovo.

[169] C. Tomuschat, 'Multilateralism in the Age of US Hegemony' in MacDonald and Johnston (eds.), *Towards World Constitutionalism*, p. 33.

[170] Bogdandy, 'Proposal from Germany', 223.

[171] 'Barcelona Traction' Case (1970) *ICJ Reports* 32, 'Legal Consequences of the Construction of a Wall in the Occupied Palestinian Territory Advisory Opinion' (2004) *ICJ Reports* 136.

[172] De Wet, 'The International Constitutional Order', 54–5.

global organisations. De Wet argues that the UN Charter cannot provide the constitution of the world community as its membership is exclusively state based.[173] In line with her own analysis, the UN's inclusion in the community does not extend the membership of the community beyond states.[174] As De Wet does not consider democracy as necessarily linked to legitimacy, in domestic or international orders, she argues that there is little need to consider how its absence affects the potential constitutionalisation process. Thus De Wet moves beyond the classical view of international community but in doing so replicates Tomuschat's reliance on domestic democratic legitimacy without explaining how the interests of both may be legitimately combined in a global constitutional order.

Far from uniform democratic legitimacy within international constitutionalisation theories appear to consist mainly of state-centric approaches with little regard to the establishment of community interests through any democratic process. Instead, these community theories remain reliant upon a state-centric view of how democracy can be established within domestic constitutionalism and either transferring this upwards with little regard for differing constituent actors and interests or relying on a predetermined notion of international community as a fall-back to legitimacy. While international community is discussed in the next chapter, its firm place within constitutionalisation theories suggests its on-going importance to global legal theory, even if it fails to satisfy the necessary constitutional norms.

6.3.2 Democratic legitimacy in global constitutionalisation theories

As with the rule of law and divisions of power, democratic legitimacy rarely sits at the centre of debate is reflected upon as an essential norm of constitutionalism or regarded as an attribute of the global constitutionalisation process. Grimm argues that the democratic element and the rule of law cannot be separated without diminishing the achievements of constitutionalism, but such emphasis on its role as intertwined with other elements of constitutionalism loses its prominence in the global debate.[175] Both the rule of law and democratic legitimacy are constitutional necessities, and their relative weakness in global constitutionalisation theories,

[173] *Ibid.*, 52.

[174] As well as individuals to the extent that they have legal personality in particular contexts; *ibid.*, 55.

[175] Grimm, 'The Achievement of Constitutionalism' in Dobner and Loughlin (eds.), *Twilight*, p. 10.

in contrast, for instance, to their place in global legal pluralism, opens up a number of questions regarding the role of constitutionalism as a normative governance structure in the global legal order. Further, the recognition that constituted, and more particularly, constituent power form part of democracy's legitimacy is all but absent from debate.

Two features commonly take the place of democratic legitimacy. The first centres on democratic deficits and the interaction at state level of democracy with international institutions. This pushes domestic democratic legitimacy beyond the state into the global realm, regardless of the fact that the constituent actors and thus interests are not necessarily analogous. Community forms the second feature, requiring a process for identifying its interests, though one not necessarily coupled to a particularly constitutional governance structure. Coupled with this obfuscation of dealing directly with issues related to democracy, the difficulty of theorising democratic legitimacy isolated from the rule of law and divisions of power emerges, as various theories acknowledge the shortcomings of the structure their propositions may produce.

This obfuscation of democracy at the point of international law was probably much aptly described by Marks. Her critical examination of democracy's utilisation at the hands of international lawyers in many ways points to an underlying difficulty that continues to exist with its invocation today.[176] What is described as the emergent right to democracy confronted by the actuality and acquiescence as to its content within states, together with a position that surrenders the potential of democracy in the midst of international law itself, is perhaps the most difficult hurdle for constitutionalisation to surmount. While Marks was not dealing with constitutionalisation, her rallying call at the end of her book, citing Marx, that 'entrenching democracy as the endlessly tantalizing, perpetually unsettling, continuously confounding *riddle* of all constitutions', naturally should hold a place in the debate discussed here.[177] For democracy requires a connection to constituent power holders and while the various propositions as to how this may be achieved within international law are beyond discussion here, the necessity of its inclusion, even beyond constitutionalisation, although perhaps even more so if this is indeed the future of international law, cannot be underestimated.[178]

[176] Marks, *The Riddle*. [177] *Ibid*., p. 151.

[178] D. Held, *Democracy and the Global Order: From the Modern State to Cosmopolitan Governance* (Cambridge: Polity Press, 1995), p. 221.

At this point, it is clear that constitutionalisation theories recognise that democracy is usually at issue, but whether any of the theories, beyond perhaps that of Habermas, recognise that to continue with constitutionalisation is in fact problematic or that would hold it back from attaining legitimacy is unclear. Democratic legitimacy should form a core tenet of any constitutional proposal. As these theories currently stand, democratic legitimacy does not appear to be entrenched to the extent necessary to properly describe global law as constitutional. Dobner argues that, '[o]n the global level, the production of law is undertaken in many fields, and those who observe and promote this production either do not care about its democratic control or they are unable to provide satisfactory answers to how it could be legitimised'.[179] While this may seem like an overly negative overview of global constitutionalisation, there is a deficit of democratic legitimacy within global constitutionalisation theories. This deficit must be overcome before the global legal order can be claimed to be constitutional or constitutionalisation theories comprehensive.

6.4 Constitutional norms in global constitutionalisation

Mosler maintains there must be core constitutional elements to any society, as without this, it would not be a community at all but a mere collection of individuals. He maintains that even before the introduction of organisations into international law there was a central constitutional element and that this was law's existing lawmaking processes. This he argues is drawn from the consensus that establishes a pre-eminent constitutional component. This chapter set out to discuss whether constitutional norms were present as part of the global constitutionalisation debates and whether constitutional purchase is noteworthy as a component of discussion. This was undertaken on the basis that analysing the global constitutionalisation debate, how it has developed and the major differences between the various propositions ought to distinguish its particular constitutional attributes.

Paulus argues for an understanding of both fragmentation and international law that is constitutional but also remains perceptibly international. This accepts that the ideal of actually achieving the rule of law, the division of power or democratic legitimacy has yet to be achieved. It could be suggested that in not maintaining the existence of a present constitutional order Paulus is stepping back from making a bold claim.

179 P. Dobner, 'More Law, Less Democracy' in Dobner and Loughlin, (eds.) *Twilight*, p. 160.

However, in acknowledging that there are faults within international law, particularly with regard to constituent and constituted power, there is at least a push towards a reforming ethic as opposed to an acceptance of the status quo as enough for constitutionalism. Agreeing that a constitutional order does exist, with the exception of Allott's reforming conception and others like it, advocates continuing with a system that according to most constitutional principles remains substandard.

The major differences between sectoral and world constitutionalisation propositions illustrate the variations within the global constitutionalisation debate. The reasoning behind sectoral constitutionalisation does not appear to give enough consideration to the overall coherence of a global constitutional order. Should sectoral constitutionalisation come to fruition, this lack of coherence may result in the term 'constitution' ultimately being erroneously applied to a governance order though ought to be recognised as based on alternative normative values. A constitutionalised system should offer levels of certainly that sectoral constitutionalisation, in its present guise, does not offer. To function, world order constitutionalisation theories require that at least some of the norms of constitutionalism must be in operation at a nascent level. World order constitutionalisation tackles the need for coherence but this leaves open the question of whether constitutionalisation theories are imbedded with the necessary aspects of normative constitutionalism.

The rule of law, divisions of power and democratic legitimacy are central to constitutionalism. As was described in Chapter 2, to ensure that constitutionalism is maintained, these three constitutional norms must be present in a constitutional order and nascent during a process of constitutionalisation. The constitutionalisation theories discussed in this chapter rarely deal directly with these three constitutional norms. This is not to suggest that these norms are not present, simply that many constitutionalisation advocates seem reluctant to directly deal with them. It may be argued that this means that constitutionalisation within global law is based on grounds other than constitutional norms, that global constitutional purchase lies elsewhere. But these three are necessary norms of constitutionalism and, as such, must at least be present in the constitutionalisation debate even if in actuality they have yet to come to full fruition. Further, such considerations would give footing to a deliberation as to whether gaining constitutional purchase may necessarily be a good thing for global law. If these theories mean nothing more than a change in the legal structure of global law, then, as these make less grandiose claims, the theories regarding fragmentation or global administrative law are more appropriate descriptions of global law's future.

The lack of a firm basis in constitutionalism in the majority of global constitutionalisation theories is a result of their origins. Thus far, the parameters of the global constitutionalisation debate have been set by international law. If, instead, global constitutionalisation theories began from a basis in constitutionalism, from a footing that recognises the depth and problems with it as a governance structure, then these norms would become central to the global constitutionalisation debate. While such a starting point may result in finding that global governance is only at the outset of a constitutionalisation process or in fact should not attempt to take up constitutionalism, it also sets an agenda or impetus for reform. Currently, normative constitutionalism remains superficial within the constitutionalisation debate. If constitutionalism was more emphatically drawn into the constitutionalisation theories, it would offer a stronger coherent basis on which to judge the advantages of global constitutionalisation and make a persuasive argument to those who doubt its appropriateness and applicability.

7

Whom does global constitutionalism address?

An essential activity of any constitutionalised order, regardless of its governance structure, lies in identifying the holders of constituent and constituted power. Yet, the global constitutionalisation debate lacks a conscious inquiry into how and whether to identify the holders of both forms of power and, more critically, their relationship to the constitutionalisation process.[1] Habermas argues that law has a specific rationale behind its existence. It is germane for establishing the subjects operating in global constitutionalism to aid in understanding its particular rationale.[2] Sidestepping this aspect of constitutionalisation excises context from the discussion; it isolates constitutionalism from reality and from the developing complexity of international law. This chapter examines the line between the governance structures that constitutionalism maintains and the subjects that ought to grant legitimacy to governance, thus asking whom global constitutionalism would address.

Political power is central to the debate over whom global constitutionalisation addresses.[3] Beyond vague references to states, community and other actors, within global constitutionalism, the link between holding and restraining constituted power through the rule of law and divisions of power, as well as between constituent power and democratic legitimacy, must be addressed. Walter argues that if constitutionalisation limits itself to states, then the global legal community must always have consisted of

[1] Besides the constitutionalisation and related debates, as already discussed, there are several other avenues of inquiry into the future of international law. For example, M. Koskenniemi, *From Apology to Utopia* (reissue, Cambridge University Press, 2006); Charlesworth and Chinkin, *A Feminist Analysis*; Allott, *Eunomia*; Anghie, *Imperialism*.

[2] R. Nickel, 'Private and Public Autonomy Revisited: Habermas' Concept of Co-originality in Times of Globalization and the Militant Security State' in Loughlin and Walker (eds.), *The Paradox*, p. 153; J. Habermas, *Between Facts and Norms* (Cambridge, MA: MIT Press, 1996), p. 83.

[3] See, for example, D. Dyzenhaus, 'The Politics of the Question of Constituent Power' in Loughlin and Walker (eds.), *The Paradox*.

states and nothing else.[4] The implication of this is that constitutionalisation must include more than states as they are no longer, if indeed they ever were, the sole subjects of international law. If states' role as the sole producers of international law lessens, then no longer are they the sole possessors of constituent power. The degree to which this shift is recognised in constitutionalisation theories varies, but here it is suggested that an acknowledgement of the gradation amongst actors within the global legal order is essential.

Thus, discourse on constitutionalisation is not simply a nation-state conversation; rather, claims for a new legal order must grapple with a broader shift in actors.[5] Beyond the global constitutionalisation debate, the degree of clarity necessary to identify the holders of constituent and constituted power remains debatable. This chapter aims to establish the remit of constitutionalism within global law. The space normally reserved for domestic constitutionalism cannot simply be transplanted in order to gain legitimacy for global governance. The holders of constituent and constituted power engaged in global constitutionalisation cannot be reduced to individuals or states, as normative constitutionalism requires more from its constituent actors. It is essential to characterise whom global constitutionalism addresses and thus determine who are the holders of constituent and constituted power.

This chapter addresses three key issues: first, how to characterise constitutional subjects within global constitutionalism; second, how to identify the holders of constituent power; and third, as a consequence of that question, how to identify them collectively as either a community or a constituency. The first section addresses the nature of international community. In grasping the nature of international community it is hoped to understand its use in global constitutionalisation. A historical overview of the use of 'community' within international law is followed by a consideration of its current place within constitutionalisation and its potential to identify the holders of constituent and constituted power. This pursues a similar model to Chapter 3, with the Stoics, Vitoria, Suárez, Hobbes and Kant setting the historical trajectory of community's development, while Franck and the Cosmopolitans are contemporary examples of its use. This is followed by a consideration of international constituency and how it

[4] Walter, 'Process of Constitutionalization' in Nijman and Nollkaemper (eds.), *New Perspectives*, p. 196.

[5] See P. Carozza 'Constitutionalism's Post-Modern Opening' in Loughlin and Walker (eds.), *The Paradox*, p. 184; and also M. Hart and A. Negri, *Empire* (Cambridge, MA: Harvard University Press, 2000).

may be used to identify the holders of constituent and constituted power. This leads to a debate as to whether it is best to consider the addressees of constitutionalisation from a basis within community or constituency. Naturally, the discussions in Chapter 3 are very much in focus herein and are the backdrop to considering the use of community and constituency beyond the state.

7.1 Community

7.1.1 Stoics and international community

Stoic philosophy centres on reason and logic and was one of the first varieties of philosophy to identify a universal humanity broader than notional human identity or what could also be described as an international community of sorts. Seneca wrote that '[t]he first thing philosophy offers us is the feeling of fellowship, of belonging to mankind and being members of a community',[6] arguing that there are two communities, the one assigned at birth and another that embraces all men. Stoicism does not distinguish between Roman and barbarian or master and slave, and this is central to its philosophy on governance.[7] This is not to suggest that the Stoic theory was as inclusive as Aristotle's theory was exclusionary. Marcus Aurelius and Cicero were not concerned with the real impact of their Empire or Republic on the masses, on women or indeed upon the slaves who in that period made up much of humanity. Yet, Stoicism identifies a conception of community and governance beyond immediate state or nation ideals.

Stoicism does not identify the *telos* underpinning Aristotle's continual development. Instead nature becomes part of reason. Rationality underpins the Stoic tradition; *logos* and reason create rational rule as the 'foundation and spirit of community'.[8] The Stoic community contends that persons are members of their home state community but also of the 'kingdom of reason', a much broader supposition with almost universal membership. Further, the Stoic kingdom of reason negates the habitation requirement of Aristotle's community. It is also, in broadening the conception of allegiance, an argument against dictatorship, and particularly

[6] Seneca's 'Fifth Letter to Lucilius', quoted in A. Rorty, *The Many Faces of Philosophy* (New York: Oxford University Press, 2003), p. 8.

[7] Seneca, *Moral and Political Essays* (trans. J. M. Cooper) (Cambridge University Press, 1995), p. 175; see also Seneca, quoted in M. C. Nussbaum, 'Kant and Stoic Cosmopolitanism' (1997) 5 *Journal of Political Philosophy* 1, 1.

[8] Douzinas, *The End of Human Rights*, pp. 52–3.

relevant to jurisprudential arguments of Verdross, which rely upon universal and unchanging norms. As Douzinas points out, this form of community creates an abstract idea of a kind of universal fraternity.[9] Although intangible, it is a concept in which all humanity may at least potentially participate. This does not mean that the Stoics were not elitist or that this community was based upon equality, but it was an understanding of community that could be global in at least the Stoic's own sense of the world.

Stoicism maintains two communities, the first a global community with equality of rights and participation, and the second consisting of the local community of birth. Stoics argue that allegiance is thus owed beyond the state towards all humanity and that there is a moral-legal duty connecting the first community's members as world citizens. This global community was not based upon a communion of states but rather on humanity's internal wrangling. Thus, it is from humanity that community gains its authority. As Cicero states 'there will not be different laws at Rome and at Athens'.[10] Here, Cicero was not arguing that all law should be identical; rather he was claiming a core law common to all. This gives a foundation to the proposition of universality.

Within the Stoic tradition a major life goal is to follow nature's rational plan ascertained through reason and achieved through community. Cicero argues that the different roles that one fulfils in society are reconcilable: 'good lives are conceived as contributing to a cooperative existence within an organized community and virtuous individuals are therefore expected to be emotionally capable of engaging in a range of common projects'.[11] This calls for individuals to be active in community, and thus a member fulfils many roles. An individual may be regarded as father, son or magistrate, with each role relating to the others and being fulfilled together.[12] It is important to state that this was a patriarchy; therefore, the roles of mother or daughter were not considered as vital to the political aspects of community. Creating a hierarchy of obligations is part of the Stoic approach to enable a participant to engage in a number of roles contemporaneously. To uniformly fulfil these roles is demanding, but it is also conceivably well suited to understanding the nature of being a constitutional subject in a global order.

[9] *Ibid.*, p. 52.

[10] Cicero, *The Republic, The Laws* (trans. N. Rudd) (Oxford University Press, 1998), p. 69.

[11] D. Rutherford, *The Cambridge Companion to Early Modern Philosophy* (Cambridge University Press, 2006), p. 198.

[12] *Ibid.*, p. 198.

In making such an analysis, Stoics certainly had individuals in mind, but this multi-stranded approach could be usefully redeployed to examine the obligations that states, international institutions, individuals and so on may have within a modern legal order. It may be particularly functional in understanding multiple levels of constitutionalism. Rarely does the subject of constitutionalism play a single role, instead it occupies a multidimensional position. For instance, a state may be subject to its own internal constitutionalism, while concurrently subject to regional and global constitutionalism. Present articulations of international community may be read as requiring multiple roles for each actor and thus resolve some of the difficulties in recognising global constituent and constituted actors. For example, constituent power holders may also hold constituted power and vice versa. If the international community is seen as something beyond a linear set of stakeholders with one and only one interest, for example, as states with only state interests, and instead as a conglomeration of members that possess different interests based upon their varying roles within global society, this reflects better the experience of constitutionalism at multiple levels. The complexities and intricacies in participants' various interests, for example, how they fulfil different and sometimes adjoining roles in different spheres, explain why, at times, a legal order community may appear incomplete. In turn, whether members manage their interests, as well as constituent and constituted power, is a question of the maturity of that community and, as such, the proper functioning of constitutionalism.

If the international community is understood not as a static body, but rather as a group that is multi-layered and possesses intricacies not easily resolved, this allows for a much more complete analysis of the global context. The question is whether the stakeholders can be expected to be capable of engaging at this level or even if the necessary machinery can be established within the international community. Franck, though statist in his outlook, argues that '[t]he difference between a rabble or even a primitive association and a developed community is that in the latter members accept specific reciprocal obligations as a concomitant of membership in that community, which is a structured continuing association of interacting parties'.[13] As obligations do not necessarily mirror each other, for each the level of interaction is imperative and must be beyond simple two-way traffic.

[13] T. Franck, *The Power of Legitimacy among Nations* (Oxford University Press, 1990), p. 197.

The multi-stranded approach appears to establish an international community where there is, at least, an acceptance of nuance. Nonetheless, there is an implicit hierarchy. While a member of the community may hold many roles and offices, the power within the community does not lie with all: not every member of the community can hold both constituent and constituted power. There is a global sense of humanity and kindred law, but this does not necessarily translate into equality of participation or even diversity of membership. This can have repercussions for democratic legitimacy. Though the Stoics would argue that the community is based upon the reason that every human being possesses, and thus moral allegiance is owed first to humanity, which requires dignity to be given to every human, this did not require the Stoics to change fundamentally how law was applied. Marcus Aurelius did not free the slaves of Rome.[14] It is a model of world community that sets aside a core in national or local characteristics and attempts to achieve some form of global feeling or community. This Stoic community is based beyond sovereignty; it is founded upon humanity, but a humanity that is implicitly hierarchal.

7.1.2 Early modern international law

Early modern writers of international law, such as Vitoria and Suárez, do not always reflect current international law; yet, similar to the Stoic tradition, they do provide early and formative conceptions of contemporary international community.[15] Understanding these models and their impact on present perceptions of international law remains instructive, and adds to an appreciation of the present role of community in constitutionalisation. The wealth of writing from these authors means that each will not be discussed in depth; rather, as with the Stoics, this section aims to describe the advancement of community in international law during this period. It is also accepted that the relationship between each of these authors is not straightforward, and while the analysis here may appear linear, this is, in fact, far from the case.[16]

14 Nussbaum, 'Kant and Stoic Cosmopolitanism', 7–8.

15 Though there is some disagreement on whether Vitoria and Suárez are late medieval or early modern, for the purposes of this work it is only necessary that they have been utilised in the development of international law. Kennedy, 'Primitive', 40.

16 See commentary by Brown on the relationship between them in his introduction to the translation of Suárez's work; Williams, Brown and Waldron, *Selections from Three Works of Francisco Suárez*, p. 15a.

Vitoria's work points towards international law's instinctive approach to new global issues.[17] In his two major studies, *De Indis Noviter Inventis* and *De Jure Bellis Hispanorum in Barbaros*, Vitoria asserts that the peoples of America, though newly located by Europeans and clearly not having participated in its creation, were bound by *jus gentium*. This was controversial at the time, as the prevailing theory stipulated that, as non-Christians, international law could not be extended to the peoples of America.[18] Thus, this extension implicitly reflects an understanding of law's remit as unrestricted by European or Christian mores and based upon the notion that universal law is applicable to all persons without regard to engagement in its creation or identification.[19] While this does not per se establish an international community, it extends law's remit to all persons, even when it is obvious, as it was here, that it would ultimately have a negative impact upon those to whom it was extended. While Vitoria would not have seen Spain's claimed civilising mission as negative, and regarded this application of law as establishing equality, his template could be considered the basis of international community as an oppressive force, that 'barbarous peoples too must be considered equal members of the universal community of peoples'[20] – a view that is clearly imperialist in character. Further, the religious aspects of Vitoria's writing should not be underestimated. Together with the notion of universal applicability of divine law, Vitoria provides a Christian underpinning to international law.[21] Echoing earlier discussions of community, to become a member of the international community one has to sign up to the previously established rules, whether or not these laws are in one's favour.

[17] For an overview see Anghie, *Imperialism*, chapter 1.

[18] G. C. Marks, 'Indigenous Peoples in International Law: The Significance of Francisco De Vitoria and Bartolome De Las Casas'(1990–1991) 3 *Australian Yearbook of International Law* 1.

[19] As Verdross and Koeck argue, the Spanish King as Emperor of the Holy Roman Empire was Lord of the World and could therefore legally occupy any part of it. This view of international law extended no rights to any indigenous population. Verdross and Koeck, 'Natural Law', in MacDonald and Johnston (eds.), *The Structure and Process*, p. 20; and G. C. Marks, 'Francisco De Vitoria and Bartolome De Las Casas', 1; Anghie, *Imperialism*, pp. 19–21.

[20] Verdross and Koeck, 'Natural Law', in MacDonald and Johnston (eds.) *The Structure and Process*, p. 20.

[21] Kennedy, 'Primitive', 15. Though Kennedy's criticism of Vitoria's lack of methodological explanation is incorrect. Certainly, for Vitoria religious doctrine without question, at the time and in the context Vitoria was writing, was largely a given. This is indeed problematic in its future application to international law, but is not an issue of Vitoria's lack of legal methodology.

Though clearly the idea of sovereignty that Vitoria recognises differs from its modern usage, its antecedent is still relevant in understanding how international law developed. Vitoria's treatment suggests that the sovereignty of states is not enough to render certain acts beyond *jus gentium*. Further, Vitoria does not distinguish as clearly as later authors would between jurisdiction and sovereignty, and this lack of distinction grants a more secure platform on which to build his international community. Its application in America illustrates that while First Nations were considered actors in law, the laws they had no hand in establishing what were, in reality, European and Christian. While the peoples of America were entitled to the same legal protection as was granted to Europeans they also had to perform similar duties for their European conquerors. Despite granting equality to all humanity and identifying a world law, Vitoria aided in establishing a tiered community.[22] If they were unaware of the existence of these systems or the manner in which the Europeans would and did enforce them, how were the First Nations, whose governance systems were not of the state model, to enforce their own rights vis-à-vis Spain? Here, admittance to the world community had an immediate cost detrimental upon these new subjects of international law.

Suárez, as one of the first international lawyers to conceive of some form of international community or society, played a central role in establishing this notion as part of the international legal discourse.[23] He argues that,

> [h]owever divided into different peoples and kingdoms it may be, mankind has nevertheless possessed a certain unity ... as a moral and political unity ... although a given Sovereign State, Commonwealth, or Kingdom, may constitute a perfect community in itself, nevertheless, each of these States is also, in a certain sense, and viewed in relation to the human race, a member of that universal society.[24]

He suggests that there is an innate and eternal universal community in existence beyond the realms of the traditional sovereign state, commonwealth or kingdom, transcending these borders.[25] These conventional

[22] Certainly, not all of Vitoria's work has made its way into international law.

[23] Though, as Kennedy has alluded to when examining early international law, it is important to consider the context and law at the time of writing, particularly the fusion of law with morality; Kennedy, 'Primitive', 4.

[24] Williams, Brown and Waldron, *Selections from Three Works of Francisco Suárez*, p. 349

[25] Suárez argues that civil power 'in the nature of things, resides immediately in the community; and therefore, in order that it may justly come to reside in a given individual, as in a sovereign prince, it must necessarily be bestowed upon him by the consent of the

groupings form perfect communities, and beyond these clusters a universal community that by its nature is imperfect may be established. Thus, the perfect community, recognised in the state, is at the epicentre of international law. This is before Suárez even begins to consider the operation of that law. In Suárez's estimation community and the natural law complement each other.[26] Importantly, while *jus gentium* is not part of the natural law, the mere fact that there is a universal society or community gives *jus gentium* a higher stature than positive law.[27] The reasons for imperfection stem from Suárez's idea of the unity required for a community that he did not recognise, at that time, to be present. The universal society bounded eternally by the natural law though not necessarily by *jus gentium*. According to Suárez, *jus gentium* may change and develop, and it is thus not a stalwart to be relied upon in the same manner as the natural law.[28] The universal society and international law are thus not interdependent, and this forms part of the former's imperfection. Accordingly, international law is not a requirement of international community but can flourish within its remit.

Suárez's universal society is not as global as it may appear. His global view does not extend much beyond Europe, and when it does it is not with the goal of extending parity amongst states or kingdoms of the wider world. When recognition did occur it was based upon imperialist notions of establishing a just government over backward peoples.[29] The sovereign state, as the perfect community, places sovereignty, in contrast to Vitoria's discourse, at the core of international law, a position that it has since maintained. This model of international law was the precursor to the issues discussed earlier with regard to imperialism and colonialism within international law. From a classical perspective this does not appear to have radically changed since their time of writing and as such is perhaps the easiest base from which to identify the subjects of global constitutionalism. This greatly influenced Verdross' theory of international law and he emphasised that it was the combination of community with international law that moved Suarez's theory beyond that of Vitoria.[30]

As their influence upon international law has been significant, Suárez and Vitoria are essential to understanding contemporary discourse on

community; Williams, Brown and Waldron, *Selections from Three Works of Francisco Suárez*, p. 384.

[26] *Ibid.*, p. 346. [27] *Ibid.*, p. 347. [28] *Ibid.*, pp. 343–9. [29] *Ibid.*, pp. 772, 825–6.

[30] Verdross and Koeck, 'Natural Law' in MacDonald and Johnston (eds.), *The Structure and Process*, p. 20.

community in international law.[31] Though they are certainly not alone, both were extremely influential. In the nascent period of the present global order's legal development through to its current iteration, they remain influential in how both international law and community have been perceived and inter-related. While community is not central to any of their theses, they both considered community to be relevant and a precursor in discussing how international law should be understood.

It is striking that although these authors were not dealing with current international law, nor was the entirety of their conceptions adopted into the modern era, their notion that global law is applicable to all and, further, that the international community was never given to equality, remains prescient. As Abi-Saab stated '[i]f there was a "community" in that period it was one represented by the idea that reined in Europe at the end of the Middle Ages until the Reformation … [t]his was the idea of the existence "of a Christian empire, heir to Rome" … [a]nd it is the disintegration of this community that led to the birth of a new structure'.[32] Arguably, the break is not as clean as Abi-Saab suggests. While the conception of international law advanced in that period is certainly not entirely comparable to modern ideas, it has had a considerable impact on current concepts of international community.

7.1.3 Enlightenment: Hobbes and Kant

Hobbes argues there is no natural organised community, no natural coming together of states in a universal fraternity.[33] He advises that '[t]he final cause, end, or design of men (who naturally love liberty, and dominion over others) in the introduction of that restraint upon themselves, in which we see them live in Commonwealths, is the foresight of their own preservation…'[34] Humanity is not made up of, as earlier writers conceived of it, naturally social creatures drawn together to form communities. Regarding the individual as the 'subject of modernity and the source of law' at the core of the social order, this perception was indicative

[31] See T. Meron, 'Common Rights of Mankind in Gentili, Grotius and Suarez' (1991) 85 *The American Journal of International Law* 110; J. L. Kunz, 'Natural-Law Thinking in the Modern Science of International Law' (1961) 55 *The American Journal of International Law* 951; Anghie, *Imperialism*; J. Brown, *The Spanish Origins of International Law* (Oxford: Clarendon Press, 1934).

[32] G. Abi-Saab, 'Whither', 250.

[33] As per the Stoics, as described by Douzinas, *The End of Human Rights*, p. 52.

[34] Hobbes, *Leviathan*, p. 40.

of a break in community between the classical and modern age, when the individual became the sole actor not limited by community or tradition.[35] For Simma and Paulus this view of law, when understood within international law, portends a realist version of community with states constantly in a state of cold or hot war.[36]

Hobbes' reason is based upon the individual, and at its core law centres on self-preservation and death. In contrast Locke conceived of an era before the social contract as a perfect age, which humanity yielded in exchange for security of property.[37] Both Hobbes and Locke dismissed Aristotle's notion of development as *telos*, and argued that man had to give up independence to create the sovereign state. The individual is the centre of reason, not the community. For Hobbes and Locke reason no longer is based in antiquity and Christianity but rather embedded in humanity. Yet, similar to the Stoic explication, it is through reason that the way forward is found; thus *telos* and community are the centre of law and society.[38]

Hobbes suggests that justice may only be achieved through the sovereign state, thus making it the ideal legal order.[39] Accordingly, sovereignty is necessary to achieve justice. There can be no justice within global governance without an understanding of sovereignty. Justice does not require an international community, as individuals gain it through the sovereign state. But rather injustice continues within inter-state relations while it subsists without global governance.[40] Since the consent of states remains a basic requirement for any global system, Hobbes would not recognise any global sovereign.[41] The state order is based upon a contract relationship between it and an individual; thus a community may not be necessary for its creation. Similarly, consent is required in the international system; thus, here also, community becomes optional.[42] Accordingly, the

35 Douzinas, *The End of Human Rights*, p. 71.

36 Simma and Paulus, 'Facing the Challenge of Globalization', 269. They dismiss the purist versions of this form of realism as reflective of ninteenth-century international law but not as descriptive of today's law. See pp. 271–2.

37 Locke, *Two Treatises*.

38 For an alternative narrative on the state and sovereignty, see M. Foucault 'Two Lectures' in Michel Foucault *Power/Knowledge*, (ed. C. Gorden) (London: Harvester, 1980), pp. 95–7.

39 Hobbes, *Leviathan*, p. 100; T. Nagel, 'The Problem of Global Justice' (2005) 33 *Philosophy and Global Affairs* 113, 114.

40 Nagel, 'The Problem of Global Justice', 133.

41 N. Bobbio and D. Gobetti, *Thomas Hobbes and the Natural Law Tradition* (University of Chicago Press, 1993), p. xiii.

42 *Ibid.*, p. 69.

sovereign will of the state is paramount and any hindrance to this, including an international community, is ruinous. Often such sentiments stand at the core of arguments for a denial of present or any future international community, though this does not infer a state of nature, but rather relations based in power politics.[43]

Kant states that international relationship 'has been everywhere steadily increasing between the nations of the earth, has now extended so enormously that a violation of right in one part of the world is felt all over it'.[44] This oft-quoted line exemplifies Kant's vision of international law and community. Douzinas notes that Kant's vision of international law includes a notion of a binding international cosmopolitan law very much linked with Kant's view of rights as the basis of international law.[45] The link between Kantian philosophy and human rights has become more tangible in the post-Charter era, though there is some debate as to whether he was arguing for a statist or human rights vision of international community.[46] Kant articulates a need for a union amongst states analogous to that between individuals, forming a similar polity to the domestic system.[47] Tesón argues that Kant was one of the first to argue that '[r]espect for states is merely derivative of respect for persons. In this way, the notion of state sovereignty is redefined: the sovereignty of the state is dependent upon the state's domestic legitimacy; and therefore the principles of international justice must be congruent with the principles of internal justice'.[48] Kant argues that international and domestic law are inseparable, the strict division creating entirely different legal systems false.[49] Nussbaum suggests that Kant's indebtedness to Stoicism is clear in that his proposals are based upon a kingdom of free rational beings equal in humanity.[50] The Stoic view of a global community of humanity is evident in Kant's writing, though other philosophical developments during the Enlightenment are also present.

43 J. L. Goldsmith and E. Posner, *The Limits of International Law* (Oxford University Press, 2005); Franck, *The Power of Legitimacy.*

44 Kant, *Perpetual Peace*, p. 20.

45 Douzinas, *Human Rights and Empire.*

46 F. R. Tesón, 'Kantian Theory of International Law' (1992) 92 *Columbia Law Review* 53, 58.

47 Kant, *Perpetual Peace*, p. 10.

48 Tesón, 'Kantian Theory', 54; see also I. Kant: *The Metaphysics of Morals* (Cambridge University Press, 1996), pp. 114–15.

49 Tesón, 'Kantian Theory', 53.

50 Nussbaum, 'Kant and Stoic Cosmopolitanism', 12. Nussbaum also points to the implicit inequality both in Kant and the Stoic writers with regard to the place of women, slaves and the imperial/colonialist project, 14.

Believing that any international community must be based upon a federation of free states, Kant argued that this would eventually achieve perpetual peace.[51] This was part of his wider philosophy based upon universalism, though not necessarily communitarianism.[52] Tesón argues that Kant believed that the state of nature amongst states progresses towards the formation of an ideal federation that would mirror the relations of men under a civil constitution.[53] However, before this can occur, states, to be eligible to join this world community, must be based on a combination of rights, ideals and republicanism. This is one of the first articulations of a basic entrance requirement to an international community not expressed as dependent upon the notion of 'civilised states'. Instead, it links to a rights-based state. Today there is no state that would argue that it does not respect human rights nor claim to be just, but Kant's standard is arguably an objective threshold. It is also clear that this ideal does not as yet reflect the current factual situation.[54]

The historical development of international community mirrors the progress of the broader perceptions of community as described in Chapter 3. Historic deliberations on forms of commonality are clear, and the Eurocentric development of international law has left its mark on what this commonality involves. In discussing the present place of community within international law, the impact of this historical analysis is important. In this period, Kant and Hobbes represent opposite perceptions of international community but both recognise its role in governance and law. They also significantly contribute to development of the roles of the state, sovereignty and community as the bases of understanding the locus of international law.

7.1.4 *Community theories in contemporary international law*

The present perceptions of international community are inculcated into the global constitutionalisation debate. Two contemporary perspectives

[51] Kant, *Perpetual Peace*, p. 15.
[52] Nussbaum, 'Kant and Stoic Cosmopolitanism', 2.
[53] Tesón, 'Kantian Theory', 54, 59. Tesón's view of Kant can be contrasted with Capps, who criticises Tesón, arguing that he does not defend to the extent necessary the methodological and justificatory basis of Kantian theory, and further that Tesón does not adequately develop the second of Kant's major theses, which concerns the maintenance of peace by international legal institutions, concluding that Tesón's approach is closer to moral foreign policy than international law. P. Capps, 'The Kantian Project in International Law' (2001) 12 *European Journal of International Law* 1003.
[54] Turner, 'Delivering Lasting Peace', 135–49.

on community, Franck and cosmopolitanism, point towards its most common use. Franck represents the traditional statist approaches to international community, while cosmopolitanism characterises attempts, similar to the earlier discussions on Nancy, to move beyond some of its negative attributes. Whilst this is far from an complete exposition, this section aims to examine how these theories connect to the identification of subjects of international law and as such the holders of constituent and constituted power within constitutionalisation.

7.1.4.1 Franck

Franck, examining the same period as the previous section, states that

> [t]he world has evolved as a community of rules, a stockade within which all states are to be found, bound together by a set of common, or at least compatible, assumptions. These assumptions have been evident for some time. Vitoria, in the sixteenth century, noted the emergence of a 'law of nations' which 'exists clearly enough' and derives from 'a consensus of the greater part of the whole world ...' and Grotius, too, based much of a work dating to 1604 on what he called 'the consensus of all nations' or 'common consent of mankind,' which he traced back to Cicero's notion of human 'right reason' and Heraclites' 'universal form of reason or understanding ...'[55]

He asserts that the Westphalian version of the historic development of international law has seen the emergence of an international community, centring upon an understanding of an emergent consolidation of communal feeling developed over an extended period.

Placing community between two other similar, though underdeveloped groupings, a primitive association on the one hand and an 'international system' on the other, Franck argues that the former is indicative of a reality where there is no empathy or concern for others. The primitive society possesses no continuity; transactions are isolated and, if occurring, are neither within an established framework nor part of a series of transactions.[56] Franck relies on Hoffman's definition of an international system as yet underdeveloped into an international community. An international system is a 'pattern of relations between the basic units of world politics which is characterized by the scope of the objectives pursued by those units and of the tasks performed among them, as well as by the

[55] Franck, *The Power of Legitimacy*, p. 205.

[56] *Ibid.*, p. 197. This is also evident in the work of Dworkin; R. Dworkin, 'The Model of Rules' (1967) 35 *University of Chicago Law Review* 14; R. Dworkin, *Law's Empire* (Cambridge, MA: Harvard University Press, 1986).

means used in order to achieve those goals and perform those tasks'.[57] Franck argues that this is based upon the notion of reciprocity, as one transaction is part of a broader pattern of transactions, which each member recognises as such.

For Franck a community is based upon a social system of continuing interaction and transactions.[58] Reciprocity, linked to moral imperatives and values of fairness in international law, remains important to the emergence of community but, unlike Hoffman's international system, is not its sole feature.[59] If this defines community, then it begs the question of what happens to those in the community who do not have the means or the clout to engage in such interactions. This opens questions regarding the parity of interactions and whether this restricts participation to a potential member's ability to contribute to the mêlée, a difficulty previously raised regarding global governance networks.[60] If interactions lead to asymmetric membership, this may also lead to asymmetry between the holders of constituent power. To Franck, in a community reciprocal duties are paramount and an integral part of membership. However, as will be explored further below, his vision of community never quite gains the momentum for it to be established fully.

Franck identifies a moral community leading to a rule-based community.[61] For a grouping to qualify as a 'rule community', it must have two vital aspects: '[i]t must have agreed on a core of reciprocally applicable rules and it must also have agreed on a process for making and applying rules and resolving disputes about their meaning'.[62] Yet, this does not presuppose a sovereign hierarchal system. To be a community there must be rules as well as a legitimate process for the creation of rules that must be fairly applied. Resulting from the dialogue as an offshoot of reciprocity, community ensures fairness in the system.[63] Community guarantees compliance with the law, as shared moral senses will, together with

[57] Franck, *The Power of Legitimacy*, p. 199; S. Hoffman, 'International Systems and International Law' (1961) *World Politics* 207.

[58] Franck, *Fairness*, p. 10. [59] *Ibid.*

[60] Franck uses the WTO as an example of this transactional continuity. A state that loses in the Dispute Settlement procedure of the WTO today will remain in the organisation, as it will recognise that it is in its long-term interests. Franck, 'Legitimacy of Power', 92.

[61] Franck argues that when power relations fluctuate amongst international actors this can have a negative impact upon international law, arguing for instance that abuse of Article 2(4) of the UN Charter is an example of when legitimacy and power lead to a struggle for the soul of the 'community of nations'; Franck, 'Legitimacy of Power', 91.

[62] Franck, *Fairness*, p. 12, though is arguably what Franck's analysis currently reflects.

[63] *Ibid.*, p. 10.

the notion that each must do as they are legally required to, achieve such aims.[64] Franck acknowledges that his conception of international law and community is not without its detractors, particularly in the positivist camp.[65] He contrasts his ideas with those of Hart, though not without acknowledging the usefulness of this particular critique.

Regarding international law and relations to have come to a point where there is now 'an emerging sense of global community', Franck concedes that at other times this may not as yet be fully formed.[66] Surveying the future of international law, he states:

> As we enter the third millennium, there is much evidence of a global community, emerging out of a growing awareness of irrefutable interdependence, its imperatives and exigencies. It may be tempting to speak of emerging 'global communities': of trade, of environmental concerns, of security, of health measures, et cetera. It would, however, be inaccurate because these regimes are linked. A state's conformity with environmental policy will have an effect on its credit-worthiness in borrowing from the World Bank ... These multiple linkages, making different regimes interdependent, are evidence of community.[67]

Similar to Suárez, who, owing to its lack of unity, saw an imperfect universal community, both regard the international community as nascent, though surely international relations have developed since Suárez's writing in the seventeenth century. Therefore, the contemporary burgeoning of global constitutional law must be of a different character to the historical changes that writers in the early modern period of international law articulated.

Importantly, Franck argues that '[c]communities can be concentric and overlapping'.[68] The global community will not bring an end to states as communities or regional bases of power; these can coexist together as there is no exclusiveness in community. This centres sovereignty as elemental to Franck's statist approach but has some echoes of the Stoic multidimensional take on community. Where an actor in a community fulfils a number of roles depending on its position, this implies a more complex community and perhaps legal order. Franck refers to a striation of identifications that has no impact or impingement upon the state.[69] But what, then, is the point of a global community if it results in no basic change in the workings and attitudes of states? Can the global community, its

[64] *Ibid.*, p. 11.
[65] This would include those in the Hobbesian tradition outlined above.
[66] Franck, *Fairness*, p. 11. [67] *Ibid.*, p. 12. [68] *Ibid.*, p. 13. [69] *Ibid.*, p. 13.

imperatives and exigencies ever trump those of states if there is no manifest change in their functions? If this is the case, then constituent power cannot be based in subjects beyond states, and in such a scenario arguably a constitutional system cannot emerge, as it would be difficult to balance state interests with the need for democratic legitimacy. State consent is not interchangeable with legitimacy within a legal order. Sands argues that Franck's view of community is a misapplied version of Dworkin's domestic community and that this state-bound account results in misdirection when examining international law.[70] If this is the case, it certainly explains why Kant and Franck, while being quite close in overall outlook towards the importance of international law, are as distinctly different in their views of sovereignty.

Franck's statist approach dismisses recent developments in international law such as the role of international organisations. It retains the ghost of Westphalian sovereignty and its exclusionary nature. Franck's community is narrow and at times moralistic, and this enables critics of international law, who do not recognise international law as a legitimate legal order, to continue with their critique.[71] Franck holds certain in his enthusiasm for an international law that is legitimate and accepted as such; however, his reliance on a statist view of community stifles any further progression of the international legal order into a more complex system. If utilising Franck's community to identify the holders of constituent and constituted power within constitutionalisation, their number and nature (that is, states) would not have changed significantly from the pre-constitutionalised international order.

In later debates, Franck argues for substantial changes to international legal norms. This suggests that he does not see community as instrumental to any development towards constitutionalism; instead he regards it as part of the legitimacy of international law itself. Kritsiotis identifies a 'triumphant claim … as international law enters its "post-ontological era" '.[72] These broad claims of constitutionalisation certainly rely on international law having moved beyond infancy. Franck develops the idea of community as part of his broader concern with future international law. In his

[70] P. J. Sands, 'Environment, Community and International Law' (1999) 30 *Harvard Journal of International Law* 393, 400.

[71] Goldsmith and Posner *The Limits of International Law*, pp. 185–204.

[72] D. Kritsiotis, 'Imagining the International Community' (2002) 13 *European Journal of International Law*' 961, 962; Franck stated in 2006 that some of the talk regarding the post-ontological era was hubris, though whether he really reflected on his commitment to the ideal of an international community is debatable. 'Legitimacy of Power', 91.

writing, community has slowly broadened and, though it has become wider than a truly statist model, it basically remains within its demesne thus restraining arguments on legitimacy. He later relies on the world community when decrying some more recent events such as the invasion of Iraq, arguing that 'a community is constituted not only by its substantive rules, but also by those institutional processes that implement the rules'.[73] At the core of Franck's argument is a community defined by the idea of continuity and reciprocity as well as a shared set of moral values and imperatives. But, as Franck did not always assert that we had reached this point, it is more aspirational than a reflection of law's operation.

7.1.4.2 Cosmopolitanism

Cosmopolitanism aims to broaden the understanding of international law and particularly international human rights to conceive of an international legal order where the subjects of international law are ensconced in a democratic order in which legal legitimacy is paramount. It offers an alternative to state-based or multiple points of community. With universal solidarity based upon a singular world community, cosmopolitan law focuses on a rights-based international law that has international institutions at its core. Contemporary cosmopolitanism comes in many varieties; however, at its core lies the claim of a global community based upon institutions of varying forms, where all humanity is represented, and justice and rights are vindicated.[74] It seeks to establish international law as intrinsically fair and participatory. However, cosmopolitanism relies on present international law.[75] The classical Stoic traditions, as well as Kant's *Perpetual Peace*, are precursors to the more recent reassertions of cosmopolitanism, but in clearly inheriting from both they also inculcate their flaws.[76] Nevertheless, the cosmopolitanism world community offers a basis on which to identify the holders of constituent and constituted power within constitutionalisation.

While the twentieth-century account of cosmopolitanism developed in the era of the Cold War, according to Douzinas, of late it has taken a more

[73] Franck, 'Legitimacy of Power', 102.

[74] Economic Cosmopolitanism in the form of Smith or Friedman does not form part of this discussion.

[75] D. Zolo, 'A Cosmopolitan Philosophy of International Law? A Realist Approach' (1999) 12 *Ratio Juris* 429, 431–2; Habermas, *Divided*; R. M. Pierik and W. G. Werner (eds.), *Cosmopolitanism in Context: Perspectives from International Law and Political Theory* (Cambridge University Press, 2010).

[76] Cosmopolitanism also has roots in the cynics and particularly Diogenes' claim to be a citizen of the world; T. Francklin, *The Works of Lucian* (London: T. Cadwell, 1780).

realistic approach incorporating theories of the rule of law and global democracy.[77] Thus, cosmopolitanism is not as statist as Franck's theory, though it is interesting to note that it does not see an end to the sovereign state, but just a weakening of power as international and transnational organisations become more influential. While cosmopolitanism does not possess new philosophical underpinnings, in that it borrows from many others we have already examined, it delivers a twenty-first-century examination of the possibilities for a world community. Habermas asserts that cosmopolitanism should end the state-bound status of international law centred upon alliances whose flexible nature would be replaced by stricter, more constitutional principles.[78] This places international law and, more particularly, human rights law above any moral code but as part of a core global legal order.

According to Douzinas, cosmopolitanism positions itself as an enemy of patriotism and nationalism, and promises a global social process resulting in institutions and world citizenship. This, he argues, is cosmopolitan globalisation with a human face.[79] Cosmopolitanism directly relates to the discussions of constitutionalism and the core elements that it encompasses, such as the rule of law or democratic legitimacy, which are included within the global liberalism that Douzinas regards as being core to the cosmopolitan approach.[80] Benhabib, one of the leading proponents of cosmopolitanism, suggests that '[w]e may need to envisage a transition from the "soft power" of global civil society to the constitutionalisation of international law'.[81] Cosmopolitanism and community meet on this ground, where the world community is called on to intervene to uphold cosmopolitan norms of human rights. Cosmopolitanism rejects attempts at imperialistic or hegemonic principles though at the same time it calls for a global moral liberalism. For example, Habermas concedes that there is a need to avoid possible imperialism in the implementation of human rights norms and seeks to avoid such a possibility.

Cosmopolitan law may be better served in eschewing community altogether in its quest for a new era of international institutional leadership and authority. It must be conceded that, similar to Nancy, cosmopolitanism attempts to establish an international community based upon engagement. Yet, the imperialist roots Habermas refers to cannot easily be escaped, but coupling the future of international law to the international

[77] Douzinas, *Human Rights and Empire*, p. 142.
[78] *Ibid.*, p. 164.
[79] *Ibid.*, pp. 134, 135. [80] *Ibid.*, p. 142.
[81] S. Benhabib, *Another Cosmopolitanism* (Oxford University Press, 2006), p. 72.

community will not hasten any fundamental change. Anghie highlights the dangers of imperialism in international law; he argues that often the price of membership of the international community was the acceptance of European standards of law that re-entrenched notions of colonial superiority, and as such international law 'remains oblivious to its imperial structures even when continuing to reproduce them'.[82] Even for those accepted members of the international community, from Anghie's reasoning their membership is based upon a dichotomy of dominance and not of full consent. Those states that fall outside the international community, as failing to meet a standard based upon a Eurocentric community, are excluded from the formation of law. This could extend to areas that are not represented in an international state-based order, such as the regions of disputed territorial control, such as Western Sahara, or where sovereignty was forgone, such as Greenland or the British Virgin Islands. Though it is a much broader point, it limits the discussion to notions of sovereignty and statehood. As has been pointed out by Yasuki, this colonial attitude is not restricted to the West, but rather is prevalent in many areas of international legal history.[83]

The cosmopolitan community exposes a variety of subjects to the international community; it moves beyond statist international law to recognise that international institutions and individuals play an important role in the global legal order. This offers a basis for the identification of subjects of constitutionalisation; however, it does not make clear who the holders of constituent or constituted power are in this cosmopolitan order. In inculcating notions of legalism and democracy within its theory, cosmopolitanism is perhaps more readily adopted into constitutionalisation than other international community theories. Cosmopolitanism reflects a more nuanced view of the present international legal order; however, its views of community also present the divergent nature of present conceptions of the international community. While cosmopolitanism attempts to ingrain a liberalism that eschews the imperialism of international law, the fact that it is bound to this discourse offers further proof of the general

[82] Anghie, *Imperialism*, p. 312.

[83] O. Yasuki, 'When Was the Law of International Society Born? – An Inquiry of the History of the International Law from an Intercivilizational Perspective' (2000) 2 *Journal of the History of International Law* 1; indeed to restrict the colonial attitude to the West is colonial in itself, as it does not recognise the imperial prowess of other regions. As Yasuki also argues, even within states that were former colonies, colonialist attitudes are often reasserted upon minority groups within the state.

conceptions of the international community, which largely remain statist and bound to the deficiencies of the present global legal order.

7.1.5 *International community in global constitutionalisation theories*

While it is not asserted that constitutionalisation theories are based upon Suárez's international community, innately exclusionary (Eurocentric) seventeenth-century assertions of sovereignty these remain prescient. The classical view of community linked to states cannot be entirely removed from its descendants. Despite major developments in global affairs, including the creation of international organisations and the place of the individual in international law, the state remains core to many conceptions of the international community. This does not suggest that this type of international community is always relied upon within the constitutionalisation debate; yet its historical understandings remain relevant.

Chapter 3 established that while the term 'community' may not have an exact content, the underlying connotations of its general use are evident; a point to be reiterated regarding international community. Community's binary nature has an exclusionary and often dampening effect on both those within and outside its remit. Extending this analysis of community to its international counterpart, it is argued that community conceals some of the lawmaking activity in international relations. Those outside the community, who may in fact take part in the creation of law, are not considered elemental. International community fails to establish a space that encompasses all the relevant interactions in the international legal order. This results in the omission of holders of constituent power from the global legal order, as they remain outside of the community. This may include states that the international community generally does not consider to be aligned with community values. Such states are not described as participants within the community and are often characterised or referred to as pariah states,[84] failed states or, in a pejorative sense, as least

[84] An interesting example of exclusion from the international community is Tomuschat's discussion of treaties in his course at The Hague. While discussing the nature of Security Council resolutions and their place as a source of international law, Tomuschat uses the example of Security Council Resolution 687(1991), which 'invited' Iraq to ratify the Convention on the Prohibition of the Development, Production and Stockpiling of Bacteriological (Biological) and Toxin Weapons. In signing the Convention, Tomuschat argues that Iraq may be able to join the community of states parties to the Treaty; '[t]he *diktat* thus spares Iraq the stigma of becoming an outcast subject to a special regime like the one reserved to the ex-enemy States under the UN Charter'. Another similar example

developed states, which are not considered to 'fully embody the nation-state form' or, in Franck's terms, are unable to participate fully on a reciprocal basis.[85] This process of exclusion is based upon notions of commonality that could very easily be traced back to the idea of civilised and non-civilised participants in international law.[86] The consequence of this is that international law is created outside of its community structure.

Chapter 3 established that, in its most common articulation, community suggests an inner harmony that precludes any suggestion of dispute, discussion or multiplicity in its governance structure. To become a member of the international community one signs up to the rules, and thereafter it is only on the suggestion of the powers within the community that any change or development may occur. This is problematic, as it is usually through disagreement and negotiation that international law develops, particularly in the case of customary international law.[87] For law to develop or change, participants have to distance themselves from the established practice and institute a new one. The inner harmony suggested by an international community can be regressive. Though often presented in opposition to individualism or atomisation, community does not acknowledge the disparate positions of its own members and, in instituting concord, precludes any meaningful discussion of development. This makes an easy argument for those who propose a Hobbesian view of self-interest in international law. If there is no community, it is often suggested that this is owing to states' self-interest and beyond this that there is no requirement for states to form a community, as the system is sufficient. By contrast, in a utilitarian 'greater good' concept '[c]ommunity is largely understood as oppositional to individualism. The result of this dualisation is that both alternatives are defined by each other, thereby foreclosing additional possibilities.'[88] Generally international community creates a two-tiered international law, which further legitimises arguments made against global constitutionalisation establishing

discussed by Tomuschat is North Korea and its treatment as a hermit state that does not engage with Tomuschat's international community, Tomuschat, 'Obligations', 272–3.

[85] Buchanan and Pahuja, 'Law, Nation', 146.

[86] M. Koskenniemi, 'International Law in Europe: Between Tradition and Renewal' (2005) 16 *European Journal of International Law* 113, 116.

[87] F. L. Kirgis, 'Custom on a Sliding Scale' (1987) 81 *American Journal of International Law* 146.

[88] D. Otto, 'Subalternity and International Law: The Problems of Global Community and the Incommensurability of Difference' (1996) 5 *Social and Legal Studies* 337, 357; *The Paquete Habana; The Lola*, 175 U.S. 677, 700 (1900), which repeatedly refers to civilised states, including 'the Empire of Japan (the last state admitted into the rank of civilized nations)'.

a coherent system. Basing constitutionalisation upon an unreconstituted international law founded upon nineteenth-century suppositions and Enlightenment ideals of state equality will simply reproduce the inequality that already subsists in current international law.

The persistence of international community serves to maintain further inequalities. Sovereign equality, protected by a statist conception of international community, determines a set of standards inapplicable to the originators of these standards. Sovereign equality enables differentiation between those states considered to be legitimate community members and those that are not; the very nature of a state-based international community reinforces the already discredited notions of civilised and uncivilised or developed and developing states as membership based upon unequal status. It also establishes a hierarchy of members, which may provide some legitimate basis for the interactions within the system, but not one linked to constituent power. This includes both state actors excluded owing to their lack of shared mores and non-state actors who, as objects of international law, are not considered to be community members on the basis of lack of commonality.

In 1948, Gross described the Peace of Westphalia as 'being the first of several attempts to establish something resembling world unity on the basis of states exercising untrammelled sovereignty over certain territories'.[89] Indeed, he goes on to argue that the Treaty itself slowed the progression towards an international community, as international law subsequently evolved beyond the parameters it set.[90] The traditional understanding of international law, which is reinforced most ardently in the ICJ Statute under Article 38, emphasises treaty and customary international law as the dual core sources of international law.[91]

This establishes sovereignty as the mainstay of international legal development and community. The consent of the state is central to its creation. This disregards any question regarding the impact of decolonisation and the role of the Global South in the choice of the principles now core to international law.[92] It also undermines the place and function of international organisations in the development of law.[93] Ignoring the role of

[89] L. Gross, 'The Peace of Westphalia 1644–1948' (1948) 42 *American Journal of International Law* 20, 20.

[90] *Ibid.*, 34–5.

[91] Statute of the International Court of Justice, 15 *UNCIO* 355, Article 38.

[92] Otto, 'Subalternity', 337.

[93] J. Kammerhofer, 'Uncertainty in the Formal Sources of International Law: Customary International Law and Some of Its Problems' (2004) 15 *European Journal of International Law* 523.

Security Council or General Assembly resolutions, the work of the WTO and to some extent the EU, the process of change in international law that constitutionalism envisages, the absence of actors such as international organisations in the formation of law questions the place of consent and, in many ways, thus the place of community itself. If community reinforces positioning based on consent and Westphalian sovereignty, it hinders rather than aids any comprehensive debate on constitutionalism.[94]

With the exception of movements such as the New International Economic Order of the 1960s and 1970s, the basic strands of the international community's fundamental order have changed little. Attempts to emerge from the long-standing basis of sovereign equality of states challenge the basis of community and, in the absence of a fundamental shift, face instituted inertia. That the New International Economic Order came to nought stresses the fact that change from within the international community is either a slow process or entirely non-existent. Members seeking to change the community risk the possibility of being ostracised as members; therefore they must remain loyal to its predetermined parameters. Pahuja describes this quite neatly as the Other, who is subjected to the West's domination of what is universal, and who is excluded from it as something different to the West and yet joins and becomes part of it: 'this paradox – of the circular self constitution of Other and self combined with the universal applicability of that claim – explains, at least in part, the impelling dynamic of international law and its puzzling containment of both liberatory promise and imperializing peril'.[95]

Furthermore, an appeal to the importance of the 'international community' often stifles action, for example, China's call for the 'international community' to respect Burma's judicial sovereignty when it had tried Aung San Suu Kyi.[96] This appealed to the traditional community's own central tenant, sovereign equality, as China attempted to dampen other members' will to produce change. This use of community in a legitimising role is part of the diminishing effect brought about by a reliance upon harmony. A state disregarding an elementary tenet of community

[94] Similar arguments could also be made around individuals, minority groups and civic society amongst others. This is presenting a traditional understanding of international law as the basis for argument.

[95] S. Pahuja, 'The Postcoloniality of International Law' (2005) 46 *Harvard Journal of International Law* 459, 461. Pahuja argues that because of this even those strategies that seek to achieve real universality or examinations of the politics of international law are destined to 'reproduce the imperializing urge'.

[96] 'China Calls on West to "Respect" New Detention of Aung San Suu Kyi', *The Times* (London), 12 August 2009.

in times of crisis or debate is not satisfying its role.[97] China, in asserting international law, and more importantly sovereign equality, is reminding those states or bodies calling for change in the form of human rights, of what being part of international law and community requires, that ultimately the core rule of the community is that of state consent and states themselves are at its heart, and that to challenge this is to challenge and undermine the community.

In conclusion, the legal context created by community is not one that serves international law's development; instead it further institutionalises the perception of the international community as a negative and hierarchal space. While the use of international community may not always seek to reinforce the more traditional elements of international law, this is often how it manifests itself, and this is repeated within global constitutionalisation theories, such as those developed by Simma or Mosler. By entangling law and community as legitimising forces, international law based upon the sovereign equality of states buttresses the status quo ante, restricting development.

The manifestation of the innate duality of community establishes a negative space both internally and externally. Put simply, it creates categories of participants in international law; those outside and those within the international community, and even those within these groups are subdivided again. This leads to critical questions. If only those within the international community create constitutional law, is it legitimate to truly claim that it is a global community? If only certain categories of actors are considered members of the community, does this establish a hierarchy of law, some elements of which are more legitimate than other elements? International community often serves a normative function in constitutionalisation. At times presented as the legitimisation of legal regimes or reform, or of a particular perspective on how international law should and does operate, it is the platform on which legitimisation of the theory of constitutionalism often occurs. The concept of the international community is founded upon self-imposed limitations, which, if transposed into constitutionalisation, will restrain its progress. These limitations include the margins that are formed by limiting constitutionalism to the ill-defined international community that establishes community as either a descriptive or normative subject.[98]

97 Buchanan and Pahuja, 'Law, Nation', 139.

98 See, for example, T. Giergerich, 'The *Is* and *Ought* of International Constitutionalism: How Far Have We Come on Habermas' Road to a "Well-Considered Constitutionalization of International Law"' (2009) 10 *German Law Journal* 31, 42.

No matter the nature of community's definitions, the perceived insistence on solidarity, compatibility or shared norms creates divisions rather than recognising sustained relations as more characteristic of the existing context in which constituent and constituted power holders interact. The central conclusion here is that within global constitutionalisation community should be displaced by another concept. To characterise constitutional subjects and the holders of constituent power as members of a community would be to carry forward the difficulties with the historical and present use of international law. Thus, an alternative must be put forward to identify the constitutional subjects and the holders of constituent power.

7.2 International constituency

Any alternative basis for identifying constituent power holders in a global constitutional order must support the operation of normative constitutionalism. International constituency proffers such an alternative even if it also possesses some potentially problematic elements. Having dismissed community as a suitable basis in Chapter 3 and its international counterpart in the preceding sections, here the groundwork for a discussion on whether an international constituency is significantly better than an international community as a basis for understanding the exercise of constituent and constituted power has been set. As discussed in Chapter 3, constituencies create spaces based upon the interaction between constituted and constituent power, ensuring the negotiation of competing interests amongst an array of participants engaged in the process of constitutionalisation. The nature of constituent power is such that its holders do not necessarily share the same mores. Constituency produces a space within which dissent and disagreement form an integral part of the process. Since it does not intimate harmony, constituency facilitates an on-going debate, reflecting the range of interests amongst constituent power holders. Existence outside the constituency is not negative, nor is holding characteristics or interests that the majority do not share. Constituency's limits are of a procedural not a substantive nature.

This section examines three contemporary uses of constituency within international law. Before utilising constituency within global constitutionalisation, it is crucial to understand its current, though limited use in wider international law. First, this section examines Henkin's use of constituency; second, global administrative law; and finally, international economic law.[99] In particular, this section focuses on whether constituency is analogous with community, and further if an international constituency is limited to states or includes other actors thus going some way to being a more credible international constitutional grouping. The limited use of constituency within international law is shown by the scarcity of examples open to analysis. As discussed in Chapter 3, within domestic legal orders, constituency often limits itself to an electorate and remains unconsidered in the context of a wider constituent power. This section considers whether it occupies a similar position in international law. Relying on the discussions in earlier chapters it may be relatively straightforward to deploy the international constituency in a limited fashion, which inevitably leads to a state model. Such a narrow approach weakens its claim to be a fully operational element in global constitutionalism, and this section aims to consider its broader potential.

Constituency's basis in process enables it to evolve; as such, international constituency should allow for an overlapping and complementary understanding of international law that is not based upon a zero-sum debate on what is or is not a subject or object of law. This necessarily should settle whether normative constitutionalism with constituent actors is potentially possible in any of the global constitutionalisation proposals. The first part questions whether constituency can be employed to define subjects of a potential global constitutional order or, in recognising it as a fully realised system in constitutional terms, the subjects of constitutionalisation and the holders of constituent power. The following section offers an alternative to international community that may lay a foundation for a constitutionalisation process.

7.2.1 Henkin's international constituency

Henkin discusses constituency as part of what he exemplifies as the interstate system of international law. Somewhat similar to Franck's discussion of international community, he uses constituency to differentiate between differing degrees of integration in the international legal order. Deciphering whether differences between the latter and constituency exist is crucial in considering whether it can be an alternative to the Frankian international community.

[99] Other examples include A. Slaughter, 'Liberal Theory of International Law' (2000) 94 *American Society of International Law Proceedings* 240, 248, referring to a constituency of NGOs.

Henkin argues that: 'the constituency of the international society is different. The "persons" constituting international society are not individual human beings but political entities, "states" and the society is an inter-state system, a system of states.'[100] Here, Henkin focuses on the individual as the sole potential subject of constituency in domestic law, a role which is difficult for the state to replicate within international law. He refers to constituency within international law as standing in contrast to its domestic counterpart, but perhaps in doing so he restricts it and arguably confuses it with constituted power. The ability to exercise power legitimately is different to establishing the group that may do so. Henkin recognises states as the sole exercisers of power within international law. Arguably, however, this fact does not establish a state's legitimate right to hold constituted power within the global legal order.

In Henkin's understanding of international law, the state holds the ultimate authority to make law with other states. This forms the roots of Henkin's argument. Yet, arguably, the state merely represents its own domestic constituency that has granted to that state the authority to exercise sovereign power and to make international law. Potentially, the state is more akin to a plenipotentiary, who has been granted the authority, or in this characterisation the constituted power, to exercise power on the behalf of the domestic constituency. This is entirely different to an international constituency, which even the most democratic state cannot legitimately represent, as its interests lie first with the state and not with the broader world. Decisions on issues of international interest, for example climate change, require states to take not only their own interests into account, but also the interests of the entire world. Democratically elected officials from countries are there on the basis of representing their own states' interests. In Henkin's view it is unclear who represents the world constituency within an international law consisting of 'persons (states) constituting the international society'. Henkin's view of international law does not appear to offer a solution to this issue. He identifies constituency with society and constituted power. As discussed in Chapter 3, constituted power in domestic law is recognised as part of a hierarchy of norms and linked to and associated with constitutional authority. Constituency based on the idea that this power is attained through delegation from the people remains central to questions of ultimate authority within a state, which seems to differ

[100] L. Henkin, *International Law: Politics and Values* (The Hague: Kluwer, 1995), p. 5.

from Henkin's view of international constituency linked to states as the subjects of international law.[101]

Henkin's position reflects his general view of international law in its most traditional Westphalian form. Yet, while asserting that this inter-state analysis reflects the status quo and will do so well into the twenty-first century, he acknowledges that there was a rising debate about whether to include more 'persons' into a broader 'variegated constituency'.[102] This leads to a further question regarding international actors, such as the UN Secretary General. In Henkin's view of international society, what constituency would the holder of such an office become responsible to and whose interests should he or she take into account when making decisions? It may be UN members collectively as states or it could be a broader understanding of the interests that a Secretary General should consider essential based within the UN Charter. This does not disprove Henkin's argument that international law is ultimately inter-state. But this question of the identification of constituent power holders does undermine the assertion that if there is an international constituency, it can simply be identified as consisting of states in an international society, as it is they who make law. The fundamental problem of how states legitimately exercise this power and further questions regarding democratic legitimacy make this problematic and, coupled with the intermixing of constituted power with constituency, ever more challenging.[103] Henkin's constituency appears to replicate many of the issues discussed regarding international community. It does not establish a nexus between constituted and constituent power and thus would not appear to be an adequate basis for understanding the subjects of global constitutionalisation. As such an alternate reading of constituency is necessary.

7.2.2 Global administrative law

As previously discussed global administrative law aims to examine transparency, participation, review and accountability within

[101] Wheatley, *The Democratic Legitimacy of International Law*, pp. 123–33; and Loughlin, *Idea of Public Law*, pp. 61–4, 99.

[102] Henkin, *Politics and Values*, pp. 5, 168. Even for the mid 1990s this is perhaps an underestimation, with writers such as Petersmann and Fassbender already proposing a constitutional analysis of international law: Petersmann, 'How to Reform the UN', 421; and Fassbender, 'The United Nations Charter'.

[103] This argument is based on the notion of some form of constitutional democratic process in domestic law; whether all states can claim such legitimacy is not within the remit of this piece.

global governance. Further, it claims that the strict barriers between international and domestic law are no longer as prevalent as they once were, requiring a new form of analysis to comprehend global governance. It 'is an effort to systematize studies in diverse national, transnational, and international settings that relate to the administrative law of global governance'.[104] Its varied objectives range from the control of government power and protection of individual rights, to the effective administration of tasks to assure governmental accountability and secure participation in the decision-making processes.[105] It is not aiming to rationalise fully the entirety of international law but rather to understand characteristics of its operation. Two aspects of constituency in global administrative law are examined, constituency in the broad debate on international administrative and constitutional law, and within the work of two academics, Macdonald and Macdonald, who directly tackle issues related to constituency in international law.

In domestic law, constitutional law establishes the boundaries and creates the norms within which administrative law operates. While it is possible to identify domestic administrative law elements that are similar or even identical to concepts in operation in international law, the transfer upwards is not necessarily straightforward. Kingsbury accepts that while the 'constitutionalist commitment to publicness' exists, and further that as international law currently operates, there is 'no coherence of structure' to constitutionalism, nor is it likely that this aspiration will be achieved in the near future.[106] His argument is that while there is global administrative law, there is no substantive international constitutional order on which it rests. This infers that an international constituency can subsist without constitutionalisation and as such can have a wider role to play within international law and governance. Kingsbury's assertion that a global administrative law is possible without international constitutional law may appear counterintuitive. It is hard to reconcile a broad notion of a hybrid law that inhabits both international and domestic spheres that is not mutually linked to constituency and constitutionalism in domestic and international law. While all elements of administrative law do not necessarily have to encompass constitutional law, administrative law is

[104] Kingsbury, Kirsch and Stewart, 'The Emergence', 15.

[105] Craig, *Administrative Law*, p. 3.

[106] Kingsbury, 'Concept of "Law"', 36. The Institute for International Law and Justice at NYU focuses to a large extent upon global administrative law. It seeks to define the concept and gather the important resources to enable research in this area to be more fruitful. Further details may be found at www.iilj.org/GAL, accessed 30 August 2013.

indelibly linked to the constitutional order that it functions to buttress. Though there is some debate as to the core purpose of administrative law in domestic law, other than a strict positivist interpretation, it is generally considered to be bound and linked to constitutional law or at the very least the system of governance, granting to it its normative form.[107]

Global administrative law in the absence of either a constituency or constitutionalism, or rather, to use Kingsbury's language, in the absence of a 'rich constitution', is from its inception limited. For example, to what constituency does global administrative law apply if, as Kingsbury and Kirsch argue, consent-based international law is no longer even theoretically provable?[108] Kingsbury recognises, as an aspect of international law, constituted power, though not constituent power. Thus, there is no contiguous constitutional law to identify the constituency on whose behalf it seeks to function. This leaves Kingsbury with an administrative law that has no normative basis and works for a non-specific assemblage of international actors. Kingsbury does not necessarily claim that an entire system of global administrative law has emerged, much as some constitutionalisation theorists point to nascent elements within international law.

Global administrative law is particularly useful in constructively conceiving of governance beyond either traditional international or domestic law. The use of constituency in global administrative law exemplifies a more useful understanding of how the subjects of international law may be understood, though the lack of nexus between constituent and constituted power limits the utility of such an understanding. Macdonald and Macdonald employ the domestic exploitation of constituency within public law to highlight the difficulties surrounding democracy and global administrative law.[109] They argue that any reallocation of power, such as in the appointment of governmental officials or officers, can only 'legitimately be delegated from one (elected) agent to another (non-elected) agent if both *share the same public constituency*'.[110] This is a critical consideration in identifying the holders of constituent and constituted power in international law. In a domestic constitutional structure, the

[107] Craig, *Administrative Law*, p. 3.

[108] Kirsch and Kingsbury note that with the development of international law over the past number of years, '[i]t is improbable that a traditional vision of international law as essentially a contractual order of equal states is even theoretically operable', 17. N. Kirsch and B. Kingsbury, 'Introduction: Global Governance and Global Administrative Law in the International Legal Order' (2006) 17 *European Journal of International Law* 1, 13.

[109] Macdonald and Macdonald, 'Non-Electoral Accountability', 89.

[110] *Ibid.*, 98; emphasis in original.

constituency of the elected agent is the same as the domestic, non-elected official appointed by the elected agent, therefore maintaining democratic accountability. The non-elected official, such as a civil servant, can be held to account and legitimated through the link to the elected official and as such to the constituency.

This is the key issue identified by Macdonald and Macdonald. They argue that this same legitimisation cannot be found in the international sphere since the constituency of the elected (or non-elected in the case of some states) agent is not the same as the constituency of the international official. The 'stakeholders' or actors that form the international constituency have an interest in the actions of an international official appointed by state agents, through a process of co-operation with other states. The domestic and international constituencies are not contiguous therefore preventing any claim to a democratic process in the appointment of the non-elected official. The international official cannot be said to be democratically mandated or to be held to account by the international constituency it now serves.

Closely intertwined with democracy, Macdonald and Macdonald's view of constituency directly links to the exercise of constituent power within constitutionalism. The assertion that the constituencies at the domestic and international levels are different and thus cannot be identified and operate through a simple inter-state theory of international law remains a point of conflict in current discussions of constitutionalisation. Domestic constituencies compose one homogeneous set of actors that, more often than not, are individuals. This cannot simply be transposed, as Henkin suggests, into international law through inter-state activity or through the representation of the domestic constituency within international law.

Macdonald and Macdonald argue that international law has overlapping 'stakeholder constituencies'.[111] Stakeholders can be identified as those with interests in a particular issue. In the case of constitutionalisation, those with an interest in the constitutional legal order could compose these stakeholders. Global legal stakeholder constituencies may be identified in substantive areas such as environmental, trade, human rights or humanitarian law. The lack of one centralised constituency, at the very least, creates an understanding of constituency linked to interest and not necessarily a domestic individualist paradigm. This mirrors the growth of the sectoral constitutionalisation debate, particularly in, for

[111] *Ibid.*, 98; the problem is that an electoral system that would take account of the varied overlapping constituencies would be overly complex.

example, trade law. For sectoral constitutionalisation, it would mean that the constituency is made up of those who have an interest or a stake in the organisation or area of international law. These stakeholders would hold constituent power. For world order constitutionalisation, it would mean that the stakeholders or holders of constituent power would encompass all those who have an interest in the global legal order.

If constituency is to offer a space in which constitutionalisation occurs, then the constitutional constituency will have to be centralised to enable the holders of constituent power to exercise their warrant. From this consolidated constituency, the other sectors may emerge and operate. These sectors may have sub-constituencies overlapping, as Macdonald and Macdonald suggest, but the core constituency linked to constitutionalism would have to be the mainstay of any global constitutionalisation process. Macdonald and Macdonald's 'decentralized non-state actors' is instructive as it recognises the innate difficulties associated with electoral democracy and other similar administrative law concerns.[112] The shared derivation between constitutional and administrative law is clear. Macdonald and Macdonald clearly identify the difficulty, particularly with regard to the exercise of constituent power, if the international constituency is limited to states. This echoes some of the discussion in Chapter 3 on why constituency should be understood in terms of process rather than substance.

While global administrative law serves a thematically similar purpose to the constitutionalisation debate, the analysis of both fails to correlate. Global administrative law is instructive in understanding constituency and constituent power within international law. The deficiencies identified by Macdonald and Macdonald regarding the differences between domestic and international constituencies are central to the argument that constitutionalisation must move beyond the state to ensure that elements of normative constitutionalism, most particularly democratic legitimacy, become embedded into any constitutionalisation process. The form of constituency identified by Macdonald and Macdonald comes very close to establishing an international constituency, which would enable constituent power holders to exercise their warrant. It also moves away from the entirely statist view represented by Henkin, and broadens the debate on constituency from an entirely statist position.

[112] *Ibid.*, 99.

7.2.3 *International economic law: constituencies within the World Bank Group and the IMF*

Constituency serves some of the organisational structures of international economic law, specifically in the management and decision-making of the World Bank Group and the International Monetary Fund (IMF). At times employed to describe the distinction between the public/private sectors or between the state and non-state actors, the use of 'constituency' in the context of the World Bank and the IMF is the most consistent utilisation of the term within international economic law.[113] As their membership grew and a system of increasingly complex decision-making was acquired, constituency's use evolved alongside the governance structures of both organisations. In both organisations, constituencies set the terms of voting for members.

Within both organisations, constituencies consist of blocks of countries with loose geographic or other fairly limited connections. While the USA, the UK, France, Germany and Japan are constituencies in and of themselves, and following recent reforms will eventually be joined by China, other states are grouped together. These constituencies change as the quota assigned to each member differs owing to variances in the member's relative economic position or as new members join the organisations.[114] These constituencies operate as a tool to allow the organisations to function effectively, while still recognising the individual needs of their members.[115] These state groupings are commonly referred to as constituencies both by the organisations and in the literature.[116] The constituencies bring states together for the purpose of voting in the plenary bodies, the Boards of Governors, and in the appointment of the Executive Boards, with the latter undertaking the day-to-day running of these organisations.

Other than occupying a very broad geographical area, though not necessarily bordering neighbours or within the same continent, these groups or constituencies have no ideological or definable commonality

[113] See, for example, Petersmann, '21st Century', 3. See also G. Teubner, 'The Two Faces of Janus, Rethinking Legal Pluralism' (1991–1992) 13 *Cardozo Law Review* 1443; Teubner, 'Societal Constitutionalism', 3.

[114] Quotas are based upon subscriptions and relative economic power. Each constituency is represented by an Executive Director who represents its relative voting strength within the organisation.

[115] See, broadly, A. H. Qureshi and A. R. Ziegler, *International Economic Law*, 2nd edn (London: Sweet & Maxwell, 2007), pp. 121–258, 507–32.

[116] *A Guide to the World Bank* (World Bank Publications, 2007), Appendix E.

as the basis of their grouping. Their linkages within the constituencies are by agreement and in an effort to maintain relatively similar voting power between the blocks.[117] The arrangements are usually voluntary, and split voting is not permitted. As such, each constituency votes as a single block.[118] This begs the question of whether there is assurance that all members of a particular constituency are represented, and, if not, whether they should be reconstituted to provide for more homogeneity in terms of the constituent members' interests, their relative power or to provide each constituency with equal power.[119] These constituencies are of import, as they directly link to both voting and distribution of power. Although such queries pertain to the operation of the World Bank and the IMF, and therefore are outside the immediate remit of this work, they also raise questions regarding the use of constituency in international law.

Two economists, Leech and Leech, argue that the composition and use of these constituencies at the IMF and World Bank means that 'each country's real voting power lies not just in the number of votes it has but in its ability to use them to determine decisions taken by voting'.[120] This, they argue, is not simply owing to the United States' influence as a global economic power, but also simply from the construction of the rules that are applied.[121] This link between constituency and voting has important

[117] Though the percentage allocated to each constituency varies from 1.92 per cent to 4.8 per cent. This does not include the five single state constituencies. See, further, 'International Bank For Reconstruction And Development Voting Power Of Executive Directors' at http://siteresources.worldbank.org/BODINT/Resources/278027-1215524804501/IBRDEDsVotingTable.pdf, accessed 3 September 2013.

[118] The United States maintains a virtual veto, as a qualified majority of 85 per cent is required for certain decisions; thus it has the capacity to block any initiate it disagrees with. Articles of Agreement, International Bank for Reconstruction and Development, 2 UNTS 39, 606 UNTS 295, Article VIII, Amendments (a) 'Any proposal to introduce modifications in this Agreement ... [w]hen three-fifths of the members, having eighty-five percent (1) of the total voting power, have accepted the proposed amendments.'

[119] A. Buira (ed.), *Reforming the Governance of the IMF and the World Bank* (New York: Anthem Press, 2006).

[120] 'In the World Bank our finding is that the 16.4% of the votes cast by the USA give it at least 19.5% of the voting power'; R. Leech and D. Leech 'Voting Power in the Bretton Wood Institutions', November 2004, *Warwick Economic Working Paper* No. 718, available on SSRN, http://wrap.warwick.ac.uk/1472/, accessed 3 September 2013. Though with recent reforms these statistics are slightly out of date, the veto remains.

[121] In the Nordic/Baltic constituency, which comprises all the Scandinavian and Baltic states, Estonia is disfranchised in the IMF as its 920 votes do not grant to it any power. By contrast at the World Bank it has 1,173 votes, which, while a relatively small increase, leads to more actual power within its own constituency. Constituency is not referenced directly in the Articles of Agreement of the World Bank.

echoes in domestic law as well as the question of general disenfranchisement within organisations, raising similar issues to those of Macdonald and Macdonald. The Executive Directors act on behalf of the organisation and as such are international actors; therefore, one of their constituencies could conceivably be that of the world. Each Executive Director also has another constituency, consisting of those states that directly appointed him or her to the office and whose interests he or she represents.

The use of constituency within economic organisations is not related to the establishment of a framework or space within which these organisations can develop, nor does it function to provide democratic accountability. Instead, it provides an operational method by which power is distributed within the organisation. Similar to Henkin, this focuses on constituted power, thus not providing a suitable basis in which constitutionalism may develop. Such an account prevents all holders of constituent power exercising their warrant and does not represent the nexus between constituent and constituted power. Nonetheless, it provides an insight into the present understanding of constituency within international law.

7.2.4 Constituency in international law

From this brief overview of constituency's use in international law, several points become clear. First, there is no legally defined constituency in international law; even the use of constituency in the context of the Bretton Woods organisations is based upon practice and subject to reform through a non-legal process.[122] Second, evident in Henkin's and the international economic law approach, constituency's use often remains similar to the international community, revealing a purely statist regime distinct from the nexus between constituent and constituted power. Third, its use by Macdonald and Macdonald questions the presence of democratic legitimacy within the global legal order, an issue that persists within international law. Whether global administrative law will supplement the exercise of constituent power within international law or will remain aloof to its operation remains an open question. Finally, when constituency is identified within global administrative law, its employment as a legal space is doubtful in a context where constitutional law, or at least a form of normative constitutionalism, remains absent.

[122] See for example reform at the IMF, 'Reforming the International Financial System', at www.imf.org/external/np/sec/misc/consents.htm, accessed 3 September 2013.

Thus, constituency does not, at this point in international law's development, have a regular place. In certain areas, particularly within global administrative law, it relates to the exercise of constituent power. The stakeholder constituency in the work of Macdonald and Macdonald, linked to interests in a legal order, enables a broader understanding of constituency in both sectoral and world order constitutionalisation theories. Its employment in the constitutionalisation debate should enable the holders of constituent power to be construed broadly and not constrained to the statist approach of Henkin or international economic law. This would not deny the importance of the state to constitutionalisation but rather recognise that other subjects of international law also have an interest and thus may be considered constituent power holders. In contrast to the common use of international community, even if disputed by some authors, there is no well-established or uniform understanding of constituency in international law.

7.3 The possible use of constituency in international constitutionalism

As already established, in the nexus between constituted and constituent power, or as the space where power is exercised and vested outside of a distinct group but on their behalf and in their interest, the assemblage may be described as a constituency. Locke argues that one of the virtues of constituent power is that it limits the actions of the power wielders, as power ultimately lies with those who granted this to them, and they are aware of their dormant authority.[123] Thus, the holders of constituted power are locked to the holders of constituent power and these are themselves bound by constituency. It is proposed that this conception of constituency proffers a superior basis for global constitutionalisation than that proposed by the proponents of international community.

Within global constitutionalism an international constituency that ventures beyond the state, centring on the identification of constituent power holders and their interests, better serves the norms of constitutionalism than international community. The processes that define who the holders of constituent power are – their legal personality, their contribution to the development of international law and their interactions with each other – should, in practice, delineate the borders of constituency. Alternatively, within a very limited state-bound constitutionalisation, the

[123] Locke, *Two Treatises*, p. 4.

constituency would consist of all states recognised as such in international law. Admittedly, this state–constituency is no better or worse than the state-bound international community, and thus this statist constituency is not suggested as a basis for normative constitutionalisation.

Using constituency over community maintains some elements of the latter, including international law's development beyond the horizontal contract-based system, which was the hallmark of the Westphalian era. It also maintains some of the binary aspects of international community; potentially there are subjects within the international legal order that are both outside and within a particular international constituency. Yet, an international constituency would decouple international law from the negative attributes that diminish international community as a useful tool for normative constitutionalisation; most notably the negative undertone associated with existing outside the international community, and its dampening effect on debate.

It is essential to consider whether constituency best serves the development of normative constitutionalism. Loughlin identifies constituent power as the force that 'drives constitutional development'; yet often it is the missing element in discussions on both international and domestic constitutional law.[124] Difficulties arise when there is no identifiable geographical or homogeneous group presenting itself as a ready-made constituency. Where constituent and constituted powers are located within global constitutionalism they cannot be identified without the recognition of a constituency directly linked to a global constitutionalisation process. The relationships between the three concepts, constituency, and constituent and constituted power, are of such a nature that they are only meaningful in a constitutional structure. Within international law, constituent power is identified with those who grant to political actors the legitimacy and authority to create customary international law, treaty law, binding decisions and resolutions, and other characteristics of the exercise of constituted power. Constituted power, on the other hand, is held by those within the system that exercise and are constrained by the authority granted to them; both the holders of constituted and constituent power form part of the global constituency. This requires the constituency to be readily identifiable.

In identifying an international constituency, constitutional norms are fundamental to the task of identifying the holders of constituent and constituted power. Despite the fact that Loughlin refers to British public law,

[124] Loughlin, *Idea of Public Law*, p. 99.

and direct analogies are difficult, the British experience is similar in some ways to global constitutionalisation, as both lack the formal constraints of modern constitutional frameworks.[125] The British experience proves that a constitutional regime is possible even where the traditional formal constraints are not clearly identifiable. For both, the identification of constituency, constituted and constituent power is made more difficult, as the context cannot be readily identified in a document or practice. The British un-codified Constitution, where the outer limits of constitutional law are debated, but the process involved in its operation is clear, is comparable. The subjects of international law, which unquestionably include states but may also extend to international organisations, individuals and other actors in global law, can aid in identifying the international constituency. Within a statist international community, the list of members limits the extension of authority and identifies the holders of constituent or constituted power as ready-made. Yet, a global constituency identifies those who have an interest in global governance and the exercise of constitutional norms, and envelops them into the constituency.

The establishment of a constituency within global normative constitutionalism must reflect the reality of global law and as such is reliant on it as it currently operates. Thus, if constitutionalisation is only in its infancy the global constituency, while identifiable, will not operate within a fully functioning global constitutional order. On the other hand, if the process of constitutionalisation has already established a constitutional order, its constituency should be readily identifiable, as the requisite processes are already underway. As discussed in Chapter 6, the absence of constitutional norms, such as the rule of law, divisions of power and democratic legitimacy, makes the identification of an existent constitutional constituency difficult. Nevertheless, if constitutional norms become entrenched, the structure that they will then lend to constituency will enable the establishment of the holders of constituent and constituted power.

As was discussed in Chapter 3, constituency's use does not result in vagueness but rather produces an understanding of how law, and in this context global constitutionalism, encompass all interactions. This does not establish a test for deciding whether there is international law, that is taken as a given, but rather as a method of best understanding its evolution on a constitutional basis. The processes involved in global law, its inclusiveness or otherwise, define constituency. Indeed,

[125] *Ibid.*

it is inherent in the process of how global law itself develops. This is not going as far perhaps as what the New Haven School or Higgins would argue is required for process to be fully operational – context and norms are also important, though entire immersion of the law is not required.[126] Combining the elements of global law that outline the parameters of its operation will itself establish a clarity that will allow for certainty in the law and aid in identifying the holders of constituent and constituted power.

Identifying the process in global law required for constituency to emerge is difficult. For the proponents of the UN Charter as international community's constitution there is perhaps an easier argument to be put forward. Within the UN Charter the elements of governance are already established. Though, as Fassbender admits, '[p]erhaps the vague character of that which is addressed as international constitutional law offers a true representation of international law as it stands, i.e. an international law characterized by the contradictions and tensions'.[127] Though these contradictions and debates are of a more rudimentary nature in international law than in domestic law, it does not have to necessarily result in vagueness.

From what can presently be observed, global constitutional law will not result, as in the domestic system, from a long drafting process. As in domestic law, unless extant constitutionalism is accepted, there has yet to be a long process of judicial, legislative and executive interpretation regarding the content of the law or constraints upon governance structures, as a constitutional debate. Nevertheless, global constitutional law can draw upon years of development of its predecessor regime. Indeed, this is the basis upon which most of the constitutionalisation debates have emerged. Even from a strictly positivist perspective, elements of international law such as sources or recognition have a significantly legal, though not necessarily constitutional, historicism attached to them.

Klabbers argues that one of the issues with the move towards global administrative law by Kingsbury is that it cannot escape the lack of an established source for its principles and thus inculcating difficulties in

[126] Higgins objects to those such as Schachter or Van Hoof who do not wish to take either one stark path or the other in discussions of process versus rules, and instead tread a middle road. However, this study suggests that this is probably the reality of how international law operates. While it may not result in the neatest arguments, it is pragmatic, as Higgins asserts, and is reliant on philosophical assumptions. Higgins, *Problems and Process*, p. 8 and fn. 20.

[127] Fassbender, 'We the Peoples' in Loughlin and Walker (eds.), *The Paradox*, p. 280.

establishing how it achieves its binding force.[128] A similar argument could be levied against constituency. However, constituency is not meant to replace a narrative or theory of international law (arguably neither is global administrative law), it is instead intended to establish the parameters within which these narratives and, most importantly, constitutionalism, can operate.

The parameters of constituency are fluid and, unlike community, are not entrenched with values or interests. This is not to suggest that global constitutionalism would be value neutral; the rule of law, divisions of power and democratic legitimacy all contain values in their operation. As such, global constituency is reliant upon global constitutional norms to operate, and these may be exclusionary to the extent that these elements of constitutionalism do not always function successfully; however, it does not force values upon the holders of constituent power. It may be convenient to exclude any possible influence of values within constituency but this would reflect neither global law nor constitutionalism. The activities of global legal actors in a constitutional process establish the borders in which it occurs. This could be seen as circular. To be involved in the process, one has to be recognised as such but to be recognised one has to be in the process. However, the process itself is defined by the law not by the participants; therefore, in the area of constitutionalisation, the space in which it is operating is defined by constitutionalism's operation. Therefore, for the global constituency to be a state-only arena, the constitutional process must revolve around states. If the international constituency is broader than this and encompasses states and international organisations, together with civil society and corporations, it is the processes that surround these actors that delineate the constituency.

As was described in the preceding chapters, the advocates of global constitutionalisation require norms of constitutionalism to be incorporated into their theories to substantiate fully a claim of constitutionalisation. The holders of constituent and constituted power are locked together within a global constitutional constituency and may be identified by ascertaining who may rightfully exercise constituent power within a democratically legitimate process. Once this is established, the holders of constituted power, whose warrant has been granted by the constituent

[128] Klabbers in Klabbers, Peters and Ulfstein, *Constitutionalisation*, p. 28. See, for example, Kirsch and Kingsbury, 'Global Governance and Global Administrative Law', 1; and D. Dyzenhaus, 'The Rule of (Administrative) Law in International Law'(2004–2005) 68 *Law & Contemporary Problems* 127.

power holders, must exercise it in line with the rule of law and a system of divested power, which incorporates a division of powers. Thus, the constituency becomes locked to global constitutionalism.

7.4 Conclusion: constituency or community?

This chapter examined the global constitutionalisation debate, to whom constitutionalism should apply, as well as the possibilities for identifying the holders of constituent and constituted power. Focusing on the historic use of both community and constituency while also establishing their present function within international law and the constitutionalisation debate, this chapter set out the space in which global constitutionalism operates. The trajectories of both community and constituency result in differing forms of binarity and indoctrination thus making their employment diverse. While within the various constitutionalisation theories questions on constituted and constituent power are most often dealt with by simple reference to the international community as a ready-made and familiar space equipped to substantiate and legitimate a constitutionalisation process, this is not apposite. Arguably this shorthand choice, without consideration of its impact or its validity, is insufficient.

To enable the imperialism of international law to be left behind, a broader conception of constituent power is of vital import. The members of a constituency are the holders of the power in the process, and since membership is fluid, there is no reliance on the Westphalian sovereign state. While it is impossible to sidestep entirely the historic development of international law without completely renewing its basis, constituency based upon legitimate and democratic participation may provide a preferred foundation to community. Constituency does not come from the Eurocentric norms proposed by Vitoria, Suárez or other historical international legal theorists. Instead, it is based upon a right of participation. This establishes a break in international law, which places it beyond its imperialist roots. It also establishes the subjects of global constitutionalism as intrinsically linked to the process involved in its operation. The discussions surrounding constitutionalism may be split between two camps. The first maintains that constitutions are apolitical and are thus based upon subsisting values, while others argue constitutionalism is based upon governance.[129] The former could arguably be based upon the notion of community, community interest and community values, while

[129] Klabbers in Klabbers, Peters and Ulfstein, *Constitutionalisation*, p. 9.

the latter is closer to constituency. Obviously, this kind of strict divide is artificial; nonetheless, it is a useful analytical tool.

The borders of constituency are delineated by each of the actors and their interactions within the global legal processes. In contrast to international community, global constituency is based upon law and its conception of constitutionalism. As such, the parameters of constituency are based on process. Constituent power limits the actions of power holders, as their authority comes from those who have granted it to them and the granters of power are conscious of their latent warrant.[130] In a constituency, the holders of constituted and constituent power are locked together. This offers a superior basis for constitutionalisation than has been recommended by the proponents of international community. To enable the constitutionalisation debate to move beyond the historical and current implications of community, and to allow constitutionalisation theories to incorporate constitutionalism, particularly democratic legitimacy, into their proposals, it is proposed that the international constituency is the best space for global constitutionalisation to operate within. This will create a global constitutionalisation process where normative constitutionalism takes centre stage and becomes operative beyond the state.

[130] Loughlin, *Idea of Public Law.*

8

Constitutionalism in global constitutionalisation theories

Constitutionalism serves the domestic realm well. Over lengthy periods of re-evaluation and redefinition, domestic constitutionalism guarantees the resilience of core norms central to constitutional legal orders. While individual constitutions do not always ensure the fairness or equity of a governance order, as a doctrine constitutionalism maintains these norms as the ideal within governance regimes. Preuss argues that the promises of constitutionalism exist to establish systems of collective action based upon equal participation, accountability and the rule of law.[1] Thus, constitutionalism offers a means to exercise governance, and the advantages gained from its utilisation provide its purchase. This constitutional purchase is at the heart of this book, which questions whether the global constitutionalisation debate adopts constitutionalism into its thesis or if it presages an entirely novel form of governance. In providing an understanding of the political, legal and social context in which constituent and constituted power holders act, global constitutionalisation ought to offer a basis to examine the setting of its governance order. Yet, as we have seen, the terms of the constitutionalisation debate fail to tackle constitutionalism to the extent necessary to assert fully that the process is underway. Global constitutionalisation provides an inclusive and coherent narrative, but one lacking in constitutional thoroughness.

Constitutionalism is as relevant to the global as it is to the domestic order. There is no justifiable reason for not considering the utility of a constitutional model beyond the state. Walker argues that '[t]he modern state, understood as the key unit within the global framework of authority, was for long the undisputed domicile of constitutionalism and the guarantor of its relevance'.[2] Nonetheless, there are no grounds on which

[1] U. K. Preuss, 'Disconnecting Constitutions from Statehood' in Dobner and Loughlin (eds.), *Twilight*, pp. 43–4.

[2] N. Walker, 'Beyond the Holistic Constitution' in Dobner and Loughlin (eds.), *Twilight*, p. 291.

to continue this monopoly. Systems of good governance are relevant to any legal order that wishes to ensure the entrenchment of norms such as the rule of law, divisions of power and democratic legitimacy. Thus questions should centre on whether constitutionalism provides the best basis for global governance.[3]

Constitutionalisation forms part of the broader debate as to the future of global governance. As the global legal order moves beyond a consensual state-based system to one based upon obligatory norms with a range of global actors, a new framework for understanding its operation becomes necessary. Global legal pluralism, fragmentation, global governance orders and global administrative law each describe part of a process underway in the global legal order. As they regularly depict trends within global law that are also pertinent to constitutionalisation, the latter embraces some of their rationales and integrates them into its own propositions. Constitutionalisation is one of the more persuasive of the current theories, partly because it so easily co-opts these other theoretical and descriptive elements. More broadly, however, what each reinforces is an accord that governance has moved well beyond the classical accounts of inter-state relations.

The constitutionalisation debate makes a valuable contribution to understanding global law and in the longer term may support the development of a more coherent doctrine of constitutionalism. The decentralised character of global law is observed through fragmentation and global legal pluralism, and the newer points of governance within global administrative law, but a deeper understanding of the system is achieved through overarching analysis provided in constitutionalisation. But much depends on the vision of constitutionalisation being advanced. As it stands, global constitutionalisation does not provide the substantial analyses that, were it to be grounded in normative constitutionalism, it would clearly offer. Few constitutionalisation theories make claim for an existing 'fully constitutionalised' global legal order. In its place, most argue in favour of a system of global law that substantiates a move towards constitutionalisation. Most constitutionalisation theorists claim the threads of this repositioning are not always obvious at the time of their development, but may be evident later. Such arguments base their rationales upon repositioning and re-examining the role of international law in global governance.

[3] G. Wallace Brown 'The Constitutionalization of What?' (2012) 1 *Global Constitutionalism* 201.

The theories underpinning constitutionalisation potentially offer a good system for comprehending the operation of global governance, but perhaps more as an analytical tool than as a basis for a firm understanding of law's current operation. From a basis in constitutionalism itself, this book sought to question the basis of global constitutionalisation theories. If global law is on a path to becoming a constitutional system this would amount to a momentous development for global governance. In seeking to understand the nature and character of constitutionalism, this work places the global constitutionalisation debate within a constitutional narrative, thus weighing up whether the use of constitutionalism is the best option for firmly establishing a legitimate governance order. This departs from the classic accounts of international community governance.

In ascertaining preliminary issues, such as the substantive content of constitutionalism and the body to which a constitutionalised governance order is attached, as necessary steps before constitutionalism, this book challenges the character of the current global constitutionalisation debate. The identification of constituent and constituted power holders ought to be at the centre of global constitutionalisation, thus ensuring that the core norms of constitutionalism, such as the rule of law, divisions of power or democratic legitimacy, form an effective part of the establishment of constitutional purchase at the global level. Each norm grants to a legal order the ability to ensure that accountability, equality and participation remain at the heart of the system. They are fundamental to constitutionalism and should be to global constitutionalisation theories. Consequently, for a legal order to be described as constitutional these norms must be present. These preliminary questions should be the focus of global constitutionalisation prior to any consideration of whether it is really occurring.

While the presence of the rule of law within international law may not be as controversial as it might have been historically, its constitutional version requires more than that it exists by the consent of the holders of constituted power (a position akin to rule by law). A constitutionalised rule of law is most clearly observable in the theories that present judicial activism or the presence of *jus cogens* and *erga omnes* norms as forms of constitutionalisation. Yet, these theories are dependent on aspects of traditional international law to affirm the presence of a constitutional rule of law. The current extent of judicial activism and *jus cogens* make it difficult to prove that they would ensure the rule of law throughout the global legal order. While it is perfectly reasonable to assert that a constitutional rule of law may emerge within international law, constitutionalisation theories have yet to present a substantial case for the rule of law's presence as an aspect of their proposals.

Like the rule of law, divisions of power are rarely explicitly referenced within contemporary constitutionalisation theories. Constitutionalism does not require the traditional tripartite division that serves most domestic legal orders. Nonetheless, a divestment of power beyond one group of constituted powers holders remains essential. Once divestment is secured, this may be achieved in a vertical, horizontal or mixed model of divisions of power. Shoehorning a domestic form of separation of powers onto bodies such as the Security Council, the General Assembly and the International Court of Justice does not establish a constitutionalised division of power. Indeed, the reliance on the UN structure remains entirely unsatisfactory, as it merely moves states' power from one body to another without divesting states of any of their authority. Alternative propositions, which recognise a geographical separation of powers based at different levels of governance, such as local, federal, regional and international, are more persuasive. Geographical separation of powers, at some future point, would better satisfy the requirements of constitutionalism by instituting a division of power within a constitutionalisation process, but this can only be in combination with other norms of constitutionalism.

The third norm of constitutionalism, democratic legitimacy, is even more problematic than the rule of law or divisions of power. Democratic legitimacy underpins the notion of formal equality within a legal order. Democratic legitimacy entitles the constituent powers holders to choose the holders of constituted power and hold them to account in the exercise of their authority. Global and domestic constituencies are not contiguous, leaving a fissure within global democratic legitimacy. States represent their own interests and rarely, at the international level, take global interests into account when making decisions. Few constitutionalisation theories have presented any meaningful manner in which this disconnect could be remedied. Indeed, some have rejected the requirement altogether. This is in error. Democratic legitimacy forms an essential aspect of constitutionalism. Until democratic legitimacy is established at the global level, constitutionalisation will remain incomplete.

Global constitutionalisation must avoid the trap of brash statements of purpose without first presenting an underlying structure to uphold claims. To ensure constitutionalisation theories maintain their legitimacy, they must adopt the core norms of constitutionalism into their theses. Rule of law, divisions of power and democratic legitimacy must be *in situ* and functioning; mere chimeras that amount to unsubstantiated claims are insufficient. As the main aim of constitutionalisation theories is to incorporate an understanding of global law as constitutional, this would imply that the norms of constitutionalism are present or will be present in the future. The foregoing analysis leads to the conclusion that at a minimum, the current debate fails to ensure that the rule of law, divisions of power and democratic legitimacy are at the core of global constitutionalisation.

Hitherto the debate has not engaged with the identification of a constitutional constituency, disregarding the key issues of whom such a process addresses and who gains from constitutional purchase. Constitutionalism requires the identification of constituent power holders. These constituent power holders make up the body that constitutionalism serves. In order for a democratic process to be undertaken the subjects of a constitutional order must be identified. Often the 'international community' is suggested as the basis by which to identify the holders of constituent power. Historically, the international community has been used to differentiate between those states that were entitled to treaty with other states and those that were not. While this is no longer the case, some of the remnants of that vision of an international community remain present. While community possesses some positive elements of solidarity and growth, it also contains negative attributes. These negative features result from community's binary nature. The international community often leaves out those states that do not conform to the values presented by the majority, but yet requires that they are subject to the law. The international community quietens proposals for change that would disrupt the traditional basis of international law. Although the international community is not always used in this negative sense, its most common understanding would incorporate these negative attributes into a global constitutional order. Thus community continues to be unsuitable as a basis for identifying the subjects of a global constitutional, or indeed any other, governance order.

International constituency could stand in the stead of community. As discussed in Chapter 7, constituency already occupies a niche within international law but one not bound by the values present in the international community. An international constituency under a process of constitutionalisation creates a space more appropriate to constitutionalism. International constituency possesses aspects of international community's binary nature. Yet, the difference between the international community and constituency lie in the manner in which a subject's inclusion or exclusion is decided. Constituency's parameters are dictated by process. Actors affected by, and who affect, other actors within a global constitutionalising order provide the members of the international constituency. Membership of a constituency centres on the effect that constituency has on the actor's interests and the impact that the actor has upon the interests of other actors in that constituency. A constituency binds the order it supports. Identifying the members of the constituency does not rely on a set of values or commonality, but rather the law itself determines who the holders of constituent power are within a constitutional process. This provides a better basis for understanding the group attached to a particular constitution than a definition based upon, as it is within a community, a common set of ideals or common character.

Starting with constitutionalism does not suggest a bias in favour of domestic law. Constitutionalism stands apart from any particular legal order. The essential elements of constitutionalism are part of the doctrine and are not particular to domestic law. Constitutionalisation theories must therefore begin with constitutionalism and work towards its application within international law. Constitutionalisation of the global legal order would create a governance system based upon equality, legitimacy and fairness. This would be a triumph for international law. As such, constitutionalism provides a worthwhile goal for global governance. Making claims for its existence before it can be substantiated, however, creates more cynics than advocates of global constitutionalisation.

Most theories discussed in this book begin in international law and work backwards towards constitutionalism. The opposite is commended to those interested in the possibilities offered by global constitutionalism. Constitutionalisation can take a footing within international law, but hitherto the theories proposed do not sufficiently tackle the core norms of constitutionalism and thus do not avail of constitutionalism's purchase. The rule of law, divisions of powers and democratic legitimacy, amongst other constitutional norms, remain essential, and while aspects of each of these norms can be identified both within constitutionalisation theories and global law itself, in not tackling these elements directly, constitutionalisation theories are easily undermined for their lack of completeness.

Constitutionalisation's account of the global legal order offers a cohesive structure within which an important debate can take place, even if constitutionalisation ultimately does not occur. It is extremely important that global governance is provided with a firm basis of analysis for performing a number of tasks, including understanding the relationship between law and politics, understanding the relationship between law and society, and understanding the relationships within law itself. Constitutionalisation is well placed to provide an insight into these interactions. Nonetheless, if the theories supporting constitutionalisation are to achieve their potential, they must tackle the hard questions posed by constitutionalism and not banish constitutional purchase from sight, in the hope that these problems simply dissolve.

BIBLIOGRAPHY

Abi-Saab, G. 'Whither the International Community?' (1998) 9 *European Journal of International Law* 248

Alexander, L. (ed.) *Constitutionalism: Philosophical Foundations* (Cambridge University Press, 1998)

Alexandroff, A. S. and A. Fenton Cooper (eds.) *Rising States, Rising Institutions: Challenges for Global Governance* (Baltimore, OH: Brookings Institution Press, 2010)

Allott, P. 'The Concept of International Law' (1999) 10 *European Journal of International Law* 31

'The Courts and Parliament by Whom?' (1979) 38 *Cambridge Law Journal* 79

Eunomia, 2nd edn (Oxford University Press, 2001)

The Health of Nations: Society and Law Beyond the State (Cambridge University Press, 2002)

'Review Essay Symposium: Philip Allott's Eunomia and The Health of Nations Thinking Another World: "This Cannot Be How the World Was Meant to Be" (2005) 16 *European Journal of International Law* 255

Alston, P. 'Resisting the Merger and Acquisition of Human Rights by Trade Law: A Reply to Petersmann' (2002) 13 *European Journal of International Law* 815

Alverez, J. 'Judging the Security Council' (1996) 90 *American Journal of International Law* 1

Anderson, B. *Imagined Communities*, 2nd rev. edn (London: Verso, 1991)

Anghie, A. *Imperialism, Sovereignty and the Making of International Law* (Cambridge University Press, 2004)

Anon. 'Hegel's Political Philosophy of the State' (1917–1918) 31 *Harvard Law Review* 78

Aquinas, T. *Selected Political Writings*, 2nd edn (trans. J. G. Dawson) (Oxford: Blackwell, 1959)

A Treatise on Law (trans. R. J. Egan) (Indianapolis: Hacket, 2000)

Arato, A. 'Carl Schmitt and the Revival of the Doctrine of the Constituent Power in the United States' (1999–2000) 21 *Cardozo Law Review* 1739

Aristotle *Nicomachean Ethics* (University of Chicago Press, 2011)

Politics rev. edn (trans. R. Kraut), (London: Penguin Classics, 1981)

A Treatise on Government (trans. W. Ellis) (London: J. M. Dent & Sons, 1928)
Aurelius, M. *The Meditations* (trans. M. Hammond) (London: Penguin Classics, 2006)
Bellamy, R. (ed.) *The Rule of Law and the Separation of Powers* (London: Ashgate, 2005)
Benhabib, S. *Another Cosmopolitanism* (Oxford University Press, 2006)
'Borders, Boundaries, and Citizenship' (2005) 38 *Political Science and Politics* 673
Benvenisti, E. and G. W. Downs 'The Empire's New Clothes: Political Economy and the Fragmentation of International Law' (2007–2008) 60 *Stanford Law Review* 595
Berman, N. '"But the Alternative Is Despair": European Nationalism and the Modernist Renewal of International Law' (1993) 106 *Harvard Law Review* 1792
Berman, P. S. 'Global Legal Pluralism' (2006–2007) 80 *Southern California Law Review* 1155
Global Legal Pluralism: A Jurisprudence of Law Beyond Borders (Cambridge University Press, 2012)
A Pluralist Approach to International Law' (2007) 32 *Yale Journal of International Law* 301
Bernstein, L. 'Opting Out of the Legal System: Extralegal Contractual Relations in the Diamond Industry' (1992) 21 *Journal of Legal Studies* 115
Besson, S. and J. Tasioulas (eds.) *The Philosophy of International Law* (Oxford University Press, 2010)
Bianchi, A. 'Ad-hocism and the Rule of Law' (2002) 13 *European Journal of International Law* 263
Bingham, T. 'The Rule of Law' (2007) 66 *Cambridge Law Journal* 67
The Rule of Law (London: Allen Lane, 2010)
Bobbio, N. and D. Gobetti *Thomas Hobbes and the Natural Law Tradition* (University of Chicago Press, 1993)
Borgen, C. J. 'Whose Public, Whose Order? Imperium, Region, and Normative Friction' (2007) 32 *Yale Journal of International Law* 332
Bowett, D. W. *The Law of International Institutions*, 2nd edn (London: Stevens & Sons, 1970)
Bradley, A. W. and K. D. Ewing *Constitutional Law and Administration Law*, 14th edn (Harlow: Pearson, 2007)
Broude, T. and Y. Shany (eds.) *The Shifting Allocation of Authority in International Law* (Oxford: Hart, 2008)
Brown, G. Wallace 'The Constitutionalization of What?' (2012) 1 *Global Constitutionalism* 201
Brown, J. *The Spanish Origins of International Law* (Oxford: Clarendon Press, 1934)
Brownlie, I. *The Rule of Law in International Affairs: International Law at the Fiftieth Anniversary of the United Nations* (The Hague: Martinus Nijhoff, 1998)

Buchanan, J. M. and G. Tullock *The Calculus of Consent, Logical Foundations of Constitutional Democracy* (Ann Arbor: University of Michigan Press, 1962)

Buchanan, R. and S. Pahuja 'Law, Nation and (Imagined) International Communities' (2004) 8 *Law, Text, Culture* 137

Buira, A. (ed.) *Reforming the Governance of the IMF and the World Bank* (New York: Anthem Press, 2006)

Burke, E. *Appeal from the New to the Old Whigs* (Whitefish, MT: Kessinger Publishing, LLC, 2007)

A Philosophical Enquiry into the Origins of the Sublime and the Beautiful (ed. J. T. Boulton) (University of Notre Dame Press, 1958)

Reflections on the Revolution in France (London: Hackett, 1987)

Speech on Presenting to the House a Plan for the Better Security of Independence to Parliament (London: Dodsley, 1780)

Cannizzaro, E. 'A Machiavellian Moment? The UN Security Council and the Rule of Law' (2006) 3 *International Organisations Law Review* 189

Caparoso, J. A. 'The European Union and Forms of State: Westphalian, Regulatory or Post-Modern' (1996) 34 *Common Market Law Review* 29

Capps, P. 'The Kantian Project in International Law' (2001) 12 *European Journal of International Law* 1003

Carty, A. 'Alfred Verdross and Othmar Spann: German Romantic Nationalism, National Socialism and International Law' (1995) 6 *European Journal of International Law* 78

'Convergences and Divergences in European International Law Traditions' (2000) 11 *European Journal of International Law* 713

Cass, D. Z. 'The "Constitutionalization" of International Trade Law: Judicial Norm-Generation as the Engine of Constitutional Development in International Trade' (2001) 12 *European Journal of International Law* 39

The Constitutionalization of the World Trade Organization (Oxford University Press, 2005)

Cassese, S. 'Administrative Law without the State: The Challenge of Global Regulation' (2004) 37 *New York University Journal of International Law and Politics* 663

Cassese, S., B. Carotti, L. Casini, E. Cavalieri and E. Macdonald *Global Administrative Law: The Casebook*, 3rd edn (New York: IIIJ, 2012)

Cassimatis, A. E. 'International Humanitarian Law, International Human Rights Law, and Fragmentation of International Law' (2007) 56 *International & Comparative Law Quarterly* 623

Castiglione, D. 'The Political Theory of the Constitution' (1996) 44 *Political Studies* 417

Charlesworth, H. and C. Chinkin *The Boundaries of International Law: A Feminist Analysis* (Manchester University Press, 2000)

Chayes, A. and A. Handler Chayes *The New Sovereignty: Compliance with International Regulatory Agreements* (London: Harvard University Press, 1995)

Chesterman, S. 'An International Rule of Law?' (2008) 56 *American Journal of Comparative Law* 331

Christodoulidis, E. A. and S. Tierney (eds.) *Public Law and Politics: The Scope and Limits of Constitutionalism* (London: Ashgate, 2008)

Churchill, R. and J. Scott 'The Mox Plant Litigation: The First Half-Life' (2004) 53 *International and Comparative Law Quarterly* 643

Cicero *The Republic, The Laws* (trans. N. Rudd) (Oxford University Press, 1998)

Collier, J. G. *Conflict of Laws*, 3rd edn (Cambridge University Press, 2001)

Conforti, B. 'The Theory of Competence in Verdross' (1994) 5 *European Journal of International Law* 70

Cottier, T. and M. Hertig 'The Prospects of 21st Constitutionalism' (2003) 7 *Max Planck Yearbook of United Nations Law* 261

Craig, P. *Administrative Law*, 6th edn (London: Thomson Sweet & Maxwell, 2008)

Craven, G. J. 'A Few Fragments of State Constitutional Law' (1990) 20 *University of Western Australia Law Review* 353

Crawford, J. and S. Olleson 'The Continuing Debate on a UN Convention on State Responsibility' (2005) 54 *International and Comparative Law Quarterly* 95

Dahl, R. A. *After the Revolution?* (New Haven, CT: Yale University Press, 1970)

de Búrca, G. 'The Normativity of International Constitutionalism', in www.ejiltalk.org/author/gdeburca/, accessed 30 August, 2013

De Wet, E. *Chapter VII Powers of the United Nations' Security Council* (Oxford: Hart, 2004)

'Conflicts between International Paradigms: Hierarchy versus Systemic Integration' (2013) 2 *Global Constitutionalism* 196

'The Emergence of International and Regional Value Systems as a Manifestation of the Emerging International Constitutional Order' (2006) 19 *Leiden Journal of International Law* 611

'The International Constitutional Order' (2006) 55 *International and Comparative Law Quarterly* 51

De Wet, E. and J. Vidmar 'Conflicts between International Paradigms: Hierarchy versus Systemic Integration' (2013) 2 *Global Constitutionalism* 196

Dicey, A. V. *Introduction to the Study of the Law of the Constitution*, 8th edn (London: Macmillan, 1915)

Dickenson, L. A. 'Toward a "New" New Haven School of International Law?' (2007) 32 *Yale Journal of International Law* 547

Dobner, P. and M. Loughlin (eds.) *The Twilight of Constitutionalism* (Oxford University Press, 2010)

Domingo, R. *The New Global Law* (Cambridge University Press, 2011)

Douzinas, C. *The End of Human Rights, Critical Legal Thought at the Turn of the Century* (Oxford: Hart, 2000)

Human Rights and Empire: The Political Philosophy of Cosmopolitanism (New York: Routledge Cavendish, 2007)

Dunn, J. *Setting the People Free: The Story of Democracy* (London: Atlantic Books, 2005)

Dunoff, J. 'Constitutional Conceits: The WTO's "Constitution" and the Discipline of International Law' (2006) 17 *European Journal of International Law* 647

Dunoff, J. L. and J. P. Trachtman (eds.) *Ruling the World? Constitutionalism, International Law and Global Governance* (Cambridge University Press, 2009)

Dworkin, R. *Law's Empire* (Cambridge, MA: Harvard University Press, 1986)

'The Model of Rules' (1967) 35 *University of Chicago Law Review* 14

Dyzenhaus, D. *Hard Cases in Wicked Legal Systems: South African Law in the Perspective of Legal Philosophy* (Oxford: Clarendon Press, 1981)

'The Rule of (Administrative) Law in International Law' (2004–2005) 68 *Law & Contemporary Problems* 127

Esty, D. C. 'Good Governance at the Supranational Scale: Globalizing Administrative Law' (2006) 115 *Yale Law Journal* 1490

Falk, R. A. 'Casting the Spell: The New Haven School of International Law' (1991) 104 *Yale Law Journal* 1991

Fassbender, B. *Security Council Reform and the Right of Veto: A Constitutional Perspective* (The Hague: Kluwer International Press, 1998)

'The United Nations Charter as Constitution of the International Community' (1998) 36 *Columbia Journal of Transnational Law* 529

Fischer-Lescano, A. 'Redefining Sovereignty via International Constitutional Moments?' available at www.fb6.uni-bremen.de/uploads/ZERP/AFL/Publikationen/Lescano_RedefiningSovereignity_Chapter7.pdf, accessed 30 August 2013

Fischer-Lescano, A. and G. Teubner 'Regime Collisions: The Vain Search for Legal Unity in the Fragmentation of International Law' (2005) *Michigan Journal of International Law* 999

'Reply to Andreas L Paulus, Consensus as Fiction of Global Law' (2004) 24 *Michigan Journal of International Law* 1059

Forsyth, C. F. and I. Hare (eds.) *The Golden Metwand and the Crooked Cord* (Oxford University Press, 1998)

Foucault, M. *Power/Knowledge* (ed. C. Gorden) (London: Harvester, 1980)

Franck, T. 'Book Review' (1964) 17 *Harvard Law Review* 1565

'Clan and Superclan: Loyalty, Identity and Community in Law and Practice' (1996) 90 *American Journal of International Law* 359

Fairness in International Law (Oxford University Press, 1995)

'Power of Legitimacy and the Legitimacy of Power: International Law in an Age of Power Disequilibrium' (2006) 100 *American Journal of International Law* 88

The Power of Legitimacy among Nations (Oxford University Press, 1990)

Francklin, T. *The Works of Lucian* (London: T. Cadwell, 1780)

Frazer, E. *The Problems of Communitarian Politics, Unity and Conflict* (Oxford University Press, 1999)

Freeman, M. and D. Napier (eds.) *Law and Anthropology: Current Legal Issues* (Oxford University Press, 2009)

Friedman, W. *The Changing Structure of International Law* (Columbia, OH: Columbia University Press, 1964)

Fuller, L. *The Morality of Law* (New Haven, CT: Yale University Press, 1964)

Gardbaum, S. 'Human Rights as International Constitutional Rights' (2008) 19 *European Journal of International Law* 749

Gearty, C. *Principles of Human Rights Adjudication* (Oxford University Press, 2005)

Georgiev, D. 'Politics or Rule of Law: Deconstruction and Legitimacy in International Law'(1993) 4 *European Journal of International Law* 1

Giergerich, T. 'The *Is* and *Ought* of International Constitutionalism: How Far Have We Come on Habermas' Road to a "Well-Considered Constitutionalization of International Law"' (2009) 10 *German Law Journal* 31

Ginsburg, T. and T. Moustafa *Rule by Law: The Politics of Courts in Authoritarian Regimes* (Cambridge University Press, 2008)

Goldsmith, J. L. and E. Posner *The Limits of International Law* (Oxford University Press, 2005)

Goldsworthy, J. 'Structural Judicial Review and the Objection from Democracy' (2010) 60 *University of Toronto Law Journal* 137

Goodhart, A. L. 'Rule of Law and Absolute Sovereignty' (1957) 106 *University of Pennsylvania Law Review* 943

Gordenker, L. *The UN Secretary General and the Secretariat* (London: Routledge, 2005)

Gould, C. *Rethinking Democracy: Freedom and Social Co-operation in Politics, Economy, and Society* (Cambridge University Press, 1990)

Griffith, J. A. G. 'The Political Constitution' (1979) 42 *Modern Law Review* 1

Griffiths, J. 'What Is Legal Pluralism' (1986) 24 *J. Legal Pluralism and Unofficial Law* 1

Gross, L. 'The Peace of Westphalia 1644–1948' (1948) 42 *American Journal of International Law* 20

(ed.) *International Law in the Twentieth Century* (New York: Ardent Media, 1969)

Guo, D. 'The State and the Society of Rule by Law, and the Society by Citizens' (2007) 5 *Journal of Political Science and Law* 3

Habermas, J. *Between Facts and Norms* (Cambridge, MA: MIT Press, 1996)

Between Naturalism and Religion (trans. C. Cronin) (Cambridge: Polity Press, 2008)

'Constitutionalisation of International Law and the Legitimation Problems of a Constitution for World Society' (2008) 15 *Constellations* 444

The Divided West (trans. C. Cronin) (Cambridge: Polity Press, 2006)

Hafner, G. 'Pros and Cons Ensuing from Fragmentation of International Law' (2003–2004) 25 *Michigan Journal of International Law* 849

Happold, M. 'Security Council Resolution 1373 and the Constitution of the United Nations' (2003) 16 *Leiden Journal of International Law* 593

Hart, H. L. A. *The Concept of Law*, 2nd edn (Oxford: Clarendon, 1994)

Hart, M. and A. Negri *Empire* (Cambridge, MA: Harvard University Press, 2000)

Hart Ely, J. *On Democracy and Distrust: A Theory of Judicial Review* (Cambridge, MA: Harvard University Press, 1980)

Hartigan, R. S. 'Francesco de Vitoria and Civilian Immunity' (1973) 1 *Political Theory* 79

Hayek, F. A. *The Road to Serfdom*, 2nd edn (London: Routledge, 2001)

Hegel, G. W. F. *Philosophy of Right* (New York: Cosimo Press, 2008)

Held, D. *Democracy and the Global Order: From the Modern State to Cosmopolitan Governance* (Cambridge: Polity Press, 1995)

Helfer, L. R. 'Constitutional Analogies in the International Legal System' (2003) 37 *Loyola Law Review* 193

Henkin, L. *How Nations Behave: Law and Foreign Policy*, 2nd edn (New York: Colombia University Press, 1979)

International Law: Politics and Values (The Hague: Kluwer, 1995).

Herdegen, M. J. 'The Constitutionalization of the UN Security System' (1994) 27 *Vanderbilt Journal of Transnational Law* 135

Higgins, R. 'International Law and the Avoidance, Containment and Resolution of Disputes' (1991) *Recueil des Cours* 230

Problems and Process: International Law and How We Use It (Oxford University Press, 1994)

Hobbes, T. *Leviathan* (Cambridge Classics, 1991)

Hoffman, S. 'International Systems and International Law' (1961) *World Politics* 207

Hofri-Winogradow, A. S. 'A Plurality of Discontent: Legal Pluralism, Religious Adjudication and the State' (2010) 26 *Journal of Law and Religion* 101

Holmes, O. W. *The Common Law* (New York: Dover Publications, 1991)

Houlgate, S. *Freedom, Truth and History: An Introduction to Hegel's Philosophy* (New York: Taylor & Francis, 1991)

Howse, R. 'Human Rights in the WTO: Whose Rights, What Humanity'(2002) 13 *European Journal of International Law* 274

Hudson, M. O. 'Membership in the League of Nations' (1924) 18 *American Journal of International Law* 436

International Law Commission, 'Fragmentation of International Law: Difficulties Arising from the Diversification and Expansion of International Law', Vol. II, Part 2, *Yearbook of the International Law Commission* (International Law Commission, 2006)

Jackson, J. H. *Restructuring the GATT System* (New York: Council on Foreign Relations Press, 1990)

World Trade and the Law of GATT (New York: Lexis, 1969)

The World Trade Organization: Constitution and Jurisprudence (London: Chatham House Papers Series, 1998)

'The WTO "Constitution" and Proposed Reforms: Seven "Mantras" Revisited' (2001) 4 *Journal of International Economic Law* 67

Janzen, H. 'The Monism of Alfred Verdross' (1935) 29 *American Political Science Review* 387

Jenks, C. W. *Law, Freedom and Welfare* (London: Stevens & Sons, 1963)

Joerge, C. and E. Petersmann (eds.) *Constitutionalism, Multilevel Trade Governance and Social Regulation* (Oxford: Hart, 2006)

Johnston, A. 'South Africa: The Election and the Transition Process – Five Contradictions in Search of a Resolution' (1994) 15 *Third World Quarterly* 187

Kalyvas, A. 'Popular Sovereignty, Democracy, and the Constituent Power' (2005) 12 *Constellations* 223

Kammerhofer, J. 'Uncertainty in the Formal Sources of International Law: Customary International Law and Some of Its Problems' (2004) 15 *European Journal of International Law* 523

Kant, I. *The Metaphysics of Morals* (Cambridge University Press, 1996)

Perpetual Peace (New York: Cosimo Press, 2005)

Kavanagh, A. and J. Oberdiek (eds.) *Arguing about the Law* (London: Routledge, 2009)

Kelsen, H. 'What Is a Legal Act' (1984) 29 *American Journal of Jurisprudence* 199

Kennedy, D. *International Legal Structures* (Berlin: Nomos, 1987)

'The Mystery of Global Governance' (2008) 34 *Ohio New University Law Review* 827

'Primitive Legal Scholarship' (1986) 27 *Harvard International Law Journal* 1

Keohane, R. O. and J. S. Nye, Jr *Power and Interdependence*, 3rd edn (New York Longman, 2001)

'Transgovernmental Relations and International Organizations' (1974) 27 *World Politics* 39

King, A. *The British Constitution* (Oxford University Press, 2007)

Kingsbury, B. 'The Concept of "Law" in Global Administrative Law' (2009) 20 *European Journal of International Law* 23

Kingsbury, B., N. Kirsch and R. B. Stewart 'The Emergence of Global Administrative Law' (2004–2005) 68 *Law & Contemporary Problems* 15

Kirgis, F. L. 'Custom on a Sliding Scale' (1987) 81 *American Journal of International Law* 146

Kirsch, N., and B. Kingsbury 'Introduction: Global Governance and Global Administrative Law in the International Legal Order' (2006) 17 *European Journal of International Law* 1

Klabbers, J., A. Peters and G. Ulfstein *The Constitutionalisation of International Law* (Oxford University Press, 2009)

Koh, H. H. 'The Globalization of Freedom' (2001) 26 *Yale Journal of International Law* 305

'Is There a "New" New Haven School of International Law?' (2007) 32 *Yale Journal of International Law* 559

'Why Do Nations Obey International Law?' (1996–1997) 106 *Yale Law Journal* 2599

Koskenniemi, M. *From Apology to Utopia* (reissue, Cambridge University Press, 2006)

The Gentle Civilizer of Nations: The Rise and Fall of International Law 1870–1960 (Cambridge University Press, 2001)

'International Law in Europe: Between Tradition and Renewal', Florence, 14 June 2004 (keynote address at the inauguration of the European Society of Law)

'International Law in Europe: Between Tradition and Renewal' (2005) 16 *European Journal of International Law* 113

'"The Lady Doth Protest Too Much": Kosovo and the Turn to Ethics in International Law' (2002) 65 *Modern Law Review* 159

Koskenniemi, M. and P. Leino 'Fragmentation of International Law? Postmodern Anxieties' (2002) 15 *Leiden Journal of International Law* 553

Kostakopoulou, D. 'Thick, Thin and Thinner Patriotisms: Is This All There Is?' (2006) 26 *Oxford Journal of Legal Studies* 73

Krajewski, M. 'Democratic Legitimacy and Constitutional Perspectives of WTO Law' (2001) 35 *Journal of World Trade* 167

Krasner, D. *Sovereignty: Organised Hypocrisy* (Princeton University Press, 1999)

Kirtsiotis, D. 'Imagining the International Community' (2002) 13 *European Journal of International Law*' 961

Kumm, M. 'The Legitimacy of International Law: A Constitutionalist Framework of Analysis' (2004) 15 *European Journal of International Law* 907

Kunz, J. L. 'Natural-Law Thinking in the Modern Science of International Law' (1961) 55 *The American Journal of International Law* 951

'Neutrality and the European War 1939–1940' (1941) 39 *Michigan Law Review* 719

'The "Vienna School" and International Law' (1933–1934) 11 *New York University Quarterly Law Review* 370

Langford, P. (ed.) *Writings and Speeches of Edmund Burke* (Oxford: Clarendon Press, 1981)

Lasswell, H. D. and M. S. McDougal *Jurisprudence for a Free Society: Studies in Law, Science and Policy*, Vols. I and II (New Haven, CT: New Haven Press, 1992)

'Legal Education and Public Policy: Professional Training in the Public Interest' (1943) 52 *Yale Law Journal* 43

Lauterpacht, H. 'The Covenant as the "Higher Law"' (1936) 17 *British Yearbook of International Law* 54

Leech, R. and D. Leech 'Voting Power in the Bretton Wood Institutions' November 2004, *Warwick Economic Working Paper No. 718 http://wrap.warwick.ac.uk/1472/*

Levit, J. K. 'Bottom-Up International Lawmaking: Reflections on the New Haven School of International Law' (2007) 32 *Yale Journal of International Law* 393

Locke, J. *Two Treatises of Government*, 3rd edn (Cambridge University Press, 1988)

Lockwood, H. C. *Constitutional History of France* (Charleston, SC: BiblioBazaar, LLC, [1889] 2009)

Loughlin, M. *The Idea of Public Law* (Oxford University Press, 2003)

Loughlin, M. and N. Walker (eds.) *The Paradox of Constitutionalism* (Oxford University Press, 2008)

Loveland, I. *Constitutional Law, Administrative Law and Human Rights: A Critical Introduction*, 5th edn (Oxford University Press, 2009)

MacDonald, R. St. J. 'The Charter of the United Nations in Constitutional Perspective' (1999) 20 *Australian Yearbook of International Law* 205

MacDonald, R. St. J. and D. M. Johnston (eds.) *The Structure and Process of International Law* (Leiden: Martinus Nijhoff, 1983)

Towards World Constitutionalism, Issues in the Legal Ordering of the World Community (Leiden: Martinus Nijhoff, 2005)

Macdonald, T. and K. Macdonald 'Non-Electoral Accountability in Global Politics: Strengthening Democratic Control within the Global Garment Industry' (2006) 17 *European Journal of International Law* 89

McDougal, M. S. 'International Law, Power and Policy: A Contemporary Conception' (1953) 82 *Recueil des Cours* 137

McDougal, M. S., W. M. Reisman and A. R. Willard 'The World Community: A Planetary Social Process' (1987–1988) 21 *U.C. Davis Law Review* 807

McGinis, O. and M. L. Movsesian 'The World Trade Constitution' (2000) 114 *Harvard Law Review* 511

Maddox, G. 'A Note on the Meaning of "Constitution"' (1982) 76 *American Political Science Review* 805

Marks, G. C. 'Indigenous Peoples in International Law: The Significance of Francisco De Vitoria and Bartolome De Las Casas'(1990–1991) 3 *Australian Yearbook of International Law* 1

Marks, S. *The Riddle of All Constitutions: International Law, Democracy, and the Critique of Ideology* (Oxford University Press, 2003)

'State-centrism, International Law, and the Anxieties of Influence' (2006) 19 *Leiden Journal of International Law* 339

Marx, K. *Capital: A Critique of Political Economy*, Vol. III, Part 2: *The Process of Capitalist Production as a Whole* (ed. F. Engels) (New York: Cosimo, 2007)

Critique of Hegel's Philosophy of Right (ed. Joseph O'Malley) (Cambridge University Press, 1970)

Meron, T. 'Common Rights of Mankind in Gentili, Grotius and Suarez' (1991) 85 *The American Journal of International Law* 110

Merrils, J. G. 'The Mosaic of International Dispute Settlement Procedures: Complementary or Contradictory?' (2007) 54 *Netherlands International Law Review* 361

Milewicz, K. 'Emerging Patterns of Global Constitutionalization: Towards a Conceptual Framework' (2009) 16 *Indiana Journal of Global Legal Studies* 413

Miraglia, L. '*Comparative Legal Philosophy Applied to Legal Institutions' Modern Legal Philosophy Series, Vol. III*' (Boston Book Company, 1912). (J. Lisle, trans., reprinted 1968)

Mosler, H. 'Book Review: Die Quellen des universellen Völkerrechts; eine Einführung' (1974) 68 *American Journal of International Law* 350

Rec. Des Cours (1974–IV) (Leyden: A. W. Sijthoff, 1976)

Mouffe, C. *The Democratic Paradox* (London: Verso, 2000)

Munro, C. R. *Studies in Constitutional Law*, 2nd edn (London: Butterworths, 1999)

Nagel, T. 'The Problem of Global Justice' (2005) 33 *Philosophy and Global Affairs* 113

Nancy, J. 'The Confronted Community' (2003) 6 *Postcolonial Studies* 23

The Inoperative Community (Minneapolis: University of Minnesota Press, 1991)

Nederman, C. J. 'Freedom, Community and Function: Communitarian Lessons of Medieval Political Theory' (1992) 86 *American Political Science Review* 977

Negri, A. *Insurgencies: Constituent Power and the Modern State* (trans. Maurizia Boscalgi) (Minneapolis: University of Minnesota Press, 1999)

Nijman, J. E. and A. Nollkaemper (eds.) *New Perspectives on the Divide between National and International Law* (Oxford University Press, 2007)

Nolan, A. 'The Child as "Democratic Citizen": Challenging the "Participation Gap"' (2010) *Public Law* 767

Nollkaemper, A. 'The Internationalized Rule of Law' (2009) 1 *Hague Journal on the Rule of Law* 74

Nussbaum, M. C. 'Kant and Stoic Cosmopolitanism' (1997) 5 *Journal of Political Philosophy* 1

O'Cinneide, C. 'Human Rights and within Multi-Layered Systems of Constitutional Governance: Rights Cosmopolitanism and Domestic Particularism in Tension' 30 March 2009 University College Dublin Law Research Paper No. 12/2009. Available at SSRN: http://ssrn.com/abstract=1370264, accessed 9 December 2013

O'Donoghue, A. 'Neutrality and Multilateralism after the First World War' (2010) 15(1) *Journal of Conflict and Security Law* 169

Opsahl, T. 'An "International Constitutional Law"?' (1961) 10 *The International and Comparative Law Quarterly* 760

Orakhelashvili, A. 'R (on the application of Al-Jedda) (FC) V Secretary of State for Defence' (2008) 102 *American Journal of International Law* 337

'The Idea of European International Law' (2006) 17 *European Journal of International Law* 315

Otto, D. 'Subalternity and International Law: The Problems of Global Community and the Incommensurability of Difference' (1996) 5 *Social and Legal Studies* 337

Pahuja, S. 'The Postcoloniality of International Law' (2005) 46 *Harvard Journal of International Law* 459

Peerenboom, R. *China's Long March towards the Rule of Law* (Cambridge University Press, 2002)

Pernice, I. 'Multilevel Constitutionalism and the Treaty of Amsterdam, European Constitution Making Revisited' (1999) 36 *Common Market Law Review* 703

Peters, A. 'Compensatory Constitutionalism: The Function and Potential of Fundamental International Norms and Structures' (2006) 19 *Leiden Journal of International Law* 579

'Global Constitutionalism Revisited' (2005) 11 *International Legal Theory Studies* 39

'The Merits of Global Constitutionalism' (2009) 16 *Indiana Journal of Global Legal Studies* 397

Peters, A. and K. Armingeon, 'Introduction – Global Constitutionalism from an Interdisciplinary Perspective' (2009) 16 *Indiana Journal of Global Legal Studies* 385

Peters, A., L. Koechlin and T. Förster (eds.) *The Role of Non-state Actors in Standard Setting* (Cambridge University Press, 2009)

Petersmann, E. 'Constitutionalism and International Adjudication: How to Constitutionalize the UN Dispute Settlement System?' (1999) 31 *New York University Journal of International Law & Policy* 753

'How to Reform the UN System? Constitutionalism, International Law, and International Organizations' (1997) 10 *Leiden Journal of International Law* 421

'Human Rights and Economic Law in the 21st Century: The Need to Clarify Their Interrelationships' (2001) *Journal of International Economic Law* 3

'Human Rights, International Economic Law and "Constitutional Justice"' (2008) 19 *European Journal of International Law* 769

'Time for a United Nations "Global Compact" for Integrating Human Rights into the Law of Worldwide Organizations: Lessons from European Integration' (2002) 13 *European Journal of International Law* 621

'The WTO Constitution and Human Rights' (2000) 3 *Journal of International Economic Law* 19

Pierik, R. M. and W. G. Werner (eds.) *Cosmopolitanism in Context: Perspectives from International Law and Political Theory* (Cambridge University Press, 2010)

Pitkin, H. F. 'The Idea of Constitution' (1987) 37 *Journal of Legal Education* 167

Pollock, F. *The League of Nations* (London: Stevens and Sons, 1920)

Posner, E. A. and D. Weisbach *Climate Change Justice* (Oxford: Princeton University Press, 2010)

Qureshi, A. H. and A. R. Ziegler *International Economic Law*, 2nd edn (London: Sweet & Maxwell, 2007)

Raz, J. *The Authority of Law* (Oxford University Press, 1979)

Rehfeld, A. *The Concept of Constituency* (Cambridge University Press, 2005)

Reisman, W. M. 'The View from the New Haven School of International Law' (1992) 86 *American Society of International Law Proceedings* 118

Reisman, W. M., S. Wiessner and A. R. Willard 'Commentary, "The New Haven School: A Brief Introduction"' (2007) 32 *Yale Journal of International Law* 575

Rorty, A. *The Many Faces of Philosophy* (New York: Oxford University Press, 2003)

Rosenne, S. *Developments in the Law of Treaties (1945–1986)* (Cambridge University Press, 1989)

Roth, B. R. *Governmental Illegitimacy in International Law* (Oxford University Press, 2000)

Rubenfeld, J. 'The Two World Orders' (2003) *The Wilson Quarterly* 28

Rutherford, D. *The Cambridge Companion to Early Modern Philosophy* (Cambridge University Press, 2006)

Sands, P. J. 'Environment, Community and International Law' (1999) 30 *Harvard Journal of International Law* 393

Sarooshi, D. *International Organizations and Their Exercise of Sovereign Power* (Oxford University Press, 2007)

Scelle, G. *Droit international public: manuel élémentaire avec les textes essentiels* (Paris: Domat-Montchrestien, 1944)

Schachter, O. 'International Law in Theory and Practice' 178 *Recueil des Cours* 2

'Self-Defence and the Rule of Law' (1989) 83 *American Journal of International Law* 259

Schmitt, C. *Constitutional Theory* (Durham, NC: Duke University Press, 2008)

Political Theology – Four Chapters on the Concept of Sovereignty (University of Chicago Press, 2005)

Schwobel, C. E. *Global Constitutionalism in International Legal Perspective* (Leiden: Martinus Nijhoff, 2011)

Seneca *Moral and Political Essays* (trans. J. M. Cooper) (Cambridge University Press, 1995)

Simma, B. 'From Bilateralism to Community Interest' (1994–VI) 250 *Rec. Des Cours* 259

The Charter of the United Nations: A Commentary, 2nd edn (Oxford University Press, 2002)

'Comments on Global Governance, the United Nations and the Place of Law' (1998) 9 *Finnish Yearbook of International Law* 61

'The Contribution of Alfred Verdross to the Theory of International Law' (1995) 6 *European Journal of International Law* 33

'Fragmentation in a Positive Light' (2003–2004) 25 *Michigan Journal of International Law* 845

'Self Contained Regimes' (1985) 16 *Netherlands Yearbook of International Law* 112

Simma, B. and A. L. Paulus, 'The "International Community": Facing the Challenge of Globalization' (1998) 9 *European Journal of International Law* 266

Slaughter, A. 'Filling Power Vacuums in the New Global Order' (2013) *36 Boston College International And Comparative Law Review* 919

'International Law and International Relations Theory: A Dual Agenda' (1993) *American Journal of International Law* 205

'Liberal Theory of International Law' (2000) 94 *American Society of International Law Proceedings* 240

A New World Order (Princeton University Press, 2004)

Slaughter, A. and W. Burke-White, 'An International Constitutional Moment' (2003) 43 *Harvard International Law Journal* 1

Sloan, B. 'The United Nations Charter as a Constitution' (1989) 1 *Pace International Law Review* 61

Stein, E. 'Lawyers, Judges and the Making of a Transnational Constitution' (1981) 75 *American Journal of International Law* 1

Steinberg, R. H. and J. M. Zasloff, 'Power and International Law' (2006) 100 *American Journal of International Law* 64

Subedi, S. P. 'The Notion of Free Trade and the First Ten Years of the World Trade Organization: How Level Is the "Level Playing Field"?' (2006) 53(2) *Netherlands International Law Review* 273

Sunstein, C. R. *Designing Democracy: What Constitutions Do* (Oxford University Press, 2001)

Suzuki, E. 'The New Haven School of International Law: An Invitation to a Policy-Orientated Jurisprudence' (1974) 1 *Yale Journal of World Public Order* 1

Tamanaha, B. Z. 'Understanding Legal Pluralism: Past to Present, Local to Global' (2008) 30 *Sydney Law Review* 375

Tesón, F. R. 'Kantian Theory of International Law' (1992) 92 *Columbia Law Review* 53

Teubner, G. *Constitutional Fragments. Societal Constitutionalism in the Globalization* (Oxford University Press, 2012)

'Societal Constitutionalism: Alternatives to State-centred Constitutional Theory' Storrs Lectures, Yale Law School 2003/2004, available at SSRN: http://ssrn.com/abstract=876941, accessed 9 December 2013

'The Two Faces of Janus, Rethinking Legal Pluralism' (1991–1992) 13 *Cardozo Law Review* 1443

(ed.) *Global Law Without a State* (Dartmouth: Aldershot, 1997)

Tomkins, A. 'In Defence of the Political Constitution' (2002) 22 *Oxford Journal of Legal Studies* 157

Our Republican Constitution (Oxford: Hart, 2005)

Tomuschat, C. 'Constitutive Elements of the Present Day International Legal Order' (1999) 241 *Recueil des Cours* 25

'International Law, Ensuring the Survival of Mankind on the Eve of the New Century' (1999) 281 *Recueil des Cours* 10

'Obligations Arising for States Without or Against Their Will' (1993–IV) 241 *Rec. Des Cours* 195

Trachtman, J. P. 'The Constitutions of the WTO' (2006) 17 *European Journal of International Law* 623

The Future of International Law (Cambridge University Press, 2013)

Truyol y Serra, A. 'Verdross et la théorie du droit' (1994) 5 *European Journal of International Law* 55

Turner, C. 'Delivering Lasting Peace, Democracy and Human Rights in Times of Transition: The Role of International Law' (2008) 2 *International Journal of Transitional Justice* 126

Tushnet, M. *The Constitution of the United States of America: A Contextual Analysis* (Oxford: Hart, 2009)

Twining, W. L. 'Pericles and the Plumber' (1967) 83 *Law Quarterly Review* 396

Van Caenegm, R. C. *An Historical Introduction to Western Constitutional Law* (Cambridge University Press, 1995)

Verdross, A. 'Austria's Permanent Neutrality and the United Nations Organization' (1956) 50 *American Journal of International Law* 61

'Forbidden Treaties in International Law, Comments on Professor Garner's Report on "The Law of Treaties"' (1937) 31 *American Journal of International Law* 571

'Fundamental Human Rights: The Journey of an Idea' (trans. J. D. Gorby) (1979–1980) 8 *Human Rights* 20

'General International Law and the United Nations Charter' 30 *International Affairs* 342

'*Jus Dispositivum* and *Jus Cogens* in International Law' (1966) 60 *American Journal of International Law* 55

'On the Concept of International Law' (1949) 43 *American Journal of International Law* 435

'Reichsrecht und internationales Recht. Eine Lanze für Art. 3 des Regierungsentwurfes der deutschen Verfassung' (1919) 24 *Deutsche Juristenzeitung* 291.

'Two Arguments for an Empirical Foundation of Natural-Law Norms: An Examination of Johannes Messner's and Victor Kraft's Approaches' (1975) 3 *Syracuse Journal of International Law and Commerce* 151

Verdross, A. and B. Simma, *Universelles Völkerrecht: Theorie und Praxis*, 3rd edn (Berlin: Duncker & Humblot, 1984)

Vile, M. J. C. *Constitutionalism and the Separation of Powers*, 2nd edn (Oxford University Press, 1967)

von Bogdandy, A. 'Constitutionalism in International Law: Comment on a Proposal from Germany' (2006) 47 *Harvard International Law Journal* 223

'General Principles of International Public Authority: Sketching a Research Field' (2008) 11 *German Law Journal* 1909

Waldock, H. 'General Course on Public International Law' (II 1962) 106 *Recueil des Cours* 20

Walker, N. 'European Constitutionalism in the State Constitutional Tradition' 58 *Current Legal Problems* 51

'The Idea of Constitutional Pluralism' (2002) 65 *Modern Law Review* 317

'Taking Constitutionalism beyond the State' (2008) 56 *Political Studies* 519

Wall, I. R. *Human Rights and Constituent Power: Without Model or Warranty* (Abingdon: Routledge, 2011)

Wall, I. R., C. Douzinas and M. Stone (eds.) *New Critical Legal Thinking: Law and the Political* (London: Birkbeck Law Press, 2012)

Walter, C. 'Constitutionalizing (Inter)national Governance – Possibilities for and Limits to the Development of an International Constitutional Law' (2001) *German Yearbook of International Law* 170

Ward, I. *The English Constitution, Myths and Realities* (Oxford: Hart, 2004)

Weiler, J. H. H. *The Constitution of Europe* (Cambridge University Press, 1999)

'Federalism and Constitutionalism: Europe's Sonderweg' (2000) *The Jean Monnet Working Paper* No. 10

'The Reformation of European Constitutionalism' (1997) 35 *Common Market Law Review* 97

'The Transformation of Europe' (1991) 100 *Yale Law Journal* 2403

Weiler, J. H. and M. Wind (eds.), *European Constitutionalism beyond the State* (Cambridge University Press, 2003)

Wheatley, S. *The Democratic Legitimacy of International Law* (Oxford: Hart, 2010)

Williams, G. L., A. Brown and J. Waldron, *Selections from Three Works of Francisco Suárez, S.J, De Legibus, ac deo Legislatore, 1612, Defensio Fidie Catholicae, et Apostolicae Adversus Anglicanae Sectae Errores, 1613, De Triplici Virtute Theologica Fide, Spe, et Charitate, 1621.* Vol. II: *The Translation* (Oxford: Clarendon Press, 1944)

Yasuki, O. 'When Was the Law of International Society Born? – An Inquiry of the History of the International Law from an Intercivilizational Perspective' (2000) 2 *Journal of the History of International Law* 1

Zolo, D. 'A Cosmopolitan Philosophy of International Law? A Realist Approach' (1999) 12 *Ratio Juris* 429

INDEX

ad hocism in international law, 157–8
administrative law, global, *see* global administrative law
Aquinas, T., 110
Aristotle, 63–6, 76
Armingeon, K., 4

Bingham, T., Lord, 22, 84
Burke, E., 66–8

Chalmers, D., 56–7
China
  rule by law, 22–3, 28
commonality
  Aristotle's theory, 63–6, 76
  Burke's theory, 66–8
  characteristic of community, 61–3
  community and, 73–7
  Hegel's theory, 68–71
  Nancy's theory, 71, 72–3
community, *see also* constituent power holders; international community
  Aristotle's theory, 63–6, 76
  Burke's theory, 66–8
  characteristics of binarity and commonality, 61–3
  commonality and, 73–7
  constitutionalism linkage, 47–8
  Hegel's theory, 68–71, 111–12
  historic concept of, 109–13
  Marxist theory, 71–2
  Nancy's theory, 71, 72–3
  New Haven School, 127–30
  problematic aspects, 62
  relationship with governance, 61–3
  role in global constitutionalisation process, 9–10, 188–9
constituency, *see also* international constituency
  binary nature, 80–3
  constitutionalism linkage, 9–10, 47–8, 84–7
  international economic law, 233–5
  international law, 235–6
  possible use in international constitutionalism, 236–41
  process, 78–80
  role in global constitutionalisation process, 10
  terminology, 10, 77
  UK, 83–4
constituent power
  absence in global constitutionalisation, 55
  definition, 55, 56
constituent power holders, 54–9, *see also* community
  identity, 55, 58–9, 200–2, 236–41, 245, 247–8
  relationship with constitutional governance, 56–9
constituted power
  definition, 55
constituted power holders, 54–9
  identity, 200–2, 236–41, 245
  relationship with constitutional governance, 56–9
constitution
  definitions, 7–8, 14–15
  terminology, 136
Constitution
  European Union, 11

UK, 19, 83–4
US, 19–20
constitutional order, 8–9, 15
domestic, 8, 243–4
global legal order debate, 8–9, 243–9
rule of law essential, 31
terminology, 5
constitutionalisation
alternatives to sectoral or world categorisation, 142
coherence debate, 151–5
division between world order and sectoral, 11
Europe, 11–12
fragmentation, 98, 143–4, 150
hierarchy, 151–5
process, 15–16
rule of law, 170–1, 245–6
rule of law necessary for process, 31
sectoral, 141, 143–8
terminology, 4–5, 136
theories, 136–40
Verdross' arguments, 118–21
world order, 141–2, 148–51
constitutionalism
arguments against use beyond domestic level, 45–9
community or constituency, 84–7
continuity, 18
democratic legitimacy, 38–43, 183–4, 246
distinction between constitutional theories and paradigms, 18–19
divisions of power, 32–8, 246
domestic, 8, 243–4
Europe, 11–12
global legal order debate, 8–9, 243–9
as goal for global governance, 248
legitimacy aspect, 17–18
normative content, 1–3, 8, 20–1, 51–3
norms, 22, 24–43, 245–7, 248
norms omitted from study, 21–2
political actors, 16
relationship between domestic and global, 44–51
relationship with global constitutionalisation, 3, 10–11, 12–14
role, 17
rule of law, 16, 20–1, 22–31, 156–71
substantive content, 245
terminology, 4–5, 136
UK, 83–4
cosmopolitanism, 217–20

democracy
concept, 38–9
right of participation, 40–2
democratic legitimacy
constitutionalism, 38–43, 183–4
global constitutionalisation, 184–90, 195–7, 246
international community, 190–5
Dicey, A. V., 27–8
divisions of power, 171–83
constitutionalism, 32–8
European Union, 34
executive, legislative and judicial, 32–4
geographical, 34–6
global constitutionalisation theories, 183, 246
organisational constitutionalisation, 177–82
state and domestic orders in international law, 172–7
United States, 35–6
domestic law
China, 22–3, 28

erga omnes obligations, 147–8, 166–7, 169
European Court of Human Rights, 161
European Court of Justice, 161
European Union (EU)
constitutionalisation, 11–12
geographical divisions of power, 34
subsidiarity, 11–12
exceptionalism
rule of law, 157–8

fragmentation, 94–8
constitutionalisation, 98, 143–4, 150
Franck, T., 213–17

global administrative law, 102–5, 228–32
global constitutionalisation
absence of constituent power, 55
community's role in process of, 9–10, 47–8, 188–9
constituency or community debate, 241–3
constituency's role in process of, 10, 47–8
content, 135
democratic legitimacy, 184–90, 195–7, 246
divisions of power, 183, 246
historical antecedents, 108–33
judicial activism, 159–64
meaning, 45
objections to, 140–1
other international law approaches, 106–7
reasons for aspiration towards, 136
relationship between domestic and global constitutionalism, 44–51
relationship with constitutionalism, 3, 10–11, 12–14
rule of law, 245–6
theories, 140–51
Verdross' and New Haven's influence, 132–3
world order constitutionalisation, 149–51
global governance, *see* international law
global governance networks, 98–102
global institutionalisation
international community, 220–5
global law
terminology, 5
global legal pluralism, 90–4
facet of sectoral constitutionalisation, 143–4
Goodhart, A. L., 28

Hegel, G. W. F., 68–71, 111–12
Henkin, L.
international constituency, 226–8, 235
Hobbes, T., 111, 209–11
human rights
judicial activities, 163–4
rule of law, 164–5
human rights law, 96, 146–7
constitutionalisation theories, 163–4

ICJ, *see* International Court of Justice
institutional constitutionalisation, 144–8
institutional law, 144
international community
cosmopolitanism, 217–20
democratic legitimacy, 190–5
early modern international law, 205–9
Franck's theory, 213–17
global institutionalisation, 220–5
Hobbes' philosophy, 209–11
Kant's philosophy, 211–12
Stoic philosophy, 202–5
theories in contemporary international law, 212–20
unsuitable for identifying constituent power holders, 247
international constituency
global administrative law, 228–32
Henkin's discussion, 226–8, 235
identifying constituent power holders, 247–8
international constitutional law, 45, 189
international constitutionalism
possible use of constituency, 236–41
International Court of Justice (ICJ), 161–2, 168–9, 191
international economic law, 233–5
international law
ad hoc nature, 157–8
attraction of constitutionalism, 3–4
consent and non-consent based, 167
consistency, 157–8
constituency, 235–6
cosmopolitanism, 217–20
current debate, 87, 88–90
current position and future development, 5
development, 205–9
elements, 189

- fragmentation, 94–8
- Franck's theory on community, 213–17
- global administrative law, 102–5, 228–32
- global governance networks, 98–102
- global legal pluralism approach, 90–4
- historical approaches, 87–8, 90, 108–33
- history of the philosophy of, 109–13
- implications of sectoral and world order constitutionalisation theories, 11
- *jus cogens*, 113–16, 165–7
- Kant's philosophy, 211–12
- neutrality, 113–16
- New Haven approach, 108, 121–33
- relationship between domestic and global constitutionalism, 44–51
- rule by law, 22–3
- sovereignty, 31
- terminology, 5
- theories, 89, 106–7
- Verdross' influence, 108–9, 132–3

International Law Commission (ILC), 97
International Monetary Fund (IMF)
- constituency, 233–5

international organisations
- constitutionalisation arguments, 177–82
- New Haven School, 130–1
- Verdross' work, 113–16

international public law, 189

judicial activism
- global constitutionalisation, 159–64

judicial review, 162
jus cogens norms, 113–16, 147–8, 168, 169
- rule of law, 165–7

Kant, I., 211–12
Kingsbury, B., 229–30
Klabbers, J., 4–5, 44
Koskenniemi, M., 24–5

Lauterpacht, H., 45
laws of nations, 189
League of Nations
- neutrality, 116, 117

legal pluralism, 90–4
Loughlin, M., 27

Macdonald, K., 230–2, 235–6
Macdonald, T., 230–2, 235–6
majoritarianism, 41
Marxism
- on community, 71–2

Nancy, J., 71, 72–3
neutrality
- Verdross' work, 113–16

New Haven School, 100, 108, 121–33
- community, 127–30
- influence on international law, 132–3
- intergovernmental organisations, 130–1

New International Economic Order, 223

Peters, A., 4, 5
pluralism
- global constitutionalism, 143–4

political actors
- constitutionalism, 16

public opinion, 40–1

Raz, J., 25–6
rule by law, 22–3, 28
- China, 22–3, 28

rule of law
- constitutionalisation, 170–1, 245–6
- constitutionalism, 16, 20–1, 22–31, 156–71
- democratic elements, 30
- essential elements, 29, 30
- exceptionalism, 157–8
- human rights, 164–5
- interconnecting constitutionalism and politics, 31
- judicial activism, 159–64
- *jus cogens*, 165–7
- necessary for constitutionalisation process, 31

sectoral constitutionalisation, 141, 143–8
  fragmentation, 143–4
  pluralism facet, 143–4
sovereignty, 118
  international law perspective, 31
  power, 32
Suárez, F., 110–11, 207–9
subsidiarity
  European Union, 11–12
Switzerland
  membership of League of Nations and UN, 117

trade law, 145–7, *see also* World Trade Organization (WTO)

United Kingdom
  Constitution, 19, 83–4
  constitutional structure, 83–4
  democratic history, 39–40
  lack of geographical division of power, 37
United Nations (UN), 131
  constitutional nature, 186
  hierarchal issues versus WTO, 152–3
United Nations Charter, 117–18, 119, 120, 121, 145, 156–7, 169
  organisational constitutionalisation, 178–82
United Nations General Assembly, 144
United Nations Security Council, 117, 162–3
  terror lists, 157
United States
  Constitution, 19–20
  divisions of power, 35–6

Verdross, A., 108–21
  constitutionalisation, 118–21
  historic influences, 109–13
  influence on international law, 108–9, 132–3
  international organisations, 113–16
  jus cogens, 113–16
  neutrality issues, 113–16
Vitoria, Francisco de, 206–7

Walter, C., 45–6
Wheatley, S., 41
World Bank
  constituency, 233–5
world constitutionalisation
  fragmentation, 150
world order constitutionalisation, 141–2, 148–51
World Trade Organization (WTO), 131
  constitutionalisation debate, 145–6, 160–1
  Dispute Settlement Body, 97, 145–6, 152, 160–1
  hierarchal issues versus UN, 152–3
  implications of fragmented systems of law, 97
  Uruguay Round, 145

For EU product safety concerns, contact us at Calle de José Abascal, 56–1°,
28003 Madrid, Spain or eugpsr@cambridge.org.

www.ingramcontent.com/pod-product-compliance
Lightning Source LLC
LaVergne TN
LVHW011523200926
848484LV00001B/131